Inspiring Leadership

Inspiring Leadership

Becoming a dynamic and engaging leader

*Edited by Dr Kerrie Fleming and
Roger Delves*

Bloomsbury Business
An imprint of Bloomsbury Publishing Plc

B L O O M S B U R Y
LONDON · OXFORD · NEW YORK · NEW DELHI · SYDNEY

Bloomsbury Business

An imprint of Bloomsbury Publishing Plc

50 Bedford Square	1385 Broadway
London	New York
WC1B 3DP	NY 10018
UK	USA

www.bloomsbury.com

BLOOMSBURY and the Diana logo are trademarks of Bloomsbury Publishing Plc

First published 2017

© Dr Kerrie Fleming and Roger Delves, 2017

Dr Kerrie Fleming and Roger Delves have asserted their right under the Copyright, Designs and Patents Act, 1988, to be identified as Author of this work.

British Library Cataloguing-in-Publication Data

A catalogue record for this book is available from the British Library.

ISBN:	HB:	978-1-4729-3207-5
	ePDF:	978-1-4729-3205-1
	ePub:	978-1-4729-3208-2

Library of Congress Cataloging-in-Publication Data

A catalog record for this book is available from the Library of Congress.

Cover design by Sharon Mah
Cover image © iStock

Typeset by RefineCatch Limited, Bungay, Suffolk
Printed and bound in Great Britain

This book is an edited collection of reflections, research and practice offered by foremost leadership faculty who work with Ashridge Executive Education at Hult International Business School. As the world's most relevant business school, our leadership faculty work across our global campuses at Boston, London, San Francisco, Dubai and Shanghai to enable and inspire leaders to fulfil and exceed their individual and business performance.

Contents

Foreword: Inspiring Leaders – and the tragic risks they run

Professor Jonathan Gosling

This volume is prompted by the intuition that being a leader has become troublesome – for those who lead, are led or have a responsibility for developing leaders. Efforts to save or transform businesses are tough enough and civic and political institutions appear paralysed by a cacophonous Babel of competing interests and identities. At the same time cherished public services seem to be allergic to the leaders and leadership culture they say they need.

The scale of these challenges, and the inevitability of at least partial failure, prompts us to think about what it is to be a leader who is held responsible for events that can turn out to be catastrophic and shameful.

This may not be relevant for all. Those leaders responsible for incremental and continuously negotiated changes, or those stalwarts sustaining continuity in the face of distractions and re-organizations, might not feel this scale of risk and challenge. Those, however, who are trying to change significantly the way things are done, or are launching a new venture, or are pressed to sign new deals and make commitments on behalf of others that move resources from one unit to another – all of these leaders are likely to feel heavy responsibility for the effects they have on those around them and the intended and unintended outcomes.

Is the leader responsible for this? How does he or she handle it? How do we, as stakeholders, treat those we hold responsible? Leaders have to take decisions that can have disastrous as well as welcome effects; moral hazard is a part of the territory, the consequences of choosing to condone or challenge ways of being that are accepted as part of the way things get done around here. This is why 'courage' is so vaunted as a quality that leaders need to have.

Taking decisions in the face of uncertainty is inherent to leadership. The leader does not know what counterparts and competitors will do, whether a predicted market will materialize, how soon disruptive technologies will come on line or whether the politicians will find it expedient to pay attention. Innumerable uncertainties make up the context within which any act of leadership takes place. There is always the risk that the leader might not achieve what they intend; but more than that, they might do more harm by misdirecting resources, landing themself and others in predicaments that will be hard to get out of. The leader might find that, in spite of their best intentions, they are perceived as a 'bad person' because of what they have done, how they have done it and/or the consequences of their actions.

How do we expect leaders to handle such responsibility? With remorse and rending of garments? Rational, forward-looking remedies? Or with blithe indifference and persistence? When things go wrong, what responses do we consider 'responsible'? In some cases we know that leaders are respected for 'falling on their sword': the Iceland prime minister exposed for tax evasion, for example. Some slip away from their misdeeds, or shrug them off as irrelevant quirks, like Berlusconi's philandering and corruption.

Often leaders appear ill-equipped to take responsibility for their actions. It is as if they are brilliantly endowed with what is required to take decisive action, but lack what will enable them to hold up their hands and say: 'I did this and it didn't work out so well . . .' Citizens are stakeholders turn instead to slower and humbler legal processes, mute resentment, or the tardy judgements of history. The Public Inquiry can be thorough and cathartic, but painfully slow – as can be seen in the Chilcott Inquiry into the UK's decision to invade Iraq.

More often the led simply shrug their shoulders and lose a bit more trust in the integrity of their leaders, and hope that historians of the present era will have the perspective, and information, to determine responsibility. This is why Aristotle felt that anyone hoping to judge the goodness of his or her life on the basis of 'achievements' is doomed to fail, because results are forever reverberating, and there is no objective point at which to say 'right that's done – let's add it all up and see how good a life he or she led'.

Many of the essays in this collection suggest that leaders might find and nurture some inner moral resource. I wonder, though, if this is consistent with the motivations that drive people to step into executive leadership roles and the hard-edged immediacy of moral jeopardy, where actions and inactions play out in an uncontrollable future.

This might be contentious. Hopefully we can all find the capacity to nurture ourselves, our ideas, our virtues, our offspring, our friends and communities, and to develop compassion for 'all sentient beings'. Yet this is easier said than done because of those life experiences that create the inner desire for leading on the edge, that feeling of being alive that comes with taking risks. This desire for edginess takes many forms: a dangerous sport, an illicit affair, a political gamble, an impossible schedule of commitments or a risk-all investment. The buzz people can get from these is often (not always and not in every case) a defence against the experience of not being adequately recognized when young.

Some of the leadership approaches that come from this experience can prove useful, especially in situations which are edgy and morally and existentially risky. But leaders who are coming from such a place are unlikely to be so functional when it comes to admitting responsibility for things that have not worked out, or have caused pain to others. Shame and remorse, for instance, are natural, proper and appropriate if one feels oneself to be responsible for something having gone wrong. But the personal resources for a nurturing response to shame and remorse are rare companions to those with a taste for power and status, because shame erodes the desire for power.

Then there are those who identify with being a leader, or having a leadership role, too much and so cannot afford to be touched by shame – as that would undermine their identity. Those for whom power is inseparable from their sense of self would find shame to be utterly devastating and so are more likely simply to deny responsibility.

These reflections reaffirm for me the good sense of leadership development that draws on culture resources that are supra-personal: myths, artworks, music. Great art somehow connects us to universal humanity, in spite of who people have become as leaders full of status.

Such leadership development helps leaders make visceral and emotional sense of the complex, ambivalent feelings that come with holding positions of institutional and organizational potency, which must then be used in situations that are bound to go beyond the limits of control of that potency. Paradoxically the experience of potency is accompanied by the experience of impotence, in terms of the ability to determine outcomes.

So is it mad to hope for leaders with the capacity for power and humility? The essays in this book can be read as constructive answers to this question – hopeful without being naïve, and rooted in long experience of leadership development. I conclude this Foreword with a perspective from the audience – what do we observers, scholars and critics of leadership contribute to its responsible exercise?

Greek and Shakespearian tragedies present us with great people whose great virtues become the cause of their downfall. Medea's love for Jason and Lear's concern for his legacy are integral to their iconic greatness – yet cruelly instrumental in their destruction. What is more, not only are the heroes destroyed – so is everyone else.

Tragedies give little credence to the kind of poetic justice in which everyone gets their comeuppance. Here the whole system is brought down by the failings of the leaders; the good suffer just as much as the bad, the innocent along with the guilty. What kind of moral lesson is this? I think tragic dramas are reassuring because they show badness is toxic. We can see how Medea's overwhelming love turns to jealousy and infanticide; how Macbeth's ambition to lead draws him on to bloody murder and then the whole civic order is poisoned by badness before it all comes tumbling down. Moral failings, even though an excess of virtue, turn out to be toxic to the system as a whole, not just to the individual perpetrator. So as an audience we must be reassured that, conversely, every act of goodness strengthens the collective moral order; it is not just a private victory – it is a public good. This is what I think we intuitively lean towards with 'responsible leadership'. This is what might strengthen the capacity for inspiration, so eloquently summoned in this collection.

Acknowledgements

KF: dedicated to my parents.
RD: thanks and love to three magic monkeys
Special thanks to John Higgins for the insights and assistance he offered so generously.

Introduction

This book offers a practical, pragmatic perspective in what might be called the great Ashridge tradition from a number of leadership practitioners at Ashridge Executive Education in the United Kingdom who collectively have over two hundred years of experience working with opinion formers, influencers, leaders and followers across the world. It offers a single publication which documents both unified and sometimes diverse voices discussing the best of leadership development and the most effective leadership practices which have evolved and are now emerging. This highly practical and effective use is coupled with a perspective and vision for the types of leadership abilities which are needed to deal with future global demands. Each contributor offers a unique perspective, which combined provide a comprehensive documentation of the practice of leadership development at Ashridge Executive Education. It offers leaders a means to bask in and glean some insights into the business school experience through a medium of print.

As editors, we want this book to help leaders translate the latest leadership thinking and offer an easy means of application to their current role as leader. A constant theme at both Ashridge and Hult is the importance of the application of theory into practice – both are and will remain determined to create work which is both rigorous and relevant. This contribution to that tradition will, we hope, offer leaders a means to develop themselves and their teams and a stimulus to think about how their organization may need to evolve in the changing environment and economies around them. It certainly offers a diverse view of leadership perspectives from which readers can choose in order to enhance their own established or emerging leadership practice.

Leadership wisdom

We also want to help practitioners to understand why and how understanding material such as the subject matter captured here really can help to make better, wiser decisions. Whether you are personally a leader or not, you will have observed leaders and been led by them. You will know that leaders think, reflect and then make decisions. What they choose to consider in that process, the things on which they choose to reflect, colour their entire *modus operandi*. Few would dispute that when it comes to the evaluation of leaders and leadership success, it is the quality of decision-making that often distinguishes the superb from the merely adequate – and as leaders there seems little doubt in the face of the empirical evidence that we are judged by the quality of our decisions and our actions and by the results that arise from those decisions. Our decisions become our legacy.

So, decision making in the world of the leader is freighted with a special significance, because so often what hangs on the decision can be life changing or career threatening. Regularly making high quality decisions is one of the hallmarks of great leaders. How do the good ones get it right so often, and what happens when they get it wrong? What can we learn from the decision-making approach of these explorers and adventurers in the VUCA landscape within which we must all now and for the foreseeable future survive and attempt to thrive? How can those of us who know, feel or fear that our decision making is not our strongest suit learn from the success of others? Let us remind ourselves of the VUCA acronym. A VUCA environment is one which is said to be volatile, uncertain, complex and ambiguous. In today's often malign and hostile business environment, some of these variables are often in play – but when an environment boasts all four, then the pressures on leaders and on those who follow them mount alarmingly fast. Mergers can create VUCA environments, as can regime change or the demand for such change; significant shifts in legislation can do so, or the social pressure to generate such shifts. Whatever the cause, the effects of VUCA environments are often calamitous.

For many parents, one of the joys of having young children is being able to read aloud to them. Today's parents are particularly fortunate as their enjoyment of this pastime coincided with the popularity of the Harry Potter adventures from J. K. Rowling. Many a dad or mum must have read the whole impressive canon aloud, from start to finish, and then wallowed in the glorious films. So it is perhaps no surprise that many an adult swears by that great modern philosopher, Professor Albus Dumbledore. In *The Philosopher's Stone*, Rowling has him suggest, in conversation with Harry, that it is by our actions and not our intentions that others judge us – for as Dumbledore points out, we all have good intentions. This goes to the heart of what decision making is about: what we do is a function of what we decide, and it seems to us that for leaders and managers, the actions by which we are most judged are our decisions and the things that happen as a result of those decisions.

Barbara Killinger, in her book *Integrity*, quotes W. H. Auden: 'Nobody can honestly think of himself as a strong character because, however successful he may be in overcoming them, he is necessarily aware of the doubts and temptations that accompany every important choice.' As leaders, we think, we consider, we evaluate and then we decide – and those things which we choose to weigh in the balance before we make a decision offer insights into our integrity. To paraphrase the language both of authenticity and of Ego and Eco Intelligence, do we think selfishly or selflessly? Do we think of the short term or the long term? Do we make contingent decisions which reflect the situation in which we believe we find ourselves, or do we only make decisions which are congruent with our inner world of values or with the values of the organization we represent or even which are aligned with the regulations which are set in place to guide or manage our actions? Do we, however much we intend to do otherwise, weigh the wrong things in the balance, or evaluate them poorly – and do we as a result make poor decisions or decisions which to others appear illogical or unsupportable? Do our decisions lead to actions and outcomes of which we are less than proud? Do we sometimes look back, reflect, regret, and wish we could be judged on our intentions and not on our actions? Yet as Dumbledore also said, in that same book, 'It does not do to dwell on dreams and forget to live.' Whatever decisions we make, whatever the consequences, we cannot forget to live. But how much better would it be to live with pride in our own integrity, knowing that the decisions we make are at the very least ones which show an understanding of what is right and what is wrong, and the courage to choose the option which is appropriate?

How leadership is changing

Leadership is the new religion. Like religion, it consumes our time, our mind space and vast amounts of space in publications of every sort, both fictional and non-fictional. Turnbull James (2011), in a commissioned paper for The King's Fund, makes the point that leadership is nowadays not confined to leaders but is more something which is important throughout an organization, leading to an attitude of collaboration and co-operation and the breaking down of silo mentalities. As she points out, Fletcher (2004) and others talk of the post-heroic leadership paradigm, where the 'who and where' of leadership are less important than the 'what and how'.

In their chapter, which is found in Section One, Higgins, Reitz and Williams also explore the premise that leadership is changing. They explore how people have experienced leadership (their own and others) in the last five years, and what assumptions they held about the future. They discuss the enormous scale of expectation that people still have of leaders, the 'heroic' breadth of responsibility for overall organizational performance, for financial contribution and for demonstrating extraordinary amounts of control. They agree with Turnbull James that at the same time, paradoxically, there is an emerging consensus that the time of heroic and forceful leadership is over. So the job of leadership remains heroic, but people want leaders to behave as if the job was ordinary. Leaders it seems, are to know everything yet be Everyman.

One clear message from the respondents in the research the authors examine is that leaders must know what to do. This is where an understanding of ethics can be as useful to today's leaders as it was to the ancient philosophers. For ethics is little other than a system of moral principles or well-founded standards of right and wrong that help us to decide what we ought to do. Ethics often concerns itself with what we believe is due to us and from us, with what will do most good for the society or the culture we are trying to create or protect, with fairness or its absence, and with specific values, which are of course no more than strongly held subjective beliefs that affect how we make decisions and lead our lives.

Stephen R. Covey was responsible for some of the hugely important early work of popular appeal in this area. His *Principle-Centered Leadership* book promoted the practice of principled leadership based on a set of 'true north' principles and 'natural laws'. Bill George's *True North* is also an accessible way into this complex subject, with some compelling and moving stories from some highly experienced leaders. Covey defined principles as the basic tenets (for example fairness, justice, honesty, integrity and trust). He talked about the things which when we examined them were clearly self-evident and self-validating (by which he meant when we followed these principles, they proved their worth), those natural laws that are always there. They are always reliable, like the 'true north' on a compass.

Covey says that real leadership begins with the humble recognition that principles, rather than people, ultimately govern. But in our imperfect and ambiguous world of business and leadership, it is hard to talk about universal principles and natural laws that are absolute, impersonal, factual, objective and self-evident, because people, particularly leaders and leaders manqué, are inclined to ask questions like who chose these principles, when were they identified and so on. Principles as described by Covey can broadly be described as values which are so obviously good and right that they are – and this is a clumsy term – akin to super-values and the unavoidable truth about values is that they are (however firmly held) subjective beliefs. This means that super-values must be open to the same criticism, however widely they are held or however self-evidently true they may seem to a majority of people. So, do they take us any further forward? In that we think deeper, yes. In that we are no closer to a binary end point – this is right and that is wrong – perhaps not.

But consider this: imagine you go into an antiques shop and as you browse, you find two things that really appeal to you. One is an illuminated map of Europe in 1714, complete with beautiful calligraphy and a carved oak frame. You admire it and negotiate a price for it with the shop's owner. As he is wrapping it for you, you continue browsing. Your next discovery is a beautiful brass ship's compass, in a wooden box which is satin lined. The compass is in full working order, the box is pristine, and the velvet lining is perfect. You negotiate again with the owner, and he sells you the compass for exactly the same price as the map. Here's our question: are either of these beautiful objects of any use to you in our contemporary world in a practical sense that reflects their original purpose? Clearly the map is not – the borders of countries have changed beyond recognition since 1714, and there are no roads indicated to guide you. Being able to read the map is not an issue: the map is simply inaccurate and out of date. However, the compass, if you know how to use it, is still of practical use, because north is still where it was in 1714 (well, unless a rare geomagnetic reversal occurs (Sagnotti et al., 2014)). Geomagnetic reversal aside, that may be a way to capture the difference between principles and values: values change while principles do (or should) not. Think back to the society that existed in 1714 and think of what their values were around issues like the right to own property, slavery, divorce, abortion, women's or workers' rights: some different to today's values. So, values are subject to societal change, and reflect where we want our society to be today. Principles perhaps reflect something deeper: those things which we will always want as part of how we live our lives and how others behave towards us. The principled compass may be a better guide to us than the changeable map of values.

In their chapter, Williams and Hayward declare that there is no perfect model of leadership, no seven steps or ten points. The essence of leadership lives within individuals. The question they identify at the heart of leadership is, 'why do people choose to follow?' If individual leaders can understand why people follow them they can build the strength of their leadership. Within this paradigm, leadership skills are helpful but they are not the essence of leadership. The key questions in followers' minds are, 'Who is this person? What are their values and beliefs? Do they care about the organization, about me personally?' When the answers to these deep questions are aligned broadly with the followers' views, then the leadership played out is 'authentic', 'real', genuine and immensely powerful. A positive cycle of energy is set up between leaders and followers. This can be (should be) challenging and sometimes uncomfortable but it is strong, unshakeable, dynamic and extremely powerful. The authors of this particular chapter offer the platform of the Ashridge Leadership Process, which is a long-standing development experience practised for over twenty-five years using a consistent philosophy of leadership as its platform, a philosophy which has been described as a 'life-changing' experience by participants as it releases the energy, belief, confidence and drive that people have within themselves to be leaders. The result is a data-based examination of what is authentic and real leadership.

To establish the frame for the next exploration, let us return to the subject of ethics – that branch of philosophy that is concerned with human conduct, particularly the behaviour of individuals in society. Nowadays it is closely aligned with what we term social anthropology – the study of human societies and cultures. Social anthropologists look to understand how we live in societies and how we make our lives meaningful. In our wider society, ethics refers to those standards that impose on us reasonable obligations, which are designed to prevent unacceptable actions or behaviour such as theft, assault, slander or fraud. In the society where we spend the largest part of our time – our workplace – we have an equally demanding set of reasonable obligations, including to behave in ways that are not ageist, racist, sexist, faithist or in any other inappropriate way prejudiced. The workplace should be a place of endeavour, not of endurance. Embracing ethics in the workplace and in wider society also encourages us to celebrate values such as honesty, compassion or loyalty, interpersonal skills such as emotional intelligence, attitudes such as authenticity or mindfulness. Ethical standards also include standards relating to rights, such as the right to life, the right to freedom from injury, the right to be treated with decency and respect and the right to privacy. Such standards represent good ethical behaviour because they are in effect the same as the principles we use or should use as a reliable moral compass. In short, at work and within the broader canvas of society, ethics covers and help us as leaders to address a number of life dilemmas which we all, to one extent or another, encounter: how to live a good life alongside others; meeting our rights and responsibilities; using the language of right and wrong; making moral decisions – deciding what is good and bad. It is hard to imagine an environment at work in which leaders would inspire to good effect without an intuitive or a learned understanding of what is 'ethical' or feels 'right'.

The leader's relationship with ethics can inform followers about that leader's values and beliefs, and will give followers some sense of how they will be treated and dealt with as individuals. So, leaders need to have a meaningful relationship with ethics if they are to retain the goodwill they require from followers. Leaders are exquisitely observed by their followers, are judged constantly and, if they are found wanting, can and will swiftly lose the confidence, the respect and the goodwill of their followers. Leaders can inspire through what they say and do, but they can only lead with the tacit permission of their followers, and the leader whose relationship with ethical standards and therefore with integrity breaks down finds themselves soon enough a leader whom people choose not to follow.

Next, Nixon, author of the recently published *Pariahs*, looks at the concepts of hubris and narcissism among leaders. One of the most critical roles – if not the most critical – that a leader undertakes is to build and protect trust in his or her organization, and by extension it seems obvious that inspiring personal trust in themselves is one of the most important things leaders do. If customers, shareholders, employees and peers do not trust you as a leader, it is inevitably harder to trust your organization. But there are some good reasons why this is becoming harder to do at both an individual and an organizational level, and why failures of trust, particularly for big brands, may be becoming more frequent, more traumatic and more damaging than ever before. Leaders who pay close attention to the risks of reputational failure can avoid some painful, expensive and damaging experiences for themselves and their organizations, and perhaps create more sustainable legacies into the bargain. For those few inspirational leaders who can actually transcend these risks without succumbing to hubris, who can combine the power of individual trust and confidence with the virtues of humility and purpose beyond self, then leadership roles of real weight and importance can and should beckon.

Nixon's chapter explores what happens to leaders who forget themselves and fall victim to their own arrogance. Nixon argues persuasively and with many an illustration from the world of contemporary business leadership that leaders in our VUCA environment face particularly pressing reputational challenges – a 'perfect storm' of pressures comprising equal parts external events and increasing psychological pressures such as the increasing trend towards the leader as celebrity and towards heavily leveraged reward systems and perverse incentives. At its worst, he suggests, the result is a leadership culture in organizations which is increasingly hubristic, where leaders are unable to hear or heed internal or external critics, and where the need to service their own increasingly narcissistic needs outweighs the need to serve other more appropriate stakeholders. As the actions of more and more leaders around personal wealth creation and protection come under public scrutiny via the leaked Panama Papers and as scandals continue to rock institution after institution across the corporate world, Nixon's central assertion, that we must fight hubris and the value-destroying and trust-destroying cultures it perpetrates, seems both timely and appropriate.

Nixon also stresses the vital role for the modern leader of transparency. But he points out that transparency is not necessarily the end of secrecy. Sometimes the best one can expect from a transparent leader is that he or she is transparent about what they must keep secret and hidden and why it must be thus and so. It is interesting to have witnessed, in this context, both the relative slowness with which the then British Prime Minister David Cameron moved from reticence to transparency about his tax affairs and the ensuing speed with which his colleagues at the time, George Osborne and Boris Johnson plus Opposition leader Jeremy Corbyn, rushed to take the same transparent position. There is a fascinating debate beginning to be had about what has to be transparent, what can be secret and what should be private. The super-injunctions of celebrities, including some from the world of business, are different examples of the same coin as well as evidence of hubris in action.

Why being a leader is always personal

Whilst our intention was not to set up challenges and then provide answers – the world of commerce is rather too complex for such a glib approach – it is possible to offer the concept of authenticity as the antidote to hubris. As Turnbull James (2011) points out, the language of leadership is acquiring new vocabulary: authentic, collaborative, collective, connected, concurrent, co-ordinated, dispersed, devolved, democratic, distributive democratic, emotionally intelligent (and who knows what will happen when we move into the further reaches of the alphabet?). Authenticity, however, is a leader concept that does appear to have some traction.

Central to the concept of leader authenticity espoused by the contributors in their own chapters within the book is the idea of leaders being real. Roger Delves starts us on the journey of the importance of being real and authentic. He suggests that helping emerging and established leaders to identify and explore their authentic selves will lead to increased self-awareness. He examines the work of established researchers into Authentic Leadership (George, 2004; Luthans and Avolio, 2003; Michie and Gootie, 2005) and pulls together the strands of Transactional Analysis, Ethical Decision Making and Authenticity to help leaders to create a sustainable approach to leadership which they find personally satisfying and enriching.

In her chapter, Fleming offers some observations on how contemporary leaders manage current environments and how emotional intelligence offers a means of humanizing leadership and inspiring followership. We all know that leadership is not what happens when the status quo is maintained but when disruptions occur. It is the excruciating time when problems arise with no obvious and immediate solutions which need to be addressed with speed and confidence. This type of leadership is not about demonstrating sparkling levels of charisma with no depth or sincerity but living and exuding honest and value led behaviours. These behaviours occur naturally for a lucky few but for most need to be sculpted from years of awareness of self and others. Fleming focuses on the importance of recognizing, using, understanding and managing emotions in order to build on your true identity as a leader, and points out the gap between what leaders need to be accomplished at doing and the skills against which organizations still insist on recruiting their leaders. The importance of understanding and managing emotions – our own and those of others – is stressed and Fleming concludes that people follow human leaders, certainly those who can lead but also those who inspire and sometimes offer a glimpse of their fallibility. These leaders have a strong self-awareness and keenly understand their values and what they stand for. They do not compromise on these values which suggests that they are tenacious, committed and honest. Emotional intelligence offers a means to capture these abilities and lead in a way which is both inspiring and intelligent in the VUCA environment.

In a broader sense, both these chapters support the view that integrity reflects on human beings and their interaction with other humans, on freedom, on responsibility and on justice. So in a very important way, integrity is concerned with human independence and human interdependence when it focuses on the relationship that exists between us and the world around us. We demonstrate independence when, in a decision-making process, we elect to ignore any and all external conditioning or influence, for example institutional or parental, and instead seek to judge objectively and to decide what direction to take. To use the language of Harris's (1979) Transactional Analysis model which Delves favours in his chapter, when in independent decision-making mode we are in our thought-through Adult self, not in the taught state of Parent or the felt state of Child. This informed independence of thought, when coupled with self-awareness and aligned with an understanding of ethical decision making, can help leaders to generate decisions which are both palatable to followers and wise within the business. These decisions will, because of the nature of Adult decision making, tend to be other-regarding, selfless rather than selfish, which will also add to their attractiveness to others.

We demonstrate an understanding of interdependence when we realize that every decision has intended and unintended consequences, and that these consequences are better understood and evaluated if we accept that in business virtually everything requires interdependent action in order to succeed. As leaders, even when we seek to inspire, we make better decisions when we discuss our decisions with some of those affected by the decision. This is complex, demanding, time consuming and often enough emotionally draining stuff, though it is certainly what is expected and increasingly demanded of leaders by followers. Today's followers may be sure of little, but they do seem convinced that inspired leadership which is based on nothing other than personal charisma has little to offer in a world which is ever more complex, increasingly ambiguous and apparently constantly creeping closer to the bounded edge of chaos. Increasingly, therefore, those who lead and who will not or cannot engage in critical conversations with those who follow, find themselves isolated and out of touch with their teams, unable to find the pulse of the unit and therefore unable to pitch the message, the question or the comment appropriately. Is it any wonder, especially when there is a pragmatic, contingent option staring us in the face, that making decisions which have integrity is difficult?

To complicate this picture further, what we consider socially appropriate behaviour, behaviour which inspiring leaders should model, can and does change over time. The generation born in the 1930s were already, as they set out to be good mothers and fathers, veterans and survivors of the worst war the world had ever seen. Had you told them that their children and grandchildren would embrace a society that took a far more lenient and permissive view of choices around marriage, abortion, divorce, sexual orientation and much more, let alone the need to conduct business in an honourable fashion that would survive any scrutiny, then that parent generation of the 1950s might have found the vision of the developed world a mere sixty years later very hard to imagine, let alone to choose to embrace. This is not about what is right, wrong or acceptable in the absolute sense; it is about what we are taught to find right, wrong or acceptable and how fast we can adapt to change. So much change has taken place in the business world over that period of time, leaving it as fundamentally altered as the broader society within which it operates – and like that broader society, some elements of the world of business are still far from sure that all those sea changes have been for the better.

What this means for the inspiring leader is that such a leader must constantly examine and challenge our standards and those of our organizations, to make sure that they are reasonable, well-founded and in tune with the spirit of the times. In other words, leaders must strive to make sure that the institutions we lead and help to shape live up to standards that are reasonable and appropriate. This is an intellectual and emotional challenge for the inspiring leader, one not to be underestimated or to be undertaken lightly.

In his chapter, Neal examines the effects of turning off emotions, using the medium of sport and the military to illustrate the impact on performance abilities. He describes experiences that offer insights on the importance of character in success and suggests three key areas to show how leaders can be developed using mind, body and spirit of leadership. In the area of mind, he examines the importance of understanding yourself and your personal values. He demonstrates the importance of goals setting and prioritization based upon the need for results and the legacy you wish to create. In body, he looks at personal image and brand and how it reflects your personal value system and suggests that physical resilience and the mind–body link is vital. In particular he considers the effect of pressure both physically and mentally on your ability to make effective leadership decisions over a long period of time. He also examines the role of recovery, sleep and mindfulness.

One of Greek philosopher Socrates' longer lasting sound bites is that the unexamined life is not worth living. Socrates believed that until we are self-aware, we are not really alive, merely existing. Neal helps us to understand that we need to examine more than just our self-awareness, more indeed than just our sense of right and wrong. Most of us do not live in a mindful way and do not examine how we live or dissect the choices that lead to how we live. Neal, by inviting us to reflect on our mind, body and spirit, helps us to attempt to answer Socrates' implied question of 'how should one live?'

Emerging practices in leadership development

In their chapter, Olivier and Hölscher challenge the notion of leadership vested only in gifted individuals and explore the idea of leadership as a shared social space. A social space is one where people live together, so the Socratic question becomes perhaps an even more important one to answer, or at least to consider. Olivier and Hölscher argue that true leadership creates a generative space of emergence and the shaping of endless possibilities towards the achievement of a vision. It is the special calling of only the chosen few to provide direction, depending on their personal skills or ability to inspire, to take decisions and to control the outcome.

In their search for 'Leadership Intelligence' Olivier and Hölscher explore the application and results of 'Eco Intelligence' and the new sets of skills that emerge from the ability to deal with incompatibility. When exploring the art of reconciliation instead of elimination, they examine how this 'leadership intelligence' enables leadership to embrace volatility, uncertainty, complexity and ambiguity as opportunities for transformation and growth rather than a dangerous threat that should be avoided. That leaders and teams will encounter volatility, uncertainty, complexity and ambiguity seems now to be a given. It is not whether they will, but how they will deal with these encounters that becomes important. In VUCA environments, followers need the reassurance that authenticity in leaders provides, and absolutely do not need the inconsistency in demeanour and in decision making that the contingent leader offers. It is, however, exactly these demanding environments, these fires of experience that cause so many leaders to lose their grip on their values, lose their sense of true north, lose their determination to ground their behaviour in ethical decision making.

In Chapter 8, Brent and McKergow offer some insight into the skill of an appreciative mind-set. This allows the shaping of the vision discussed in the previous chapter and they offer some tools such as SOAR (Strengths, Opportunities, Aspirations and Resources) and examine the importance of exploring weaknesses. They examine solution focus, which demonstrates how we can use the power of future perfect conversations. The conversation may be about an imaginary future, but the conversation is happening right now and influences people in the here and now. They also offer and use positive psychology to offer gratitude practices and exercises which include the practice of mindfulness.

What these two chapters, from Olivier and Hölscher and from Brent and McKergow show is that when it comes to the actual practice of leadership, the gap between action and intention can grow disconcertingly fast. In the hurly burly of the ever present need to act, in the face of the incessant stream of what Covey famously termed both urgent/important and urgent/not important tasks, the sheer weight of urgent imperatives can drive us away from the hard questions of ethics towards the welcoming arms of the contingent. What will generate action and apparent progress seems so much more attractive than what appears only to generate more questions. The ethical too often withers in the face of the feasible.

In her contribution, Hind builds on the work of Higgins, Reitz and Williams and writes about the common misconception that CEOs and senior managers should be pretty good at everything (as indeed some expect themselves to be), and argues that trying to be good at everything wastes effort and takes the focus from the really important and inspirational objective of developing strengths into excellence. She offers the concept of 'spiky leadership' to explain that the leaders most likely to drive growth are those who have real 'spikes of excellence' on some of those key competencies, standing out starkly, even if they are much less strong in the others. So-called 'spiky' leaders must be capable of building up, and working within, a great team made up of other leaders with different 'spikes'. In order to be comfortable relying on the expertise of others, a good deal of real and honest self-awareness is needed, acknowledging and accepting personal 'gaps' of capability. This self-awareness, combined with the determination to 'get things done', reinforces the need to have great, but different, people in the senior leadership team. Leaders must therefore develop the confidence to hire other strong people without feeling threatened. To deliver growth, spiky leaders must build a circle around them of other people who are at least as good as they are, but in other areas. Hind's chapter explores ways in which this concept can be used to enable more effective and inspirational leadership in current and future organizations through the alignment of strategy and leadership strengths.

So our inspirational leader should be spiky, should think holistically, should be able to shape a vision, deal with a VUCA environment, should be able to develop mind, body and spirit, with emotional intelligence and authenticity, the sort of person others are inspired to follow because they do the leader job heroically. If all this were not enough, they must model behaviour to which others will aspire, live life well in that Aristotelian sense of being prepared and able to live virtuously – by which is meant living a life governed by a set of admirable personal values – despite temptation.

It should be the case that individuals acting in a professional capacity take on an additional burden of principled responsibility. Professional associations have codes that identify required behaviour within the context of a practice such as medicine, law, accounting or engineering. These written codes provide rules of conduct and standards of behaviour based on professional principles which often include concepts such as impartiality, objectivity, openness, full disclosure, confidentiality, due diligence, a duty of care, fidelity to professional responsibilities and avoidance of conflict or apparent conflict of interest. These principles must be applied by everyone to everyone, so they represent a universal standard which can be practised in many different ways and which is subject to cultural variation. They grow from informed debate and are as far as possible acceptable to anyone, anywhere. Where we can successfully expand this concept of codified principled behaviour with penalties for transgressions beyond associations and into organizations, beyond the structured and externally exposed and into the selected and internally imposed, then we have the basis for a strong culture, one within which inspired leadership can flourish alongside confident followership.

Our hope is that practitioners will find much between these pages to engage them. We want to stimulate discussion, or at least reflection. We, as editors, and Ashridge Executive Education as a centre for leadership practice, want to acknowledge and embrace the challenges that face the leaders of tomorrow. It seems to us that the alternative – ignoring those challenges – is likely as a choice to be both ineffective and unsupportable. We hope that this book will help leaders wherever they are on their leadership journey. We believe – because we see the evidence before us every day of our working lives – that any leader can change and that all leaders can benefit from thinking about their leadership practice rather than simply executing it. We believe that ideas are at the heart of change and change is at the heart of leadership. So we offer this book to the leaders of today and of tomorrow in the hope that something here will inspire and in the knowledge that everything found within is sourced from a shared desire to help leaders do what they do with more skill, more confidence and more success.

Dr Kerrie Fleming, Associate Professor of Organizational Behaviour.
Roger Delves, Ashridge Dean of Qualifications and
Professor of Practice in Leadership

Setting the scene

How being a leader is and is not changing

Leading from the inside out; lessons from thirty years of the Ashridge Leadership Process

Colin Williams and Ian Hayward

This chapter explores how individuals can develop their ability to provide inspiring leadership by reflecting on their personal approach through three lenses: past, present and future. The challenge is to identify what caused past successes and difficulties, to explore the impact of being fully present 'in the moment' as a leader and to build confidence and clarity of ambition for the future. While it is fair to say that many leaders think about these things intuitively, we believe that providing a framework to support this 'ongoing work in progress' is beneficial.

The material laid out is based on our experience with hundreds of leaders who have participated in the Ashridge Leadership Process (ALP). The ALP provides the structure, challenge and support required for in-depth learning about 'my' leadership. The flow of the chapter follows the logic of past, present and future and invites the reader to reflect on their personal experience through the three lenses (Figure 1.1). A number of characters (Ray, Susan, Andy, Isabella, Ted and Maria) are introduced to provide practical illustrations of learning. Their stories are based on true events.

Although it is perhaps an unlikely comment from people who design and facilitate leadership development programmes, we do not believe that leadership skills are the essence of leadership. It is, of course, helpful to be a good listener, to act as a coach, to inject energy, to speak engagingly, to challenge constructively etc. but that is not what people choose to follow. Perhaps surprisingly most people are quite forgiving of leaders who demonstrate an absence of some of these skills – on one condition, and that condition is critical, 'Does the leader care?' Care about the organization, its purpose, its goals and ambition, its history and traditions; and do they care about me as an individual?

The essence of leadership is within individuals. Management is about organization, logic, rationale: it is tangible and therefore easy to measure. Managers choose people to recruit, set objectives and ensure compliance with processes. Leaders cannot choose followers, quite the opposite in fact. Leadership is more about emotions and feelings. It is not very tangible and thus is harder to measure, which sometimes causes people to demonstrate less leadership whilst continuing to 'manage'.

The question at the heart of leadership is, 'why do people choose to follow?' If individuals can understand why people make this choice, they can build the strength of their leadership. The key questions in followers' minds are; 'Who is this person? What are their values and beliefs?' When the answers to these deep questions are aligned (broadly) with the followers' views, then the leadership played out is 'authentic', 'real', genuine and immensely powerful. A positive cycle of energy is set up between leaders and followers. This can (should) be challenging and sometimes uncomfortable but it is strong, unshakeable, dynamic and extremely powerful.

Given this, the starting point for leaders should be a high level of self-awareness in order to build effective relationships with others, quite literally leading from the inside out. The leader must have the ability to establish a healthy, adult-to-adult connection with people. This depends on the leader having a sufficiently high self-esteem (to feel good or comfortable about who they are) and the self-confidence to accept challenge and disagreement as well as agreement and support. This builds an ongoing relationship that lives and thrives, or sometimes takes a battering, in the interactions between leaders and followers.

Groysberg and Slind (2012) describe leadership as a *Conversation*. Although at first glance this appears to be a relatively benign statement, the assumptions underpinning it are quite radical with challenges to traditional ideas of control and communication in particular. Consider one of the frequently asked questions in organizational life. Often asked quite casually, a leader will say to a subordinate, 'Is everything under control?' The almost automatic response is, 'Yes, absolutely.' At this point both parties can relax. Imagine how the conversation might develop if the answer was a casual, 'Actually, no.' Would the leader respond by exclaiming: 'Excellent, so we must be experimenting, innovating, challenging current thinking.' Or would she be more likely to respond, 'So what do we need to do to get things under control?' It is clear that some processes in organizations need to be firmly under control (a production line for example), however Groysberg and

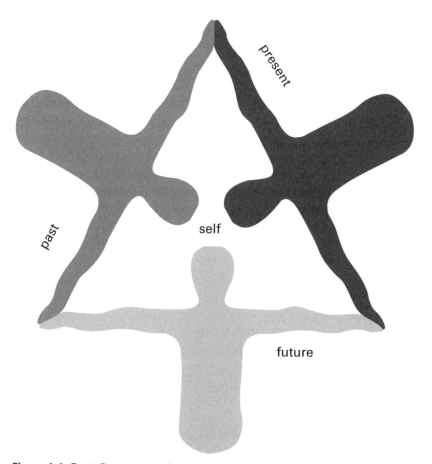

Figure 1.1 Past, Present and Future

Slind challenge the illusion of control over processes like strategy development, brand management, innovation and recognition. They argue that leaders need to engage with people, not try to disseminate information, police conversations and enforce compliance. They state that the nature and quality of conversation is what determines the effectiveness of the leader. In her book *Dialogue in Organisations* our colleague Reitz (2015) explores how leaders should attempt to reduce status differences and actively promote interaction. It is not enough to say, 'my door is always open' if there is an unspoken fear of going through that door.

An understanding of 'who I am' (as a leader), what I stand for and believe in, what drives my behaviour, starts with a look in the rear-view mirror. The poet laureate Philip Larkin, famously, describes the impact of parents on their children as unintentionally messing them up in his poem *This Be The Verse*.

His may be a particularly negative view of parenting but it illustrates the point. We copy behaviours, we adopt values, we assume some things are right and others wrong – and this is a normal part of growing up. However, it is important as a leader to be conscious of the assumptions we hold, to ask ourselves what is driving our behaviour, 'Am I taking this action thoughtfully or am I just doing it because it is "what I do"?' It is no easy task to tease out these assumptions. They almost form our life philosophy, so are buried quite deep. Just as the fish does not realize it needs water until it has none, so we are sometimes unaware of our own assumptions about how the world works. For example, one person may see a company rule or regulation as something to be followed to maintain order and equity of treatment, another sees it as unnecessary bureaucracy, stifling initiative and clearly there to be ignored. These two interpretations are based on different assumptions about the nature of authority. We do not challenge or change these assumptions lightly, perhaps they have allowed us to be successful so far. However, as we move through our career and take increasing responsibilities so we may need to become more flexible, more adaptable in order to meet different conditions and different challenges. A step on this journey is to think in a structured way about the factors that influence our view of life (and therefore leadership) in both our past and our present.

The ability to be really 'present' is not as easy as it may at first appear. Being fully present means giving your undivided attention to what is happening in that moment. It enables more honest conversations to take place, it encourages more rigorous use of data and effective challenge to break through assumptions and hearsay, it means leaders establish meaningful connections (relationships) with others. The challenges to being present are the myriad of distractions assailing us from all sides: invasive multi-media communications, the challenge of the next meeting, random thoughts that pre-occupy us, always living in the future, to mention but a few.

And yet leaders have also to be focused on the future. They are responsible for the ongoing success of their organization; for growth, for change, for profitability. Anticipation and preparation are critical. Lewis Carol said in *Alice in Wonderland*, 'If you don't know where you are going, any road will get you there.' That is not an acceptable vision for most organizations: they should have a sense of purpose and therefore need direction. Anticipation and preparation are critical. Albert Einstein also put it well: 'Learn from yesterday, live for today, hope for tomorrow. The important thing is not to stop questioning.'

Case study

Scrolling through the pre-course information he had been sent for his forthcoming ALP at Ashridge, Ray's eyes alighted on the framework underpinning the programme: 'building on the past, attending to the present, an eye on the future'. He recalled the words of a consultant he had once worked with who had opined that the most effective leaders were those capable of working in three time frames at once: past, present and future. Ray had kind of dismissed it at the time but the statement was resonating now. In his role as salesforce manager, almost all of his time was spent dealing with day-to-day operational issues, 'crisis management'. He rarely had time to think longer term about the future direction and strategy for his department and reflecting on lessons from the past was even more seldom undertaken. As a consequence, he was often frustrated by the frequency with which he and others engaged unconsciously in 'wheel reinvention'. And then there were questions about what the future held for him personally, in terms of career and life beyond work, together with what had got him to where he was now. These were important questions he spent very little time reflecting on. The forthcoming five days did indeed present a valuable opportunity to begin to correct this imbalance and he was of a mind to give it a go. If he didn't address the imbalance now, when would he?

Exploring the past

Increasing self-awareness comes, at least in part, from being open to feedback, but this does not mean accepting every comment at face value. Feedback requires filtering and interpreting. Leaders can be swamped by feedback if there is too much, too often. It is important to be open, to look to understand what is being said, and, importantly, why it is being said – particularly if we find it challenging or annoying. But data should be considered as data, material from which we can draw conclusions and make decisions and choices. However, to ignore feedback is dangerous. It means we are only operating from our own perceptions, perhaps misjudging our impact or misinterpreting other people's behaviour. This tendency can easily develop if a leader has been successful over a period of time. As a consequence of being successful and making good decisions we may finish up with Hubris Syndrome (Owen, 2009), believing we are always right. We stop listening to others because we are always right. Being open to feedback is critical in understanding what that overplayed strength may be.

While facilitating an ALP group, Williams tells the story of a baby spitting out its first teaspoon of solid food, encouraging people not to do the same with feedback. Keep it in your mouth (head) for long enough to make sure you understand it, verify it and consider it seriously. Then you may spit it out. Giving feedback does not come easily or naturally to most people. If we want it, we have to look for it, ask for it and make it easy for people to deliver it. Do not assume it will happen, or at least do not assume people will give you the 'bad news': it is frankly much easier not to.

Case study

Susan re-read the statement attributed to her line manager in her AIMS[1] 360 feedback. According to his opinion she needed to be more effective at raising her profile across the company and increasing her impact on others within her network which she should also look to extending. It was towards the end of the first day of her ALP, a full day that had given her much to think about, and this statement, in the verbatim comments section of the report she had just received from the tutor, had certainly got her thinking. The AIMS feedback in general, from her manager, peers and direct reports was not bad, in fact she had been anticipating lower scores, particularly from her peers. But this statement from her manager did accord with his lower scoring in two areas within the 'making the most of people' section: 'managing reputation' and 'building networks'. She was not denying there was some substance to the feedback but it did raise some key questions for her; what exactly did he mean by the feedback and what could she do to address it? After dinner there was an activity that involved discussing the feedback in pairs, with a 'feedback buddy', and the following afternoon there was the first meeting with her Ashridge ALP coach, who will have read her AIMS report. These were two conversations, perhaps the first of a number, where she could seek the views of others on these key questions.

Our colleague Higgins (2009) has developed a diagnostic inventory to help participants surface their assumptions about the world. This is designed to encourage participants to be conscious of the choices they are making in their leadership style. If we do not reflect on our own actions, in terms of possible reactions and repercussions, we will frequently be surprised by what appears to be unreasonable or unanticipated consequence. Higgins' approach is based on a number of factors that shape our world-view from both an early age and throughout life. These include family, vocation, religion, culture, gender (sense of), self and (attachment to) concepts. Many people have not given a significant amount of thought to the

---

[1] AIMS stands for Ashridge Inventory of Management Skills and is a '360 degree' feedback tool inviting feedback from those all around the participant's work setting, i.e. their line manager, the peers they work alongside, and their direct reports.

question: 'Why do they lead the way they lead?' Often decisions are made on the basis of 'common sense' or 'it worked last time'. It is helpful, in our opinion, to be able to step back and look at a given context or situation with a critical eye and ask yourself what is the best thing to do here There are always options, the challenge is to select the best one with as much objectivity as possible, recognizing one's own assumptions and prejudices.

Learning from success and building on strengths is important. The school of positive psychology spearheaded by Peterson and Seligman (2004) in particular, encourages people to look at their strengths and see how they can best use them rather than focusing on weaknesses or failings (often described as 'pathologies' in traditional psychology). Supporting this philosophy, we encourage people to reflect on and share a moment from their past in which they feel they provided really good leadership. Some find it rather strange to engage in this kind of personal 'trumpet-blowing' but there is real value in articulating why you think you did a good job and have others help you 'unpick it' to understand what it was that you brought or did that contributed to the success. After doing this many people comment along the lines, 'Oh I didn't consider that' or 'Now I understand better.' This contributes not only to greater understanding but also building confidence. It also represents an opportunity to reflect on those leadership characteristics and strengths, deployed in that moment from the past, that could be leveraged when faced with future leadership challenges and choices.

Brittain and Van Velsor (1996) undertook a major research study for the Centre for Creative Leadership (CCL) as to why some leaders fail to live up to their perceived potential early in their careers. When presented with some of the data from the derailment studies it is helpful to reflect on what one's own potential 'derailers' might be. One of the key findings of the studies is about the overplayed strength: paraphrased, 'what got you to here will not get you there'. There is a risk that if the only tool we have is a hammer, every problem looks like a nail. This often causes participants to pause for thought about what they may be overdoing. Another key finding from the research highlights the need for constant adaptation, or even self re-invention, in order to keep a career on track within the ever-changing context within which we are leading. Changes in the work environment, both within the organization and outside, need to be constantly monitored and responded to.

Case study

Following the discussion on derailment, what the concept meant, the forms it could take and its potential causes, Andy mused on the questions for reflection he had been given. What had led to his success so far? What might he have to give up to get on? What new skills might he have to acquire? These were key questions to contemplate to keep his career on track and avoid the risk of derailment. Andy was a sales representative and his good work had been noticed by senior management. His boss encouraged him to apply for a Team Lead position in Sales, which he was selected for, and promoted to Local Sales Manager. The next logical step for Andy was to become Area Sales Manager. He reflected on what had got him noticed in the first place. For one thing he was a natural when it came to sales. He never found it difficult to build the right kind of relationship with customers (his boss frequently described him as a 'people person') and he had understood early on how to pitch effectively and put forward a compelling sales proposition. What's more he enjoyed the challenge of selling; closing the sale and meeting the stretching sales targets he was set. He also had the reputation of being an opinion former who was capable of being a positive influence among his sales colleagues. On becoming Team Lead he noticed he had less opportunity to sell, as he became more focused on the other aspects of the role, like dealing with customer problems and complaints and also keeping his team motivated and helping meet their development needs. With his next promotion to Local Sales Manager this trend became even more marked, with less time for sales and customers and more time for managing and leading others engaged in sales. What he was having to give up was the very activity that had attracted him to the company and that he had enjoyed so much in the early stages of his career. Any further promotion up the chain would create further distance and this need to further 'let go', a shift of mind-set that he will need to adjust to. In terms of new skills for a further move up the ladder, Andy was conscious of his need to further develop his strategic thinking ability. It was something he had been working on for quite a while in his current role but with a further move it would become even more critical. Also, he was aware of the importance of leading change within the company and the need to develop his skills in leading others through change; making the case for change, keeping motivation levels up and, where necessary, managing resistance to change. He had a lot to reflect on between now and the personal vision session on Thursday.

Living in the present

The ability to provide leadership 'in the moment' is critical to success. Leadership is not all about planning the future (although this is important), it is about connecting with the reality of a given situation as it emerges or develops. It is about taking the necessary action, having the right conversations in the moment and making sense, sometimes with others, of the options available and then choosing what to do. Leaders have to be adaptable – moving between apparent opposite stances and perhaps more importantly reconciling apparent opposites or taking different position on different aspects or elements in any given situation. The ability to tolerate ambiguity is critical. To know when to move to action and when to wait – or sometimes do both – act quickly on some things and wait on others. This ability to recognize and work with paradoxes is explored by Binney, Wilke and Williams (2012) in their book *Living Leadership*. They refer to seven Zones of Choice:

1. Understanding – Enquiring while knowing.
2. Direction – Acknowledging limits while imagining a better future.
3. Timing – Waiting and seeing while accelerating progress.
4. Relationships – Getting close while maintaining distance.
5. Loyalties – Putting your own needs first while serving the organization.
6. Authority – Letting go while keeping control.
7. Self-belief – Showing vulnerability while being strong.

In order to navigate these, and other, paradoxes leaders need to be both self-aware and adaptable. Low self-awareness may cause people to operate with insufficient exploration of the reality (realities) of a situation and to assume that what worked before will work again. Some leaders work in this way – they have one style or approach and use it all the time. We believe it is important to think more broadly. For example, take the dilemma 'should I accelerate progress here or slow down?'. Speed is of the essence in many situations and yet we are aware of projects in which millions of pounds have been wasted by leaping into action without sufficient thought and analysis being done in the early stages. Leaders need to know their own preferences and their levels of adaptability/flexibility.

Sometimes it is important to be able to do the apparently impossible: to operate at both ends of the scale or paradox at the same time. This might mean, for example, being imaginative and ambitious about a desired future state while investigating current reality openly and thoroughly. Leaders can develop their adaptability through experimentation. The challenge for leaders is to think clearly, particularly under pressure, which our colleague Neal comprehensively deals with in Section Two of this book. This requires leaders to test situations for clarity of logic, exploring assumptions, and seeing things from a variety of perspectives. It develops the connection between logic and passion, exploring the importance of emotion used to reinforce and support logic rather than clouding judgement. In her book *Focus: The Art of Clear Thinking*, Pearce (2014) encourages people to put themselves under pressure and to have to demonstrate that they continue to think clearly, exercise good judgement and present arguments that are convincing. The test is – is the other party convinced? Lessons can be drawn from the experience around staying focused, working facts, using passion not emotion and building a persuasive argument using the other party's interests.

Experiential learning creates the opportunity (and need) for people to think clearly and to 'live in the moment'. They are required to take the lead in a number of unfamiliar contexts. With little preparation time participants are required to build and share their understanding of the challenge, organize and motivate the other team members and respond to difficulties that are thrown at them along the way. This requires excellent communication skills, a good sense of organization, the ability to engage others and to 'live in the moment' dealing with issues as they emerge. The debriefing of these sessions often provides valuable insights into the assumptions people hold about the nature of leadership and their own adaptability. It prompts questions as to how they responded to the onset of leadership required in the moment Through this concept shared leadership is explored. Is leadership the sole responsibility of the nominated leader or does everybody carry responsibility for their personal leadership, thus contributing in various ways to the leadership of the group?

Looking to the future

A vital step in moving from the present to a desired future is the ability to lead change. Exploring personal change is an essential ingredient in moving towards fulfilling a vision someone has created for themselves. Time should be taken to ensure there is no 'disconnect' between someone's current reality and the beginning of their journey towards achieving their personal vision. Castles built on sand have a habit of collapsing.

It is also important to look at organizational change, i.e. how to bring other people with you in a change process. Individuals must explore their own personal assumptions about change: what motivates them to change, what scares them, what makes them cynical, i.e. their own interpretation of 'how change happens'. Returning to the theme of self-awareness, if leaders do not clarify for themselves the assumptions they hold about change they tend to assume that 'what works for me will work for others'. Almost inevitably this will be true: for some people. Change initiatives requiring teams of people to engage need to be designed to respect a range of reactions: some people are mostly inspired to change by the thought of new horizons and opportunities, the potential for growth. Others take a more pragmatic view and welcome change when it allows them to solve a problem, reduce frustration and eliminate wasted time and cost. Some see it as exciting, others as terrifying. In reality, everyone finds all of the aforementioned somewhat appealing but the relative strength of the draw is important. Leaders need to create messages and meaning that appeal to a range of different motivational sources – and recognize different definitions of success.

A realistic view of change is explored by examining the different moods and states of mind individuals experience at different stages in a change process: looking at the nature of energy in organizations and the sources of motivation and resistance. Change is a 'personal journey' and at different stages people feel a wide range of emotions; excited, afraid, lost, confused, angry, to mention but a few. Janssen's (1996) *The Four Rooms of Change* is a helpful framework that lays out an 'emotional journey of change' through time.

The framework attributes certain feelings and emotions to different rooms. People in change may well start their journey in the 'contentment room' where they are broadly unaware of any need for change and feel pretty positive about their situation. The next step is often to go into the 'denial room'. In this room people often recognize that a need for change has been identified but feel either that the overall need has been erroneously diagnosed and therefore the change is unnecessary or that they personally do not need to change and that any problems or difficulties are being caused by other people. In this room people may feel very strong emotions that range from anger to sadness. There is usually an underlying climate of fear. The third room on the journey is the 'confusion room'. The fundamental step that has been made by people to move from denial to confusion is a personal acceptance that they need to change in some way. Feelings are sometimes mixed in the confusion room: enthusiastic and optimistic about possibilities and opportunities balanced by anxiety about the ongoing uncertainty. The final room in the house is the 'renewal room' in which most people feel energized and enthusiastic about the new/changed context.

By using this framework leaders can prepare for and respond to their (sometimes strong) personal feelings in a change process and, importantly, prepare to empathize with how others feel – and to design actions that help others change.

Case study

Isabella was leading a major overhaul of her department in the insurance company where she worked in Rome. Mobilizing her team was proving a challenge. The session on leading change had provoked her to reflect that she might need to modify her approach to managing her team and maybe even look at her own attitude towards the change. She had been managing all her team members in the same way: emphasizing what was needed in the future – the goal that all should aspire to. Frankly, this approach was not working. Some of the longer serving members of her team were unpersuaded of the need for change. In fact, they were clearly of the view that if things were going well, why tinker? Others felt that the main problems facing the company lay at the doors of those in other departments. If her long serving team members were unconvinced about the need to let go of current ways of working how could she expect them to embrace new ways and the future goal?

Isabella was now aware that she needed to make a much stronger case with these team members of the need for change: a compelling case with robust benchmarked data that was more likely to get their attention. She also needed to be clearer about the consequences of not changing – for the company, the department and for individual team members. That meant being prepared to share some pretty tough messages. However, some of the younger, more recent joiners on her team faced a different challenge. She detected in them an acceptance of the need for change but some confusion – possibly about the goal itself or the means of getting there. They were working hard, coming up with a range of ideas (some of which were way off the mark) that they were following through to execution. However, Isabella was finding it hard to co-ordinate and align the different activities. She wondered if they found the goal too remote and unachievable. Could she break it down into a series of steps or milestones, with some relatively quick wins which could be celebrated? Then the realization hit. This too was the difficulty she faced, the goal seemed far removed from where she stood now. She decided to define a first step that was more attainable. She smiled as she recalled the expression coined by an American General 'When eating an elephant take one bite at a time' (Creighton Abrams, Chief of Staff US Army).

Although somewhat out of fashion, the need for vision is as important as ever. We believe people should be encouraged to reflect on their ambition – personally and professionally – to build a sense of what they want to do with their lives over the coming three to five years. From this they may consider the steps necessary to move towards their ambition: who is involved, what resources will they need, what obstacles they will encounter, what opportunities and threats may emerge along the way. The vision should be broad enough to tolerate change in circumstances and practical difficulties, and important enough to ensure motivation and momentum.

Some people may not actually know what they want to do with their lives or they may discover, somewhat uncomfortably, that there are aspects of their lives they are unhappy with. Others may see themselves as 'realists' not 'dreamers' and so find it hard to engage with this activity. Almost without exception people find this visioning process uplifting by the end if they stick with it.

Case study

Ted contemplated the challenge that lay ahead. Chris, the ALP tutor, had just finished introducing the personal leadership vision exercise and Ted knew that he was going to struggle with this. Chris had done a good job of introducing the topic of 'vision', highlighting the importance to both organizations and individuals of having a sense of what their desired future holds and how to realize it, together with what a valuable opportunity the ALP represented to reflect on the future in a way that is seldom easy day to day. But it felt to Ted that it was taking him way outside his comfort zone. By background he was a structural engineer, was in his mid-thirties, and was now Operations Manager with a team of Engineers for a small company based in his native Leeds that specialized in the conservation and restoration of listed buildings. Ted had been interested in the results of a psychometric inventory earlier in the week where he learned that he had a high need for control. He disliked situations that felt ambiguous and unpredictable. Reading the report he was struck by the fact that he needed relatively high degrees of structure within situations in order to perform at his best. He certainly felt the need for structure now. Chris had been clear. There was no one best way of approaching the crafting of a personal vision, there was no 'template', since that kind of prescription was too constraining. This was an exercise in creative thinking with an open mind: what were the things that were most important in their lives, their hopes and aspirations for the future? But Ted simply did not know how to get started. He resolved to approach Chris over the difficulty he was experiencing during the break.

The following morning Ted was with his Ashridge Coach for his second and final coaching session of the week. They began by viewing the film where Ted shared his personal vision with his support and challenge group. While they watched he felt a warm glow within. Unlike most in his group he chose to stand while sharing his vision and the animation with which he pointed to the various components of his vision around the picture he had drawn was testimony to the passion he felt. His follow up conversation with Chris the previous day had certainly paid dividends. With a few carefully chosen questions Chris had certainly got him thinking about those things that were most important in his life, both at work and outside – and with family and friends in particular. Prompting him to fast forward, Chris had enabled Ted to articulate the essence of the future he sought – a light bulb moment. In terms of his career, he had been at a crossroads. Should he go for a Board position, as his CEO was suggesting, or move to a different business? He had been uncertain about the impact of either both for him and his family. Suddenly he had felt the way ahead was clear, his heart was with the business – renovating old properties. He would discuss it with his family later that same day.

Conclusion

We believe effective leadership starts from the inside out. Understanding who you are and what drives you are the building blocks that enable you to connect well with others and demonstrate leadership in action. It is an ongoing project being a leader. People change, contexts change, the world changes: the desire to be curious and willing to explore are also essential ingredients. Perhaps most important of all is the desire to learn. Leading and learning are almost synonymous: the one cannot happen without the other. The practice of working with the past, the present and the future, at the same time, helps ensure reality and connection and effective leadership.

Case study

Taking a long last look at Ashridge House before getting into her car for the journey home Maria reflected on the questions she had arrived with. She had expected the ALP to be 'interesting' but with hindsight that was not the right word. Working throughout the week with the others in her table group (support and challenge group the tutors had called it) had culminated in a round of in-depth feedback on the last day. Each person received thirty minutes of feedback from others around the table focusing on what they should 'keep doing', 'do more of' and 'do less of'. For Maria, this had been one of the highpoints of the week. She valued the diversity within her group (gender, nationality, function, industry sector – both public and private) and yet was struck by the similarity of issues and challenges they faced. The feedback she had received had been relevant and insightful. She had wondered how difficult she might find the week and it had been challenging, even tough in places. Some exercises and activities had taken her way outside her comfort zone. The programme had been described as a safe environment in which to experiment and she felt she had benefitted as a result of taking the plunge on a number of occasions. The final action planning session had allowed her to focus on the critical actions she should take, drawing on what she had learned about herself as a leader. She felt able to consolidate her recent career progression and prepare for the future. Most importantly, she felt she had found some clarity about her leadership ambitions over the coming years.

Chapter 2

Pariahs: hubris, reputation and organizational crises

Matt Nixon

Introduction – reputation and trustworthiness

Leaders today face a perfect storm of pressures that will test them to their limits – and beyond – on reputation and trust. Their reactions to this storm could redefine what it means to inspire those we lead. Successful leaders will have to move beyond traditional models of charismatic leadership, and much of the rest of this book illustrates how we can address these challenges. This chapter focuses on six major features of the 'VUCA' environment that make leadership more challenging:

1. Decline of institutional trust and deference.
2. Globalization and sustainability.
3. Transparency.
4. Technology and democracy.
5. Celebrity, narcissism, rewards and isolation.
6. Physical limitations.

The *Panama Papers* data leak in 2016 revealed the existence of offshore accounts held by some of the world's richest and most secretive individuals and companies. The scandal illustrated most of the features noted above:

- The increasing lack of respect for those in positions of power and privilege meant that many expected the worst of 'important' people and assumed they lacked moral scruples.
- The scandal revealed the way legal and banking systems enable money to move easily around the world, and the consistency of the

techniques used by elites of many countries to manage their wealth and avoid tax.

- The shock of the sudden, unexpected transparency of these arrangements when the data was revealed demonstrated that established and legal practices can become rapidly untenable when under the microscope.
- The way that technology enabled the original massive data leak to occur in the first place, then to be exploited, analysed and discussed on social media and the immediate implications for any democratic politicians involved; at least one had to resign immediately.

Such shifts in the background conditions for power mesh – often unhappily – with some of the changing psychological pressures and impacts on the leaders themselves which are analysed here under two headings:

1. Many have noted our increasing cultural <u>focus on individualism and celebrity</u>, with associated risks of narcissism and isolation, all fuelled by reward systems and sometimes perverse incentives that were never originally designed for organizations of global scope and scale.
2. These pressures combine with leaders and workers operating at their <u>personal physical limits,</u> suffering from insufficient sleep, too much stimulation and data overload masquerading as 'always on' communication.

Together, these issues enable or exacerbate other drivers of hubris. Hubris is a word from ancient Greek meaning 'arrogant overconfidence', which we largely know through its appearance in tragedies in which heroes are laid low by the gods for their arrogance and lack of respect for the gods. Hubris can of course appear – falsely – to be highly inspirational before its inevitable nemesis, so it is worth learning to spot it as a false friend.

This chapter notes what we can conclude about the lessons for inspirational leadership that can transcend these risks without succumbing to hubris, combining the power of individual trust and confidence with the virtues of humility and purpose beyond self, themes which will be prevalent throughout this book.

The problem – trust, brands and leaders

Probably the most critical role a leader undertakes is to build and protect trust in his or her organization. One of the best ways to do this is to inspire trust in the leader as an individual; if your customers, shareholders, employees and peers do not trust you as a leader, it is inevitably harder to trust your organization and its brand(s). Leaders who pay close attention to the risks of trust failure can avoid some painful, expensive and damaging experiences for themselves and their organizations, and create more sustainable legacies into the bargain. Brands provide simple, memorable signals – even for the illiterate – of which products and companies can be trusted. It is axiomatic that if we cannot build trust in our product and organizational brands we cannot expect to command loyalty or repeat business, let alone premium pricing, from our customers. Successful brands fulfil the promises (explicit and implicit) that they make to customers, and this signalling has become even more important in a world where we are bombarded with images and information from the moment we wake up. At their best, brands simplify life, by reducing the work we have to do figuring out who or what to trust.

Despite all the work to build trust in product brands, trust in well-known organizations that once were trustworthy mainstays of our societies has weakened, particularly since the financial crash of 2008/9. The most recent data from the Edelman Trust Barometer (2016) shows improvements in trust in 2016 over 2015, but a deeper look at this data highlights a growing gap between the trust of 'informed publics' (a term that basically refers to the educated elite in societies) and the 'mass publics' who represent the rest of society. Increasingly, and across multiple countries, the Edelman data suggests societies are at risk of fracturing, as people in lower socio-economic groups often fail to see their situations improving:

- The majority of mass publics in 19 out of 28 countries do not think they and their families will be better off in five years' time.
- In 18 countries there were double digit differences in trust scores between high and low income respondents.
- In 15 countries there were double digit gaps between the informed and mass publics.

The widest gaps were in the US and UK, countries where income inequality is on the rise and a source of heated political debate. Business leaders (and by extension, leaders of other significant institutions) are becoming more like politicians, whom we expect to be visible to us and accountable to us, even if we do not get to vote for them or even own their stock. The role of businesses and their CEOs as trustworthy agents is therefore of increasing importance, and 80 per cent of the general public in the Edelman study want to see CEOs discussing societal issues and want to know what their personal views are on issues of public policy.

Perhaps that is understandable given our disappointment in politicians themselves. Back in 2014, the same annual Edelman study highlighted the disturbing reality that we trust business more than government. Although the scores for both business and government leaders are disturbingly poor, it is business leaders who have the edge when it comes to credibility on some big trust issues (see Table 2.1).

Some people suggest that this trust gap is rather illusory; we clearly often manage to separate our disgust and lack of trust for organizations and their leaders from our decisions to use their products and services – only in the most severe circumstances do we boycott them altogether. But we are quick to connect the dots between corporate behaviour, especially the behaviour of leaders, and the products and services those companies provide, and then act accordingly. For example, sales for almost all models of Volkswagen cars were negatively impacted globally (and especially in the USA) in Q4 2015 and Q1 2016 by the reputational impacts of the 'dieselgate' emissions software scandal. This is typical; a study by Freshfields (2012) indicated that behavioural crises damaged share prices more in the short term than any other kind of scandal (although operational crises have the biggest long-term impact). The

Table 2.1 Trust in Leaders, Edelman data (2014)

Trust to do the following:	Business leaders	Government leaders
Correct issues within industries that are experiencing problems	26%	15%
Make ethical and moral decisions	21%	15%
Tell you the truth, regardless of how complex or unpopular it is	20%	13%
Solve social or societal issues	19%	16%

Table 2.2 Impact of trust and distrust in companies on stakeholder behaviour

	From trusted companies	From distrusted companies
Chose to buy (trusted) vs Refused to buy (distrusted)	68%	48%
Recommended (trusted) vs Criticised (distrusted) companies	59%	42%
Shared positive opinions online (trusted) vs shared negative opinions (distrusted)	41%	26%
Bought shares (trusted) vs sold shares (distrusted)	18%	12%

Edelman data (2016) suggests that this is a widespread effect and that trust and distrust markedly impact customer behaviour: 68 per cent choose to buy products from companies they trust, while 48 per cent refuse to buy from those they distrust (see Table 2.2).

This gap between trusted and mistrusted organizations, and the perceptions of elites and masses, was echoed in my own research and practical experiences as an HR executive. There seems to be a substantial growth recently in reputational crises that, even if they do not threaten the existence of the organization directly, weaken and undermine its licence to operate in a significant way. Some might suggest this trend is an almost inevitable outcome of capitalism (see Poole, 2015). However, it seems to be affecting both private and public sectors alike, and well-intentioned charities, NGOs and new start-ups are far from immune. We should all be concerned at the cumulative impact of these crises and their impact on our mutual ability to trust each other. As leaders we should be working hard to avoid them and their toxic impact on trust in society. Inspirational leaders have to achieve visible presence and identification with organizational brand values, without encouraging a personality cult that places them in a position where they will not hear the signals that tell them all is not well with the very brand they project and protect.

Decline of institutional trust and deference

Trust in institutions generally has weakened; the social contract that encouraged and buttressed deference to authority took a massive battering over the second half of the twentieth century, and in the opening years of the new century the great crash and subsequent global economic slowdown undermined faith in the new, allegedly more meritocratic and democratic institutions that were supposed to replace those that went before. In the UK, faith in and deference to centuries-old institutions such as the monarchy, the Church of England, and even paternalistic capitalism is no longer a requirement of the aspiring middle classes eager for acceptance and preferment. The UK, like the US and other developed economies, has changed the social contract with employers in important ways:

- Job security and long term reward structures, such as defined benefit pension schemes, have been eroded or removed, as work goes wherever it is cheapest or most convenient to do it and rewards are re-designed to focus resources onto current employees, based on their current economic contribution rather than past loyalties.
- Union membership and power has been slashed, and the economic gains of a more flexible and free labour market have seemingly been achieved at the expense of considerable individual and collective security.
- New job creation in developed economies is now typically in small, often start-up organizations that may (and usually do) fail, or even if they survive, merge and re-form.
- Many jobs are part-time, often at or close to minimum wage, particularly for women, who often continue to have to balance paid work with key roles as parents and carers.
- Economies with less flexible labour laws may give some greater job security, but pay a price in higher levels of entrenched unemployment, particularly among the young, with consequent impacts on social stability.
- The more successful economies of the world attract migrants from distant countries, adding to social strains, most recently in Europe where an estimated million migrants entered the EU in 2015.
- Although a lucky few in these rich economies become personally wealthy in successful tech start-ups or as financiers, most young millennials are predicted to struggle to generate the standards of living considered normal by their parents.
- Even in the largest companies there is little stability as they constantly re-organize and change to deal with an unstable operating environment.

Mergers and acquisitions in particular, as well as some spectacular company failures, have meant few organizations have been able to deliver what many employees still want – secure and well paid employment.

As well as this economic background, anchored in an increasingly connected and competitive world (see 'Globalization and sustainability' below), there have been important societal changes too. Our assumptions, especially in the UK, about deference, particularly to authority figures such as the monarchy, have changed dramatically. Views and jokes that would have been borderline treasonous in the 1930s were merely risqué by the 1960s, and mainstream by the 2000s. Tastes change, and yesterday's scandals about, for example, swearing on television, look curiously dated. So we should not be surprised to see such shifts – but it is not inevitable that they only move in one direction. We should certainly not assume that because tastes change power has necessarily moved much; very few countries can convincingly argue that they have no Establishment (see Jones, 2015) or elite who control a disproportionate amount of wealth and power. There are good reasons why Edelman and indeed companies such as Shell look separately at the attitudes of elite groups who hold most of the power and make the key decisions. In the UK recent research confirms that a disproportionate number of senior jobs in political, legal and financial institutions are held by those who have attended the private schools and elite universities to which the richest have equally disproportionate access.

It is for electorates to decide if they want to see these changes continue or try to reverse them. But it seems obvious there is a disconnect between these facts of power focused in a privileged few and a popular demand to open up access on a fairer basis. It would be a foolish leader who ignores that gap and the role their own organization could play in changing things for the better. For example, when I worked at Barclays Bank we made choices as a business to recruit thousands of apprentices in well-structured programmes providing meaningful jobs for unemployed young people. We also invested in conventional 'social investment' programmes such as Life skills programmes for children to help them into employability. Both these approaches provided real benefits to the business as well as to its bruised reputation. Anyone who is serious about leadership needs to ground their view of the power they intend to wield within the contemporary power structures and practices of the countries in which they want to operate. Leaders are almost invariably seen by others – if not themselves – as part of the elite of their societies. But they usually employ – and sell to – the mass public, or are at least influenced via politicians or regulators who answer to such a public. In other words, leaders have to make hard choices. If they work in the largest and most powerful organizations they will discover they face deep challenges about whether to collude in the existing structures or to challenge them, to survive comfortably or be a maverick, to join the club or stay outside it.

Even within the cosy establishment, business leaders are rarely able to hide from difficult public positions. Senior leaders in the UK at the moment need to pick sides on topics as diverse as whether the UK should actually exit the EU, whether to build a third runway at Heathrow airport, whether and when to build on the green belt, and the wisdom of building a new nuclear power station to ensure security of energy supply. These are hardly trivial challenges, and as the Edelman data suggests, the attitudes of prominent leaders to these questions are of the greatest interest to their customers and other stakeholders. All this suggests that the background, education, character and political persuasions of leaders are going to be of increasing importance in creating diverse and healthy organizations that can not only gain power but manage it sustainably. Leaders who inspire lasting trust rather than shallow admiration will be those who can demonstrate that, even if they themselves are privileged, they understand how to open up to input from those who are different from them, and are prepared to defend their views on controversial topics.

Globalization and sustainability

No one doubts the significance of globalization as a force in modern leadership. Of course global trade is nothing new, but the global village predicted by Marshall McLuhan is now upon us. Most of us are more globally connected, both socially and professionally, than ever before. Although only about 3 per cent of the global population lives outside the country of birth, many more of us travel abroad, or have to work in international teams, often in different time zones. Domestic manufacture and even customer services have been outsourced to wherever it is cheapest and most convenient. Jobs move around the world with these decisions, and along with them go a cadre of global managers and leaders who have had to learn how to get things done in this new world, whether that be negotiating a Chinese manufacturing joint venture, drilling a gas well in Russia, or financing a complex derivative trade in New York.

Few of us work in worlds untouched by international mergers and acquisitions. Apart from some government work it is becoming increasingly rare for me to work with clients whose sole focus is on a single country or market. Indeed, modern trans-national business leaders often complain about governments' parochial level of interest. Politicians are answerable to their domestic electorates, not stateless owners or the needs of employees in other jurisdictions. Although widely predicted, globalization has had effects we could never have dreamed of, including a massive boost to brands that can transcend boundaries of language and culture – think of Apple, or Coca-Cola, or Shell, or Vodafone. But it is not just the ability to build massive brands and powerful companies that comes with globalization. External expectations of these companies mirror their massive scale, power and complexity. Most leaders in these organizations privately admit that meeting these often conflicting expectations is impossible, but usually cannot say so frankly for fear of the fallout.

There are few purely domestic scandals and news items any more. With this globalization of village gossip goes a new risk for leaders: violation of norms you never knew were there. In the past, organizations managing reputations in mono-cultural environments faced relatively stable sets of norms and cultural groupings in their home markets where conflicting needs could be managed via multiple connections. They became adept at managing customers, regulators, investors and suppliers in that context. But all that has changed. If your culturally appropriate advert offends people outside its intended target market, that can be a big issue for you. If you have an industrial accident causing environmental damage in a distant and inaccessible location, it will be headline news everywhere. Local views on everything from facilitation payments to child labour used to be managed locally and in a cultural context. Now policies are crafted centrally to be legally and ethically acceptable to a wide range of stakeholders, including what Fine (2001) usefully calls 'reputational entrepreneurs' who control what various constituencies will learn about what is happening. This opportunity to offend across geographic and cultural boundaries has increased with changes in technology, and in particular social media. Mirroring the growth of transnational organizations is that of transnational NGOs and protest movements.

Globalization, as well as bringing us closer together has – not accidentally – been contemporaneous with a growth in the centralization of power in large organizations, largely to enable speed and clarity in decision making. It has also coincided, less obviously, with organization designs that create fewer general managers below the CEO who need to make balanced judgements across the whole enterprise appropriate to one locale or external stakeholder group. More and more people in larger and larger organizations hence risk having delusions of their own importance, without the learning opportunities to bring them face to face with the real implications of their decisions, especially in the longer term. Globalization has therefore acted as an accelerant to factors that create both tremendous opportunities and massive risks for organizations that they need to understand equally well. Globalization enables power to operate differently, for money and people to move more freely, but also for people to feel controlled by organizations run from far away by people who may not understand them at all, let alone care about their best interests. This can be particularly acute where the activities of a global company appear to put sustainability of vulnerable populations at risk, as is the case in so much of the developing world.

Global companies try to manage these risks, but can become hubristic if they believe they have superior understanding of the world beyond the narrow boundaries of national regulation or governance. Such cleverness has rebounded badly on, for example:

- Royal Dutch Shell in the 2004 reserves crisis;
- Amazon, Google and others trying to optimise UK tax payments;
- numerous banks, including HSBC and UBS, providing services for internationally wealthy clients who turned out to be criminals.

Hand in hand with the globalization of world trade, media and technology has gone a growing consciousness of the serious strains growth is putting on the planet. Whether it is the stresses of climate change and water scarcity, the impact of resource extraction where supply is finite, or the destruction of ecosystems by an increasingly wealthy and polluting global population, organizations of any complexity and their leaders cannot ignore they now play a part and need to assert a point of view in a long term future that lies far beyond their direct control. The unintended consequences of your own firm's actions past and present, as well as those of others, are becoming of the greatest importance in managing trust and reputation. Sustainability claims have to go beyond 'greenwash' and become part of a meaningful narrative that works alongside your brand and its promises. The apparent skill with which some leaders such as Paul Polman at Unilever have achieved such a nuanced positioning in Fast Movement Consumer Goods (FMCG) makes him one of the most admired and inspiring leaders of our time, but he and his organization remain keenly aware how close they could be to crisis if their claims prove hollow or superficial.

The absence of a global government means bodies such as the UN, the G8, G20, World Economic Forum and international trade bodies start to take on transnational coordinating roles instead, mediating power across the world. It is not always recognized that global companies have to talk to someone beyond individual governments to establish meaningful rules and norms, and these bodies play important roles. However, they are not accountable to electorates, and can strengthen the appearance of secretive, even devious behaviour by leaders of the political and business elite as they congregate in Davos or at the latest Bilderberg Group meeting. In the past we either did not know about these meetings or accepted a degree of secrecy from attendees. But such assumptions are unsustainable given wider shifts on transparency; either such elite meetings will have to become more transparent (as they are doing, largely), or they and their participants will be tainted. However, if that transparency can demonstrate that the leaders we see are honourable, intelligent people capable of listening to each other and to their opponents, then they could turn out to be more inspirational than they can even imagine.

Transparency

Expectations on transparency have shifted massively in recent years, and leaders are having to react to these changes in real time. Increasingly, we expect to be able to see what is going on, everywhere, all the time, especially in a crisis. If we do not, conspiracy theories rapidly surface. It is almost as though the phrase 'that's none of your business' has become redundant, an unthinkable thought. The traditional secrecy of decisions made 'behind closed doors' may not be acceptable in the future. Equally, we are in the middle of fierce debates about how private data may be shared, whether with commercial entities or governments, and to what extent we get to choose. There is every sign that tomorrow's leaders need to be much bolder and braver about transparency. It is too easy to look shifty and untrustworthy by refusing openness, but we should not fall into the easy trap that confuses secrecy and deception.

The philosopher Onora O'Neill (2002) rightly pointed out in her Reith lectures on trust that 'Transparency certainly destroys secrecy: but it may not limit the deception and deliberate misinformation that undermine relations of trust.' This is a key distinction too often lost in public discourse, but all too real to modern leaders. Secrecy is often demanded as a legal requirement (we cannot share medical or employment records at will, for example), or as a commercial necessity (our negotiation strategy for a competitive bid is legitimately no one else's business). So transparency will not always be possible or warranted. Nevertheless, to earn the right to be secretive one must first perhaps demonstrate that one is not habitually deceptive. And leaders need to recognize that the publics who judge their behaviour may not recognize the distinction between justified secrecy and unjustified deception.

Although greater transparency may not be sufficient for trust, a new breed of more radical transparency may be required to save organizations with difficult reputations – I call them pariahs – from themselves. One of the most interesting of these companies is Google, because it both creates and suffers from technology-enabled transparency, and the new ethical and leadership challenges these create.

The arguments around Google and its role in the world are closely allied with political points of view around openness, transparency and secrecy. On the one hand, the benefits of transparency are considerable; if I share my travel data with Google, then others can benefit as I do in turn from accurate information and insights. But few of us are truly aware of quite what a Faustian bargain we are getting into. Do we really want a record of everywhere we have ever been, everything we have ever done, every picture ever taken of us, recorded and catalogued and stored for ever? How do we know such data is not being (or subsequently going to be) used against us?

Recently it has fallen to art to mirror back the problems of such a society; plays such as James Graham's *Privacy* or novels such as *The Circle* (Eggers, 2013) revel in the double edged nature of these challenges, and the conflicts they are creating between those who believe in radical transparency and those who want to retain notions of privacy outside of the public domain, and free from the risks of state control and interference. In Eggers' dystopia, *The Circle* is a tech company that wants everyone to belong to its privatized internet as the price of identity in society, in order to be taxed, or vote, or do just about anything. This is presented as part of the great project symbolized by the slogan: 'All that happens must be known.' Compare this exaggeration with the Google reality. Google's mission is stated on its website: 'Google's mission is to organize the world's information and make it universally accessible and useful.' With that mission, it is not clear where Google would choose to stop, or curtail its activities. Certainly such an ambitious (and potentially intrusive) goal leaves plenty of scope for 'evil' by some definitions, but does it inherently set Google on a collision course with philosophical and practical objectors? Is it inevitable that it must become a future established pariah, tiredly defending itself and managing political processes to give it freedom to operate?

It would be lazy to suggest that a play and the book cited are the same as measured, reasoned critiques of Google – they are works of art exploring the ideas and challenges of the new world we live in. But inspirational leaders will need to watch for forms of backlash against the excesses of the internet society and somehow remain on the side of the angels – perhaps as advocates of transparency yet able to protect the privacy of their employees' and customers' data. This is going to take some real political skill to get right. Google is inevitably going to be a prime focus for such opposition, and their leaders would have been well advised to explore the ethical issues involved before they suddenly had to deal with them in person. There is existential and philosophical/political opposition to the organizational, cultural and legal clashes about privacy and other topics, and alongside that Google will have to 'grow up' even further than it has already done. Tech companies cannot pretend to be innocent if they are really becoming important to our lives; along with great power does indeed go great responsibility.

But what are the lessons for our purposes? Certainly we learn that every time increased disclosure occurs, independently verified, we learn useful information about what is going on. Should not investors have the same option to know what is being done with their money, just as much as voters? Perhaps therefore there will be calls for more freedom of information rights over the private deliberations of companies. In a digital world, what is clear is that norms of privacy and secrecy are changing rapidly, and leaders are going to have to stay wide awake to keep ahead of developments. Inspirational leaders need clear values and principles to help them decide where to fight (as Apple CEO Tim Cook fought the FBI over hacking the IPhone of a deceased terrorist) and where to give in, and to explain their rationale as they do so.

Technology and democracy

Technology is perhaps the single most powerful force of all accelerating challenges for future leadership. It is going to do this in a variety of ways, some more predictable than others:

- Technology has always speeded up processes and replaced workers through automation.
- Technology has always enabled communication across time and space (printing, and later the telegraph and telephone transformed trade and opened up access to information centuries before the internet and mobile phones did the same for the developing world).
- Technology enabled both centralised control as well as democratic accountability and transparency through newspapers, radio and television many decades before Twitter.

So to some extent a good deal of the rhetoric around how different modern tech is lacks a sense of proportion and history. But it seems certain that the sheer pace at which new tech is changing whole industries, and the simultaneous shifts of mass behaviour and working patterns that are going with these shifts, are very significant indeed, and may indeed unleash social change on a par with the shifts brought on by the first Industrial Revolution in the nineteenth century as robots and Artificial Intelligence (AI) replace knowledge workers, cars become electric and driverless, and business processes continue to simplify and speed up. Where there are moments of political change and uprising, technology is potentially now a critical tool for change movements. The Arab Spring uprisings in 2010/11 sparked a chain reaction of protest and regime change across North Africa. The role of Facebook and Twitter in organising protests, spreading news outside the control of the regimes concerned, and enthusing fellow activists was an accelerant, if not a critical factor, in these movements. A survey conducted by the Dubai School of Government in 2011 found that between 32 per cent and 51 per cent of respondents felt that 'Social Media played a role in empowering me to influence change in my community/country', and nine out of ten Egyptians and Tunisians used Facebook to organize protests and disruptions. During the riots of 2011 in England, Twitter provided both protesters, looters, police and citizens with the most accurate picture of what was happening live in a fluid situation. So we can argue whether technological change is unprecedented, but it is certainly not something leaders can just ignore.

The challenge for leaders

Leaders will therefore have to pay attention to at least three spheres of technological change if they want to manage their reputations effectively. Firstly, they will need to be able to embrace the fact that well-executed tech can subvert existing industry incumbents surprisingly fast. Experts enjoy arguing whether Uber is really disruptive or not (Christensen et al., 2015), but there is no question that consumers love what it provides just as much as vested interest local taxi firms hate it for upsetting the status quo. Without the technology of the smartphone and the app, Uber would not have a business. As it is, it has grown to be worth potentially over $50bn, despite a number of controversies surrounding the business ethics, tactics and behaviour of

Uber and its executives. It remains to be seen whether Uber's arrogance will become fatal hubris, but there is no doubt it represents a new breed of tech-enabled, fast growth companies that are attractive to the young and ambitious. Leaders who can align disruptive tech with their own disruptive agendas stand to gain massive followership as others seek to see how they can ride the next wave (and perhaps get rich, or at least change the world, doing it).

Secondly, leaders will have to recognize the challenges and risks posed to even established businesses by hacking and data theft. The comprehensive hacking of Sony in 2015 by persons unknown (widely assumed to be North Koreans or perhaps even Chinese government hackers with political motives) was a wakeup call for executives. Not only were unreleased Sony movies made available online for free – a massive theft of valuable intellectual property – but also the firm suffered reputational embarrassment as frank emails about 'the talent' were shared globally. All the major firms I have worked with suffer such data breaches regularly, though they usually do not discuss them. In my own taxonomy of reputational crises, I treat data as a (currently novel, but soon to be well-understood) form of operational (vs behavioural or financial) crisis, but I agree with Freshfields, the law firm, who forecast that it will be the fastest growing area of crisis management for some time to come because the risks are insufficiently understood or defended against. The *Panama Papers* scandal and the Snowden Wikileaks further underline the power of stolen data to have profound political implications. Inspirational leaders will have to demonstrate clear moral principles with regard to intellectual capital ownership, and choose whether to respect the law when opportunities arise to gain advantage from competitor embarrassments.

Thirdly, leaders need to recognize that technology has changed the game on communication about the company. When it comes to reputation, we are in a world where increasingly we have the capability to gather data ourselves (think of pictures of terrorist incidents, dramatic weather or other news) and share our views on social media such as Twitter and Facebook or via messenger apps. News (true or not) can massively propagate in minutes or even seconds that would in the past have taken hours or days to report (see Freshfields, 2014 and Miller, 2016). Critically, and to the continued dismay of traditional journalists and governments, news is no longer owned and controlled just by the professionals in the newspapers, radio and television; the notion that a story can be spiked by a 'D notice' or a quiet drink with an editor is long gone. Expectations continue to shift:

- We now expect high quality, live video of what is going on, and apps such as Twitter Periscope allow us to deliver such feeds to the world.
- We expect polished spokespeople who can explain what is happening and why, especially from big organizations or governments, even though they may be just as hard pressed as we are to understand what is going on.
- We tend to digest our news faster and are impatient to get not just to the facts but the analysis of those facts and the allocation of responsibility and blame.

As we discussed above, organizations are collecting and using vast amounts of data about us, with as yet unexplored knock-on effects into privacy and reputation. Modern technology and social media certainly create new opportunities for the dissatisfied to air their grievances, even if there are no mechanisms to do so internally. For example, Shell's corporate lawyers have struggled for years to manage the stream of anti-Shell sentiment on the royaldutchshellplc.com website, much of it emanating from their own employees. Some people are worried that social networks have changed our interpersonal dynamics, and perhaps also our moral behaviour. A recent study (Mishna et al, 2015) in a Canadian school district found that 10.8 per cent of students report being victims of cyberbullying, with 2.8 per cent admitting to being perpetrators, while 24.4 per cent admit to observing such behaviour. It is becoming clearer and clearer that we are quicker to blame and bully companies and their leaders too. Ronson (2015) investigates this phenomenon by looking at the cases of a series of unfortunate people whose lives have been shattered by the reaction to their perceived missteps online. The last sentence of that book is one to think about: 'We are defining the boundaries of normality by tearing apart the people outside of it' (Ronson 2015: 269).

Ronson is not alone in having these worries. My colleagues at Demos, the think tank, are using Twitter's open API to track millions of voter comments and conversations as a way to try and predict voting intentions. Carl Miller, Research Director for the Centre for the Analysis of Social Media, Demos notes the importance of continuing to educate tech-savvy young people in online behaviour.

> Power is changing as hackers, tech geeks and mathematicians become the architects of our new social worlds. But alongside this, we also need a new concept: digital citizenship. Kids learning coding also need to learn how we actually treat people decently in online spaces, what our new responsibilities are, and how they should use these new skills in ways that are socially beneficial.
>
> Quoted in *Daily Mirror* newspaper, 23 March 2016

So we worry about whether children know how to behave online, and we need to consider how inspirational leaders behave too, including how they treat their customers online. Politics may provide some insights about the future. A recent *Economist* survey noted that politics adopts new online technologies almost as fast as the online porn and gambling industries. There are risks that the increasingly clever use of internet analysis and online polling may not – ironically – be good for democracy, as interest and focus surrounds only a minority of the potential electorate who are both active and open to being convinced. As we increasingly customise our news and other digital stimulus to our personal likes and dislikes, the danger will be that we cut off all sources of dissent, while politicians play only to their own electorates and ignore their obligations to wider masses. As the *Economist* puts it:

> When the internet first took off, the hope was that it would make the world a more democratic place. The fear now is that the avalanche of digital information might push things the other way.
>
> *Economist* Special Report, 2016

And yet, the internet gives us lofty expectations about democracy, because of the relative ease of access and participation compared to traditional activism. In particular, we have strong democratic expectations about our right to information and access. We don't accept deference any more to authority figures from the Establishment telling us not to worry, or that things are safe, or to vote for the party's chosen winner. We expect to take part in the crisis if we want to, as commentators, activists, and even as actors. And we think we can change the world by clicking to like opinions or online petitions

(Morozov, 2013). Meanwhile we worry about the balances of power that let the government read my email, and whether that is privacy worth giving up if it enables the state to prevent acts of terrorism. Edward Snowden has opened quite a can of worms, and few leaders of the future will be able to avoid the consequences of these debates.

What does all that mean for inspirational leaders of the future? They will have to remain as cognisant as ever about the possibility of new entrants and new technologies disrupting their industry and its assumptions about how business is done, costs, prices, and access to customers, suppliers and political power or influence. At the same time, they need to be mindful and on their guard about the risks to their own data and intellectual capital, which needs to be safeguarded in what amounts to a war of attrition with criminals and hackers. But the 21st-century challenges will come from the expectations of social engagement, both as an opportunity to connect directly with customers and clients, but also the chance to air points of view and sidestep conventional press relationships, yet with a new risk of instant shaming and judgement that could prove highly personal and damaging to leader and organization alike.

Getting the balance right between luddism and digital overload will not just be a challenge for the older generations; millennials face all the same risks, and may discover that their digital native status is no guarantee of success. Leaders will have to be wary of the pull towards narcissism or even demagoguery that new social media enables. Demagogues who opt for personal brands that keep things overly simple and echo and amplify only their audiences' more basic aspirations and fears will thrive for a while. But many will still be attracted to leaders of integrity and character, who can demonstrate independence from corruption and the capacity to engage with ordinary people. In the future, the best leaders will connect successfully with both the elite and the 'masses'.

Celebrity, narcissism, rewards and isolation

One of the most frequently discussed shifts in contemporary culture is the growth in pure 'celebrity' (that is, people famous for being famous) and attendant concerns that we are becoming more narcissistic and self-obsessed. In the United States, these concerns are nothing new, and commentators such as Jean Twenge have made careers from discussing the 'epidemic' of narcissism. In the UK too we see an increased set of worries that the broader celebrity culture, and the easy access we have to it via Twitter, newspapers, magazines and reality shows, is dragging down our sensibilities towards a facile, self-interested and childish set of norms which is unhealthy for us both individually and collectively. As Twenge and Campbell (2008) put it: 'Our social fabric will tear under the weight of egotism and incivility. The Chinese will eat our lunch economically as narcissistic American consumers spend themselves into permanent debt and entitled employees demand more money for less work.' Except, of course, the Chinese turn out to have been doing something rather similar.

Whether or not one accepts the claims about celebrity culture (often voiced in the same newspapers that encourage such a culture in the first place), we should be interested in the relationship between leaders, celebrity, narcissism and hubris. Both narcissism and hubris are words which are prone to challenges, even though they have quite widely understood everyday meanings that are likely adequate for our needs.

It is quite widely accepted now that major leadership roles are extraordinarily taxing, and that many (if not most) people's mental and physical health takes a battering under the stresses of life at the top. Books such as Owen's (2012) *Hubris Syndrome* or Ghaemi (2011) suggest that mental illness may be both common and, to some degree, even helpful for certain types of leadership in a crisis. Ghaemi in particular notes that the increased levels of realism, creativity, resilience and empathy seen in moderately mentally ill people may be helpful to dealing with crisis leadership conditions, whereas Owen suggests that hubris is a disease that should be in the psychology manuals, and that it is brought on by exposure to power. Both authors find stunningly high rates of illness in famous presidents and prime ministers (Owen 2011).

The nature of these powerful roles often attracts extreme personalities and those with psychiatric dispositions towards hubris. We should also note that Owen is not the only one to have diagnosed extensive narcissism in politicians. Hill and Youssey (1998), for example, noted that politicians outscored librarians, university professors and clergy in narcissism. Furnham (2010) reviews much of the key literature on the subject.

Senior leaders and Hubris

To those vulnerable to hubris, their existing tendencies to self-confidence (bolstered by being right a lot of the time), their high intelligence (which also often equates to being right before others have figured out the issue), their drive, their egotism and even outright narcissism, their need for praise, their manipulative natures, even their religious faiths may combine with what I call hubris-accelerating conditions (Nixon, 2016: 90). These conditions are more common in senior leadership roles than other roles in the organization, and hence may start to point our way towards not only what can trigger unhealthy and risky behaviour in our leaders but also some cures. In particular, in my work I have noted the following conditions (think of them as risk factors implicit in many senior roles):

1. *A need for frequent, rapid decisions* – present in all big jobs, tends to reinforce a frequent feedback loop that the leader is correct and has great judgement, and does not therefore need to listen to naysayers or doubters.
2. *Access to resources* – being able to mobilise resources enables leader whims and personal needs to be met without the difficulties or need for teamwork or compromise essential lower down the organization.
3. *Requirement to present oneself as a strong leader internally and externally* – reinforced by press and PR professionals, can result in something close to a personality cult with an unhealthy lack of challenge to the leader's view of their own success and righteousness. Even naturally self-effacing individuals are now driven down this route to 'personalise' the brand of their organization.
4. *Isolation for reasons of wealth and security* – leaders mix less and less over time with 'normal' people and start to live their lives in a bubble away from normal society and those who might challenge their world view. High rewards only increase this effect.

5. *Isolation by nature of the office* – the most senior roles have tough accountabilities but others manage access to them and their calendar to isolate them from diverse opinion, challenge or input.
6. *The glamour of power* – leaders can become enamoured of the trappings of high power jobs, especially if they are highly remunerated, and their personal hinterland of friendships lacks connection with 'normal' life in their society.

These conditions are hard to guard against, so we should be doing more to screen leaders for the personality traits that might make them prone to hubris when exposed to them. Sadly, we have all too often known leaders who suddenly lost humility on achieving a really big promotion. Inspirational leaders who can be of lasting impact will have to be more than Machiavellian psychopaths who manipulate their audiences; transparency will 'out' them all too fast. Some readers may be sceptical whether being prone to narcissism or hubris is really a new problem. It seems that the very ancient words we are using suggest otherwise. Perhaps this is a fair critique, but the counter-argument is that we have turned up the volume on all six of the hubris factors above in our current societies, and so we are going to see more leaders from all walks of life suffering from these problems. And on hubris in particular we should note that Athens in the fifth century BC was a society like ours that was struggling with how to contain individual power and manage a new, democratic world. Familiar concepts these may be, but the risks are increasing again.

We should also mention that the very high rewards now seen as normal for many senior leaders in the UK and US models may have a further multiplicative effect on hubris syndrome, particularly if these rewards lead to further social isolation in communities of the wealthy elite, and/or where the rewards are oriented towards the short term in large, complex organizations. This is not an argument for state intervention in high pay, but boards and others in positions of governance power need to recognize the challenges, particularly for longer-serving leaders; many believe extended periods in power are toxic to leaders, and there have been calls for term limits for CEOs to mirror those for politicians in senior roles.

What is certain is that we should be wary of all cultural tendencies that isolate senior leaders or encourage them towards excessive and immodest feelings of being special or different. They are just human beings, and they need people around them who can keep them realistic and grounded, and occasionally oppose them. Owen talks about what he calls 'toe holders'; figures who perform these roles for leaders. Perhaps boards and regulators should be asking who is holding the toes of all CEOs, and HR professionals (who can often be well placed to perform this role themselves) should document who is capable of challenging the CEO and other senior leaders, and factoring this into decisions about talent management and team selection.

There are four areas where executive and non-executive leadership need to focus to avoid creating the conditions that enable hubris and then crisis. These are the precursor conditions which – though potentially benign – together may allow a potentially hubristic leadership to develop:

1. Growth, although necessary in all organizations to some degree, must be questioned as an unalloyed good or goal, especially where the leadership, infrastructure or experience of the organization cannot keep pace with its financial growth. Additionally, we cannot all grow on all dimensions if we actually care about the planet we live on.
2. A powerful and well-known brand is potentially easier and quicker to build than ever before, but exposes the organization to profound embarrassment if its promises cannot be met by the products, services or people.
3. Success and praise are great to receive, and we are very much wired up as animals to enjoy them and to want more of them. But an adoring press or self-love in the form of excessively positive internal and external communications is often a half step from a state where important information that could cause a course correction is ignored or suppressed.
4. Finally, weak governance is more lethal than ever. It is surprising how often investigations into crises reveal that those whose job it was to watch over the executive have failed to do so effectively. Again, our human frailties and the need to preserve good social relationships can be at odds with asking the tough questions or insisting on a suitable level of detachment by boards or regulators.

Physical and mental limitations

The rapid pace of change noted so far contrasts with the speed at which we human beings are evolving. Leaders need to be reminded that however hard they try, they are unlikely to be able to perform physical and mental feats greater than those of leaders in centuries past. They are still essentially Mark 1 human beings.

We have not evolved nearly as far from the apes as we like to think we have. Indeed, one of the most intriguing questions about the human species is why our brains ever needed to get as big as they have. For some people that is a sign that we have not yet fully exploited the potential of our brains, but for others it is a sign that they mainly evolved the way they did to accommodate our tremendous need for social processing (Lieberman, 2013). Apes live in large family groups, and are keenly aware of their social status within the group. Being cast out from such a family group is often fatal, and is obviously not good for either mutual social support or the opportunity to pass on genes via procreation. As humans have evolved ever more sophisticated societies, our science suggests we still operate most comfortably in small groups of dozens of colleagues or family (Schultz et al., 2011), that we feel the social pain of exclusion or loss as we do physical pain of serious injury, and that our civilised, suit-wearing, book-reading behaviour is a relatively thin veneer on top of a thoroughly animal set of passions and drives. Any HR generalist will tell you that the animal needs for status management, expression of feelings and desire to mate continue to be at odds with the needs of most idealised workplaces, and therefore at the cause of many of their problems.

Although we have perhaps become more and more conscious of these similarities between ourselves and other animals on the planet in recent years, the similarity is of course nothing new. What is new is the amount of stress so many of us are putting on ourselves, the sheer physical and mental demands on the human brain and its ability to process data and information and make good judgements. We might argue that serious and important jobs have always been exhausting and have always therefore attracted exceptional people who felt they could rise to these challenges. No one could read the wartime diaries of senior commanders such as Field Marshal Lord Alanbrooke (Danchey, 2011) without realizing there have been times of far greater strain than most of us live in today. Reflecting on his own terse entries around the time of the Battle of Britain in 1940, when invasion seemed imminent, Alanbrooke confesses a sense of inadequacy and fear that many would recognize:

> The full knowledge of all that depended on my preparations for, and conduct of, the battle to repel the invasion, combined with the unpleasant realization as to the deficiencies in equipment and training in the forces at my disposal, made the prospect of the impending conflict a burden that was almost unbearable at times. Added to it all was the necessity to maintain outward confident appearance. There was not a soul to whom one could disclose one's inward anxieties without risking calamitous effects on lack of confidence, demoralization, doubts, and all those insidious workings which undermine the power of resistance.
>
> Danchey, 2011: 106

Similar feelings of being overwhelmed and exhausted punctuate the diaries and correspondence of leaders throughout history, including most cabinet ministers. And much further back, Plato in the *Republic* notes that 'weariness and sleep are the enemies of study' and therefore does not allow the young to even commence their serious education until the age of twenty (and by most scholars' calculations, Plato thinks you would need to be about fifty years old to take on the burdens of serious political leadership after a lifetime of preparation). So concerns about tiredness are nothing new, but recently we take on the complexity of the world while struggling with less and less sleep.

Ashridge colleagues have been at the forefront of connecting established medical, neuroscience and psychological studies on sleep deprivation with original research on the consequences for leaders and organizations. Culpin and Russell's (2016) work looked at the negative impacts of insufficient sleep on participants' social and emotional life, physical health and work performance. Their conclusions were worrying, and not least for senior leaders. At all levels of organization and across all age groups, sleep deprivation is an issue. On average, survey participants secured only 6 hours and 28 minutes of sleep per night, almost half an hour (or 7 per cent) less than the recommended minimum amount. In some industries we go to great lengths to enable workers to secure adequate rest before undertaking critical tasks such as flying planes or making key decisions. In other industries there are no such protections, and research, anecdote and experience alike suggest that things are getting worse, particularly with the rise of the smartphone and the 'always on' world of the internet and email.

Those who have worked in globalized companies know that the assumptions that used to prevail, and allowed a degree of relaxation and rest from intense working days, are becoming worn away in an increasingly insecure workforce that dare not even stop for a decent lunch break. The two weekend days of Saturday and Sunday are a cultural construct of the West that was largely created through the efforts of organized labour in the nineteenth century. Recent changes to legislation and work habits are beginning to seriously undermine these norms, and for those working in global companies, may not be held to in other parts of the world anyway (particularly the Middle East, where the weekend falls on different days). The same goes for national or religious holidays, which are often ignored by head offices or clients, who can be equally insensitive about 'good' times for conference calls or virtual meetings. Global travel plans for workers often start or finish on private or family time to ensure productivity is maximized, while even for domestic-focused employees the assumption in many organizations is that ambitious and successful workers and leaders will come in early and/or leave late to demonstrate their enthusiasm for continued employment. Even part time workers or those who 'work from home' or virtually are affected too; the need to be visible rapidly becomes a baseline expectation even for those who may have explicitly sought to avoid such office politics that may not be connected with meaningful productivity or useful work. Culpin and Russell suggest that, as well as the physical and mental performance price being paid for the sleep debt created lower in their organizations, senior leaders themselves are suffering in several key areas, including ability to adapt management style, ability to analyse information, formulate opinions, be mindful of their impact on others, make decisions and hold strategic conversations. Hardly what you would prescribe for a VUCA world!

Ashridge's Erik de Haan and Anthony Kasozi also note that modern leaders have many other pressures on them that are beyond human.

In a word, you have to be incredibly present to a great many people. You have to be erudite and action-oriented; reflective and initiating; flexible and warm in relationships and decisive in your stance. This means you have to embrace quite a few paradoxes and transcend as many contradictions. It appears superhuman, yet around the globe entire hierarchies of executives are engaged in precisely this tough yet flexible dance.

De Haan and Kasozi, 2014: 20

Many of us who work closely with the most senior leaders, in capacities which allow us to see them in action frequently and closely, recognize that these performance pressures are often unhealthy for the leaders concerned. Although a few people have incredible physical and mental capacities, as well as the personal drive and learning agility needed for success in the most complex roles, even they are often cowed by the sheer Catch-22 of a world which will require one thing of them one minute and castigate them for that same quality the next. De Haan and Kasozi note, as have others, that biology is not on our side when it comes to producing such capable yet humble superbeings on a reliable basis:

So undoubtedly we bring a lot less flexible, adaptive, learnable and malleable a person to the table than our 21st-century working environment is calling for. It would be no exaggeration to say that the main obstacle to meeting the challenges demanded by our present-day context is . . . us.

Ibid, page 10

To defend themselves against such unreasonable demands, leaders and workers find ways to cope, ways which, under the pressures of permanent sleep deprivation and limited feedback in which most of them live, often can become negative and destructive to themselves or others. At their worst, leaders succumb to hubris and start to become over-confident in their own decisions and righteousness, and contemptuous of those who would dare to oppose them. Soon, these leaders start only to hear the good news, as others either give up or are removed, and surround themselves with sycophants under the guise of loyalty. These cultures almost invariably succumb to crises that can destroy the organization and the leader alike, and it is essential that boards and others in positions of governance do more to defend against these negative outcomes by taking the risks of hubris as seriously as they would safety risks, compliance risks or the physical security of the organization's assets. There are two good reasons for worrying about the excessive focus on leaders as individual superstars in a VUCA world. Firstly, focusing on individual leadership when the systems they lead are so complex and can only be understood (if at all) by some sort of 'group mind' is clearly not sensible. Secondly, excessive focus on leaders as the source of answers and wisdom is disempowering and disrespectful to the rest of the workforce, who actually have valuable knowledge and understanding.

We therefore ought to be highly focused on ways to generate a wider and more diverse leadership capability for the future which will enable organizations to remove pressures on leaders that may have once been appropriate for those in charge of ships, industrial plants or even small companies, but are too risky for large multinationals or complex systems with mutual interdependencies. This will mean challenging some of the basic assumptions that have been in play for centuries. At the core of this new leadership must be a greater ability to enable leadership in diverse teams, and to downplay the natural tendency in hierarchies to place excessive and impossible demands on the leaders at the top, and to value and learn from local and focused experiences while holding an overall enterprise view.

Conclusion

As well as this list of areas for continued pressure, it seems clear from the above that the other area that will need more attention in the inspirational leadership of a VUCA world is the topic of diversity and, particularly, inclusion. The evidence is mounting that measurably more diverse companies perform better. What ought to concern us is that so few organizations can really mobilize the very challenging range of diverse experiences (not just of race or gender or sexual orientation, but of age, origin and life experience) that can, where led well, insulate them from groupthink and low quality decision making. It is quicker, cheaper and better to have the necessary debates in the boardroom than half way through a botched implementation that failed to understand critical stakeholder viewpoints. As the world becomes more complex, we might reasonably assume that this complexity can only be matched by putting in place leadership, governance and representation that starts to match that complexity without somehow causing all progress to grind to a halt.

Ultimately, leading in a world of more complexity while protecting personal and organizational reputation is going to be very challenging. Only by recognising the shifts in the external world and managing personal behaviours accordingly will leaders be able to inspire followers by avoiding the pitfalls of hubris and its toxic impact on trust. By embracing diverse inputs and learning humbly (Day and Power, 2009), the inspirational leader will not only find themselves being given more power by a variety of stakeholders, but also decrease the risks of crisis and failure of trust. Balancing that edge will require character, courage and challenge from above and below, as well as a continuing healthy scepticism about the leader's own uniqueness and value.

Those who succeed in this endeavour will indeed be inspirational, but one suspects they may be surprisingly unconventional and untraditional figures. Clement Attlee, the Prime Minister of arguably Britain's most radical reforming government of the twentieth century, was so unassuming and uncharismatic, so shunning of the press limelight, that he is said to have bumped into an old friend soon after he became Prime Minister; the friend, after sharing his own news, politely enquired in genuine ignorance, 'And what have you been up to?'. A story from a different age, but one is reminded that huge ego and a high profile is not a prerequisite for inspirational leadership.

Chapter 3

The hero is dead . . . long live the new hero

John Higgins, Megan Reitz and Colin Williams

The heroic leader has been with us for hundreds, if not thousands, of years. Sometimes in the guise of a warrior king and often in the form of myths and legends – archetypes that people turn to when they try to explain what a good or strong leader should be like. Yet we live in an age of reason, the Enlightenment tradition is one of the great achievements of Western thinking and should mean that the logic of leaders and leading would have won through by now. In this chapter we explore the unexpected persistence of the heroic ideal, despite all of our best efforts to dethrone this apparent hangover from our more instinctive past.

The strange persistence of heroic expectations

Over ten years ago Williams and his fellow authors of the highly successful *Living Leadership – A Practical Guide for Ordinary Heroes* (Binney et al., 2012) were coming to the conclusion that the heroic paradigm for leadership had run its course. In the company of many other respected workers in the field, such as Henry Mintzberg, they assumed that people would realize that modern organizations were far too complex, and the world far too unpredictable, for people to stay attached to the belief in the strong individual leader, capable of controlling the world and shaping an organization's performance through their individual will.

In 2014 the three authors of this chapter launched a major research study (Williams et al., 2014) to explore if and how leadership was changing and whether or not these assumptions about the impending death of heroism were true. We received over two hundred responses to a comprehensive attitudinal survey, which looked to find some data to answer the question we were frequently being asked, namely: Is leadership changing? We wanted to tease out the assumptions people actually held about the nature of control and responsibility (and not the assumptions we thought they should have). We wanted to understand who people saw as having responsibility for overall organizational performance. We wanted to get a sense of how people saw this developing over time from the perspectives of life as it used to be before the big recession of 2007/8, as it is now and as they imagined it would be five years into the future.

The results surprised us – this sample of middle and senior leaders from across all sectors revealed that the heroic model had most certainly not gone away. People absolutely expected their organizations to be led by people who had all the traditional attributes of heroic leadership, of being able to exercise strong judgement and execute well-informed strategies, but there was a modern twist to it. The modern heroic leader had to take on all this responsibility, while at the same time embracing a much more modest demeanour.

Heroic leadership has not gone away – but what counts as good heroism has. The leader is not ordinary, but they are expected to be modest, not to lose their sense of connection to the day-to-day. They have to be accessible and personable heroes, rather than distant and forbidding ones.

The paradoxes experienced by senior leaders

To hold a senior position in an organization is an invitation to lose personal perspective – to retain a sense of modesty and connection to others is in itself a heroic endeavour. One of Colin Williams' clients told him of the thrill of being invited to a Royal Wedding in his home country, of rubbing shoulders with all the great and good that made up the establishment of a significant world power. The temptation was to believe that the invitation to attend was attached to him as an individual, rather than his status as the CEO of a large multi-national domiciled in the country. This temptation to take personally the respect and deference, or fear and jealousy, that comes with a senior role can be overwhelming. A banker, whom Reitz and Higgins are currently working with, is transitioning out of a major and very high-profile global role, and is surprised by how much of his sense of self has become wrapped up in the role and the trappings that come with it – security guards used to know instantly who he was, receptionists stood up and would know immediately what room he needed to be in when the lift doors opened on the floor where the executive suites were. His guests would be treated with the highest regard and his standing in the social hierarchy of the banking world reinforced – whereas now his visitors wait with the motorbike delivery people, a public statement of his demotion from, as Robert Fuller (2004) puts it, a somebody to a nobody.

Over time it would be all but impossible for someone not to be seduced into a sense of their own importance. In the case of a senior military leader Higgins recently interviewed, he spoke of the battle he faced to retain a sense of his own ordinariness while being chauffeured around in his staff car, with people saluting as he passed by – they may have been saluting the pennant on the car's bonnet, but over time you can begin to believe that it is you they are saluting. The divide between the role and the person performing the role begins to dissolve and everybody can be tempted into becoming their own local version of Louis XIV, that famous French Sun King who declared that he was both King and State (*L'etat c'est moi*) as there was no difference between the two.

There is little to offset this with organizational systems and experiences shielding senior leaders, and those identified as stars in the making, from the experiences of those viewed as less important. It takes a super human, a real hero, not to begin to believe that they are the 'dollars' in a world filled with others who are the 'dimes', especially in a context where the 'dollars' that are paid to successful leaders are growing in leaps and bounds, compared to the remuneration packages of those around them. The novelist L.P. Hartley (1953) once observed, in his classic work *The Go-Between*, that the past is like a foreign country, they do things differently there – a sentiment that can be readily re-expressed to describe the life and work experiences of well rewarded leaders; being comparatively rich is like a foreign country, when you come across it people do (and know) things differently there.

To be a senior leader is to inhabit a different world to the vast majority of others, it gives a different set of experiences on which to base judgements and it creates a distance between them and most others. Over time it is very easy for the executive elite to mistake their seniority, which is an inevitable and vital function in an organizational hierarchy, as being about their general superiority as human beings, creating an all but unbridgeable disconnect between leaders and led, what Fuller (2004) identifies as the curse of rankism.

Those who are recognized as leaders, or leaders in waiting, really have their work cut out to be the modest and accessible human beings that our research told us people widely want them to be. Once you become senior people speak differently to you, there are rules that are followed when engaging with those who occupy positions of authority – as one of Reitz's clients experienced on his elevation from 'Managing Director in waiting' to actual Managing Director. His office, always buzzing with people popping in and out, felt energized and alive in his 'MD in waiting' days. He called Reitz two hours after the announcement that he was now the actual MD and told her: 'My office is empty!' Power creates distance and senior leaders have to work really, really hard to counter its effects. If they are not countered then the old heroic personality is all set to flourish, fuelled as it is by all the conventional trappings of success and the hubris (that inflated sense of personal pride) it all but inevitably fosters.

It is very rare, as one activist investor told us, to find established members of the corporate elite who purposively take steps to stay in touch with the experiences of the ordinary world, outside of their gilded bubble. An example of someone who does take such steps is the Chair of 'BigCo' – he travels around London by bus and has in his head every route that will help him get to his meetings and appointments. Embracing the importance of getting out of the executive world can be hard for some to take seriously, especially when their time is so valuable. In the case of 'BigCo', the CEO played the bus game whenever travelling with the Chairman but would have his chauffeur driven car parked round the corner to pick him up once he and the Chairman had finished their joint business. What the CEO may have seen as an affectation in the Chairman, the Chairman saw as an essential requirement of being a senior leader. Riding the buses was something he did to stop himself disappearing into a sealed world of privilege.

The activist investor, already mentioned, also saw the professional advisor industry being part of this world of chauffeurs and Personal Assistants, who actively maintain and reinforce a *cordon sanitaire* around the C-Suite, ensuring that they stay apart from the ordinary messiness of the day-to-day. This investor likes to know whether or not the leaders of the firms they invest in 'ride the subway' or not – to them it is material data about the leadership mind-set and culture.

To summarize – our research and anecdotal experience points to a world where leaders are still expected to take on gargantuan responsibilities and accountabilities, while at the same time maintaining a modesty of nature and approachability to all. These leaders, with their heroic responsibilities, are surrounded by behaviours, attitudes, organizational processes and advisers guaranteed to reinforce hierarchical distance and any meaningful sense of accessibility or approachability. It is sobering simply to read through the job descriptions of the senior leader posts that are publicly advertised: they speak to an extraordinary range of attributes rarely found in normal human beings. This is further documented by Fleming later in this book.

The changing nature of heroic leadership

One of the first things we have to accept is that the heroic is with us to stay. However much we may want to wish it away and stay true to the guiding light of reason, the desire to see someone as being in charge, of having responsibility for the whole, would appear to be an enduring feature of the culture of our organizational leadership. We seem to have a basic human need to see a human face representing the authority of an organization, rather than accepting that an organization is something that cannot be personalized, an insight supported by a recent article in the *Wall Street Journal* that showed people engage with organizations as if they were actual people, not abstract entities (Sapolsky, 2015). We may want to rationalize away this desire, but it is much more useful – we now believe – to work with this reality, whether or not we would like to classify it as a fantasy. Leadership resonates when it can be seen in terms of flesh and blood.

The challenge is how to work with this need for humanization, without creating a context in which the human face of leadership is achieved while creating leaders who are utterly disconnected from the ordinary. The old heroic view accepted this as inevitable – heroic leaders were indeed special people who needed to be seen as a breed apart. Much leadership development still actively fuels this sense of specialness by designing programmes that stratify an organization's leadership, rather than to see leadership as something to be understood within a wider social dynamic. If we accept the finding that our future heroes also need to be connected and accessible people, then we need organizations to find new ways of creating a collective understanding of what heroic leadership looks like in their context.

But much as we may wish to pursue this noble ambition, and many organizations are actively exploring how to create a more systemic approach to developing their leaders, many of the recent developments in technology and fashions in management are reinforcing the old model of the isolated and all-powerful heroic leader.

The forces at work that reinforce the old heroic model

Leaders have the capacity to know what is going on to ever-greater levels of detail – the potential for micro-management, or engaged connection, between tops, middles and bottoms (to borrow Oshry's (1986) terminology) can lead to the heroic leader taking on ever more responsibility and having the technology to be ever more present in the minds of people. Sales figures can be tracked in real time, organizational performance interrogated with bewildering detail and sophistication. For leaders there is the real potential to track results, and enforce standard business practice through IT-enabled business processes. The sphere of control has expanded dramatically, in line with the thinking of Zuboff (1988) in her seminal work *In the Age of the Smart Machine*, opening up opportunities for control and supervision unimaginable to leaders from only a generation ago.

The potential for demonstrable control is great and growing greater, creating a positive feedback loop and so reinforcing one of the core tenets of traditional heroic leadership. The tools for all but totalitarian levels of control are now available. At the same time the checks and balances on senior leaders are in practice notoriously light, as was discussed at the book launch of Ashridge's Erik de Haan and Anthony Kasozi (2014) work on *The Leadership Shadow*, most corporate leadership teams have more in common with medieval courts than any other power structure. Senior leaders operate in settings of great asymmetries of power, giving them huge licence compared to those under them. Combine this with technologies that have great potential for control and investigation and the modern organization can be seen as being a socio-technical setting ripe for old-fashioned, heroic command and control, a modern re-imagining of Jeremy Bentham's (2010) 'Panopticon' (all seeing) prison design. This was a carefully imagined proposition of the late eighteenth century, in which prisoners would be kept apart and invisible from each other, while always being in direct supervisory sight of the improving eyes of the warders and prison authorities.

The challenge for modern leaders is how to work with this capacity well; to hold the tension between having enough of a grasp of the detail of organizational performance, while at the same time ensuring they do not undermine the authority of other managers by setting up lines of communication and instruction that bypass them. And that is not the only tension the senior leader of the social media age has to hold; they have to be highly conscious of how their well-intentioned emails and personalized commentaries land on those they reach out to. When a relatively junior person receives a direct piece of feedback, or a suggestion, from a very senior other, who they have no personal knowledge of, that communication carries great weight – as one boss told us, he has to be very careful that his helpful suggestion does not get interpreted as an unchallengeable order. What is meant as wise counsel may be experienced as the long arm of the executive law.

Looking at this world with a psychological hat on, we can see how this type of setting could help evoke the feelings of dependency described by

Wilfred Bion (Symington and Symington, 1996), in which people feel in such awe of the great leader they become passively dependent on them – treating them as all but a god, a psychological invitation that you would need to be godlike to walk away from! Higgins (2009) describes just such a pattern of the 'leader as god' in his book *Images of Authority*, where he explored the experience of a communications consultant (who also happened to be a qualified Freudian psychoanalyst) in their dealings with an omnipotent senior leader during a major merger in the banking industry.

The story describes how people unconsciously use organizations to manage a sense of wellbeing, giving away to senior leaders what makes them feel bad. The challenge for this senior leader, as he oversaw the merger, was how to live with all these unconscious hopes and fantasies being pinned, or projected, onto him. A leader can act as a psychological lightning rod for people in an organization during times of high stress and anxiety. In the end the organization did well by him, as he surrendered any sense of independent identity, but after the merger mayhem subsided he was left feeling empty – no longer the centre of adulation of the group, and over time both his personal and professional life collapsed. Being an old-fashioned hero is not all sunshine and roses.

The forces at work that drive us towards a new heroic model

But the world never simply flows in one direction; there are always counter-currents, paradoxes and contradictions. As discussed by Nixon in Chapter 2, while the development of social media and the potential for internal policing has never been greater, so the potential for collaborative connection and creative exchange is also growing as never before. The positive potential of the senior executive being able to be in contact with anyone and everyone, is to be in touch with all the liveliest minds in the organization – to be a cheerleader for those who are willing to see things differently. Never have senior leaders been able to touch corporate culture so broadly and directly. Much as internal control may grow in its potential, organizations are of course much less in control than they ever have been in terms of how they are seen in the market and the wider world. People are no longer reliant on the internally generated truth of how things are in their sector and their organization's relative performance – people can find out for themselves what is going on, outside of the official lines of communication. Leaders throughout the organization can no longer control the corporate narrative in the way that they have been used to; they have to become active agents in creating the story of the organization.

The three authors of this chapter share an understanding of leadership as a distributed quality of organizational life, a relational process that takes place and gets its meaning and energy in specific encounters between people as they go about their work – independent of the organizational chart. This leads us to advocate the need for all leaders to engage in an adaptive and responsive fashion to the realities of what is actually in front of them (rather than what they believe is meant to be in front of them). Never has it been truer that the map of organizational life, in the form of plans and formal hierarchies or objectives, is very different from the territory of what makes organizations actually tick (with apologies to Alfred Korzybski (2003)).

Leaders at all levels have to be out there in the workplace, in conversation, negotiating the meaning that people are making of their organizational experience – which is why so much attention is now being paid to the idea of conversational leadership, which Reitz (2015) explored in her doctoral thesis and her latest book *Dialogue in Organisations; Developing Relational Leadership*. At the same time there is the shift in Western economies to a much greater emphasis on knowledge workers – where their contribution exists within their heads and much less so in terms of their visible, behavioural contribution. Many of the mechanisms that reinforce the old controlling model of heroic leadership come from an era of clerical or visible work – they are good at monitoring the quantity of work, but very poor at saying anything sensible about its quality. The current organizational measurement paradigm has more in common with the dying days of the Soviet system, where its lorry manufacturers would create deliberately heavy lorries that would help them readily meet their tonnage-based output targets. The old hero paradigm draws people to measure what can be measured, rather than noticing and paying attention to the subtle characteristics of people's internal state and the qualities of their work.

One of the tensions at the heart of the co-existence of the new and old hero paradigms is an attraction to the mantra of 'what gets measured gets managed', which co-exists with the emerging observation that 'what cannot be measured still happens – and determines the quality of what happens'. We can redeploy the assessment of one of the fathers of Total Quality Management, W.E. Demming, who was known to observe that if you want to explain why people behave the way they do in an organization, go and look at how performance is rewarded. Within organizations many performance reward systems encourage old-fashioned, individualistic heroic leadership – with a fixation on individual performance and reward, which is of course anathema to the Total Quality Management movement, and indeed to organizational leadership that seeks to include the many, rather than the few.

How we talk about leaders, leading and leadership tells us a lot

There are many different frames of reference in common use when people talk about leaders, leading and leadership – and they point us towards very different types of heroism, all of which co-exist at the moment and have the potential to contradict each other.

Heroic Leadership (the thing)

One of the most established ways of talking about leading is to talk about a thing called 'Leadership'. When people see leading and leaders in this light they tend to focus on a disembodied set of virtues, such as authenticity, honesty or directness.

The heroic leader is a vessel for disembodied goals and lacks any active connection to the social processes within which their leadership takes place. For such a leader, engagement with the messiness and complexities of the day-to-day becomes problematic – and so they can be found to operate through a series of abstract mantras, which people often find difficult to connect to the realities of their actual working context. If this abstract conception, of leadership the thing, takes hold and then combines with dominant cultural assumptions such as US universalism (Trompenaars and Hampden-Turner, 1993), you have the recipe for much of what passes for good leadership practice in organizations, the application of universal truths. These find expression in such organizational processes as standardized competency models, mandated values statements and talent management via a one-size-fits-all template – fine for a predictable and homogeneous world, less so for one that is a heterogeneous permanent work-in-progress.

This desire for universal truth, and the sense of certainty it brings, can be very compelling. For some it locates leaders and their leadership within a moral framework of great truth, but as with any upholders of great truths this creates a distance between its standard bearers and its followers. The hero is a virtuous hero, but not one who is likely to meet the needs of connection and social presence. Moses represented a rather distant and forbidding figure when he came down from the mountain with the tablets containing the Ten Commandments in his arms.

The Heroic Leader (the role)

The use of the term standard bearers and followers takes us into a second form of the heroic leader – with a focus on roles, especially those of leader and follower. The abstraction in this case is the removal, or diminishment, of individual presence and the importance given to the job description of the leader and the job descriptions of those around them. The focus on role frames heroes in terms of the tasks they are responsible for, and the way in which they need to work through the instrument of those around them to achieve these tasks.

As a form of engagement with others it fits within Buber's (1958) I-It form of relating, where leaders and followers are encouraged to see each other as transactional objects, interested only in what each can do for the other. Heroism is an economic activity devoid of personal consideration, a state of mind ideally suited to a world defined in terms of shareholder value and mandated targets in constant flux – where there is no time to build meaningful, long term relationships. In this context the world becomes full of abstract heroes, who will not be able to meet the needs of those who wish for a more connected and human form of leader–follower exchange.

Heroic Leading (as relationship)

A third way of understanding the different contexts for the heroic focuses attention on processes of human relating and connecting, drawing heavily on the thinking of the dialogue movement – popularized in organizational circles in the work of Isaacs (1999) and more recently by Groysberg and Slind (2012). Isaacs is particularly influenced by Buber's alternative frame to I-It relating, a form of human connection he calls I-Thou relating. This form of relationship sees people turn towards each other with the intention of being in touch with the other as a fellow, living human being, not as a thing to be manipulated or used instrumentally. These are relationships where people see each other as part of a shared community of humanity first, rather than through the restrictive lens of an organizational title.

At this moment of connection, labels such as leader and follower melt away and in the moment people both see, and feel seen, in a way that the old language of roles and leadership cannot describe. This is the new heroism, where leaders and followers are drawn to be present with each other and know the world differently, even if it is only for that moment, before the labels reassert themselves.

Some conclusions and pointers to the emerging future for heroic leaders

First up, the expectation of heroism has not gone away and does not look like it has any intention of going anytime soon. The heroic would appear to be something we might like to rationalize away, but to apply reason would seem to miss something at the heart of the human psyche. We would appear to be hero-seeking (or hero-needing) by nature. But even if we are at heart hero-seeking/hero-needing entities, how the heroic gets expressed is not a constant. We appear to be living in a time of flux in which the distant, abstract and ideal hero – the remote father figure – is being replaced, or rather supplemented, by a much more connected, human and accessible hero figure.

In making sense of this reality we have realized that different, even contradictory, definitions of what it is to be heroic co-exist in the organizations we encounter. Some people continue to hanker after the classical archetypes of leaders as Warrior, Parent and Rescuer – while also expecting these archetypes to co-exist with a world of collaborative adult-to-adult, human scaled connection. These various and conflicting definitions vary according to the extent to which people see leaders in terms of being a collection of abstract virtues, a role within a portfolio of roles, a practice within a set of organizational practices and/or people capable of being in profound mutual connection.

These different experiences and expectations have come about through the shifting socio-technical context within which leaders, leadership roles and inter-personal relating take place. What is striking about the shifts in this context, in the last ten years or so, is how much they make possible a great and growing degree of directive control *and* at the same time a previously unimaginable potential for collaborative connection.

People who occupy positions of authority, and people who are part of the social setting within which that authority is exercised, have more choice than ever before in terms of creating leaders, leadership and personal relationships. To be a leader in the future requires a much greater degree of mindfulness, a capacity to step back and see how taken-for-granted socialized assumptions are present. These unconscious norms are frequently disconnected from robust contact with the world as it is in the here and now.

When the world is in flux, simply trusting what has worked before is not enough because there are no simple accepted ways to fall back on. Every organization has to engage in a continuous creative process in which the practice of power and authority is negotiated and renegotiated – while working with the reality of our need for heroes, ancient and modern, who we also want to connect with at a human scale.

Putting the human experience centre stage

Why being a leader is always personal

Chapter 4

Understanding why the authentic leader leads better

Roger Delves

Introducing the terminology

Authenticity and authentic leadership are increasingly heard and used terms to describe the type of leaders and leadership required in today's ever more fraught, complex and ambiguous business landscape. Like many another phrase, authenticity or authentic leadership has expanded in meaning to embrace a number of related concepts and ideas. According to Howell and Avolio (1992) we should only consider as authentic those leaders who are concerned for the common good. Bass and Steidlmeier (1999) suggest that the personal virtue and moral wisdom of authentic leaders is what helps them avoid the pitfalls associated with power accumulation and self-aggrandisement. Hartner et al (2002) require thoughts and feelings to be consistent with actions if the leader is to be considered authentic, and that one acts in accordance with one's true self. This presupposes that one's true self is aligned with a worthy set of values, so perhaps more useful is the definition offered by Michie and Gooty (2005) that the authentic leader is driven by high-end, other-regarding values. Luthans and Avolio (2003) require authentic leaders to be transparent about their intentions and maintain a seamless link between espoused values, behaviours and actions. For them, authentic leaders need the moral capacity to make selfless judgements.

What is consistent across the academic literature is both that the bar for authentic leadership is set high and that the majority of leaders are not reaching that bar. The evidence, touched on later in this chapter, is all around us in depressing detail. Leaders or nascent leaders have a personal responsibility to explore the challenges of leading with authenticity and the difficulties and pitfalls of leading without it. There is a further requirement to decide whether their own sense of authenticity needs deeper examination and to explore tools and techniques which might help them so to do. This chapter will probe aspects of what may be lacking in leaders and managers who have no ready access to enough authenticity to resist the day-to-day temptations of the workplace. It will examine what such individuals can do to help provide better defences against those temptations – such as the pursuit of personal power, wealth, gratification or other reward – and suggest that authentic leadership, challenging as it is, is a better alternative than the current popular model of broadly self-interested leadership.

The challenge for leaders

Leaders do not do enough to examine their approach to integrity in decision making (to balance the objectivity of principles with the subjectivity of values, to examine their values and decide which are core and which peripheral, which are self-directed and which other-directed) to understand authenticity and its importance in building trust and confidence amongst others. This is important not just for the leaders and their sense of an ethical self, but because followers require a degree of predictable integrity from leaders. They need to feel that their leaders can be relied upon to choose a response to any given situation which is within certain bounds, and which at minimum is predominantly other-directed rather than self-regarding. If this reassurance is not present, team members find it hard to trust leaders or to believe that the leader's decisions or choices are going to be appropriate. This predictable integrity is most likely to be missing when leaders are relying on peripheral or unexamined values, have poor values and/or have no ready understanding of concepts such as universal principles, ethical decision making or integrity. In short, when integrity is lacking, the perverse imperative of temptation is hard to resist.

The pressures facing leaders, at every level within organizations, are increasing and will continue to do so. Whether you lead Volkswagen and find yourself in a hole of sizeable proportions dug by the organization's own management, or you lead a British steel producer and find yourself at the mercy of decisions made in India or China, or you lead one of the many SMEs which make up over 60 per cent of organizations which operate in the UK, and you are struggling with the ramifications of the Brexit decision in 2016, leadership outside times of outright war has probably never been tougher. As Hannah, Avolio and Walumba (2011) point out, modern organizations have been characterized as morally complex environments that impose significant ethical demands and challenges on organizational actors. High levels of character are needed to promote and maintain ethical behaviour. Often leaders feel they inhabit a world where they are judged solely by results; how they achieve those results is entirely situational. With no ready access to a set of values in which they believe, too many feel they have no option but to embrace the 'ends justify means' philosophy which powers results-driven cultures. This undermines any impetus to act with moral purpose, or integrity.

Leading through ambiguity, uncertainty and constant change is a necessary skill for every leader today. We can see stark evidence of what happens to leaders in this challenging environment who do not have access to integrity when it matters: the governmental bail outs of RBS saved an entire banking sector from failure, yet many of these same banks are now implicated in a rate-fixing scandal, while elsewhere hugely inflated senior executive remuneration packages suggest a disconnect between the moral reality of senior management and that of everyday life, while cover-ups in our own national broadcasting corporation as well as within the broader entertainment industry show an endemic failure of management leaders to provide programme-making staff and celebrity talent with a suitable set of standards within which to work. Phone hacking brought a number of journalists to court in what was seen as a massive betrayal of trust, whilst elsewhere 2016 saw the long awaited publication of the Chilcot Enquiry and a damning verdict on the actions and decisions around the Iraq War of former Prime Minister Tony Blair, a man and an office in whom and in which we all placed trust.

As discussed by Nixon in Chapter 2, the biggest ever leak of confidential documents, eleven and a half million separate documents leaked from Panamanian offshore agents Mossack Fonseca, and colloquially referred to as *The Panama Papers*, in just five days led to the fall of the Icelandic prime minister, the embarrassment of the British prime minister, calls for the resignation of the Russian president and the revelation that Mossack Fonseca themselves were complicit in laundering cash from Britain's biggest gold bullion robbery: the Brinks-Mat raid. In addition to the scandals already engulfing it, FIFA found its new president, elected to replace the disgraced Sepp Blatter, caught up in suggestions of corrupt wrongdoing. The children of the serving Pakistani prime minister were named in leaked documents, as were close colleagues of Robert Mugabe, in each case using offshore companies to avoid tax.

Behaviour of such stark inauthenticity is not uncommon, even if usually played out on a smaller stage and less scrutinized *post facto*. It seems that what prevents the organizational actors acting with moral purpose or integrity is a lack of moral courage – what Kidder (2005) defines as a 'commitment' to moral principles, an 'awareness' of the danger involved in supporting these principles, and a 'willingness' to endure these dangers. Increasingly, as formal investigations are made into business and social scandals, what transpires is not that nobody knew, but that nobody who knew had the courage to speak out. It is not generally a lack of understanding right from wrong which holds us back, but a lack of courage to act on what we understand. There is no reason to believe that what plays out on the larger stage of the public scandals does not play out on a daily basis on the smaller organizational stages of businesses across the country, the region, the world – we may not know Sepp Blatter, Robert Mugabe, Vladimir Putin and their fellow travellers, but we know them writ small, in the offices and corridors of organizations the world over, doing the same thing on a lesser scale. What holds such people back is lack of opportunity, not lack of intent.

Linking emotional intelligence and authenticity

If then authenticity and authentic leadership is the sum of many parts – integrity, virtue, wisdom, underpinned by courage and principles, values-led – then self-evidently many of these constituent parts are informed by self-awareness, one of the four central tenets of the theory of Emotional Intelligence (EI). The point has long been powerfully made (Goleman et al., 2003) that emotional intelligence is a better differentiator than is IQ of great leaders from the merely adequate. The compelling point in this argument is that intellectual capability, knowledge and even technical ability are, as leadership qualities, threshold. In an increasingly competitive and educated leadership market, these factors are not differentiators but hygiene factors. IQ offers little to no competitive advantage and Goleman's argument, that the differentiating factor in leadership success is emotional success, is compelling.

Businesses spend time, effort and money attempting to identify as best they can those who are most likely to succeed, most likely to meet the expectations held of them by employers paying them considerable sums of money to contribute to the goals of the corporation. Often all under consideration are intellectually capable – some extremely so. But over time and frequent exposure to them, evaluators with experience will find that those most likely to succeed catch the eye not because they are brighter than the others, but because they are more articulate, or more persuasive, better able to influence, or better able to control themselves under pressure – in short they manifest many of the skills of the emotionally intelligent individual: self-awareness, self-management, social awareness and the ability to manage relationships. These are the leaders who show the beginnings of an authentic leadership style – a sustainable, supportable approach to leadership grounded in something solid and valuable to followers.

Goleman also noted that some very intelligent people 'walk blindly through the realms of human emotion and interaction, stumbling along a path of reason without sensitivity'. This is something else that can be regularly noted among aspiring professionals. The right thing, said in the wrong way, is frequently either unheard or misinterpreted. From the mouth of a leader, the right thought, insensitively offered, is worse than silence because it can demotivate not just an individual but an entire team. Leaders are exquisitely observed by others – by team members, by members of other teams, by peers, by senior management. They are discussed – indeed dissected – in endless post mortems of incidents long past. Every utterance can be freighted with significance.

So the thoughtless word, the insensitive remark, the obvious left unsaid or the bizarre thought aired can and will come back to haunt them, undermining their authenticity by divorcing their behaviours from their espoused values. Maybe there will not be criticism to their face, but criticism there will certainly be, in the endless conversations about them held in their absence. Here the emerging caricatures of their true selves become the way in which they are recognized within the organization. These sometimes grotesque misrepresentations are sketched, acknowledged and then established not as an exaggerated version of reality but as truth incarnate. None who are leaders want to become their own caricatures, so each must learn to season reason with sensitivity.

Being sensitive to others is, in EI terms, about social responsibility or awareness of others. Social responsibility is an important construct that aids perceptions of an individual's authenticity. It has to be owned somewhere within the team, and the obvious home for social responsibility is with the leader. It is not the only source, but it is probably the primary source, and if leaders lack social responsibility it is difficult for the rest of the team to fill that gap. This talks to the leader's primary or overt responsibility within a team, which is to make decisions. To be socially responsible is to be other-regarding, and to be other-regarding is a central element of authenticity.

Increasingly, social responsibility means understanding and taking responsibility for attitudes towards diversity within a team. Diversity is irreducibly associated with the 'isms': ageism, racism, faithism, sexism. The true embracing of diversity of course involves much more, including not just understanding others' rights to be different but welcoming those differences and using them to make the whole greater than the sum. The degree of social responsibility and the resultant attitudes towards diversity which a leader has will hugely affect that leader's decision making approach and ability. Imagine, for example, a leader who, for unconscious reasons of which she is naturally unaware, or for conscious reasons which she cannot seem to challenge or change, cannot place genuine trust in young people. In many industries or many teams this particular 'ism' would represent a dead hand on the wheel of progress and would significantly limit the team. This leader's decisions, coloured by her attitude to a certain group of individuals (in this case, young people) will inhibit progress. Her attitude would undermine her apparent authenticity, because she would demonstrably not be other-regarding, nor would she be acting in line with high-end values, or making selfless judgements. The high bar of authenticity does not allow for overt prejudice.

The value (and danger) of moral particularity

We have established then that leaders think, consider and then make decisions. We know that these decisions, if they are to be authentic, cannot be self-interested but must be for some collective good. So, how leaders think, what they choose to consider and what criteria they use in making decisions will inform every aspect of the organization's success, or otherwise, in its endeavours. MacIntyre is a Scottish philosopher whose book, *After Virtue* (1981) is a long established modern classic of moral and political philosophy. He is well travelled, Emeritus Professor of Philosophy at the University of Notre Dame, and a past professor at Brandeis, Duke, Boston and Vanderbilt. He points out that what the leader brings to this decision making process is very particular: 'I am someone's son or daughter, someone else's cousin or uncle. I am a citizen of this or that city, a member of this or that guild or profession; I belong to this tribe, that clan, this nation. I inherit from my family, my city, my tribe, my nation, a variety of debts, rightful expectations and obligations. These constitute the given of my life, my moral starting point. This is in part what gives my life its own moral particularity.'

Moral particularity can be both a barrier and a conduit to authenticity. It can be a conduit if those things which give my life its own moral particularity, my own particular inheritances, encourage me to require my actions to be consistent with my thoughts and feelings, or require me to be guided by explicit and conscious values that enable me to operate at higher levels of moral integrity or with the necessary moral courage to do the right thing. Examples would be inheritances around faith-based principles or around values, a strong sense of right and wrong. But of course this may not be what I inherit and what I have not been able or willing to put aside. I may carry a set of prejudicial beliefs which distort values and make me, perhaps, intrinsically self-interested, less well equipped to deal with the ethical challenges of the workplace, less able to meet targets or goals without compromising values. Or indeed my entirely well-meaning faith-based principles or my personal values, strongly flavoured by the culture which nurtured me, may cause me to be a divisive influence within a team.

In an increasingly global business world, the moral particularity which exists in any given meeting room will be hugely varied. Part of the social responsibility of the leader may well be to persuade team members to lay aside that moral particularity. On the face of it, this is a difficult, if not insensitive thing to ask. But imagine attempting as a leader to try to find common ground between assertive, determined individuals from markedly different cultural backgrounds – not two different backgrounds, but twenty individuals with a dozen or more different moral particularities. One might find this challenge in any international organization – and in such a place, the team could perhaps only unite and collaborate with success when each individual lays aside their own moral particularity. Yet it seems likely that nobody will do this willingly unless each is offered an attractive alternative to this cultural wallpaper with which they have grown up and with which they are achingly familiar.

It is the leader who needs a united team, so it is the leader who must offer that attractive alternative – a common culture not simply to overarch at work what has been embedded over years at home, but to replace the moral particularity of each individual. This culture can be team specific, naturally, but it must be at minimum aligned with the values, culture, rewarded behaviours and other signposts by which the organization measures, observes or otherwise remarks on interpersonal and individual behaviour.

This offering of an alternative culture to be embraced by all is a huge challenge because the leader needs to find cultural foundations which can transcend the 'isms' of age, gender, nationality, faith and so on. One aspect of authenticity which can overcome the moral particularity of clan, tribe, nation, debts and inheritances, and which seems to have over-arching, multi-cultural appeal, is emotional intelligence. Moral particularity can be blind and insensitive (generally values based, though not always grounded, in 'good' values), it will at minimum be deeply subjective, and the objective self-awareness of emotional intelligence, when coupled with awareness of others, will act as an antidote to the insularity of moral particularity. For the leader of culturally diverse teams, this may indeed represent common ground.

Integrity: a transcending concept

Integrity comes through emotionally intelligent self-awareness and is at the centre of an individual's developing authenticity. Emotional intelligence in action is a practical barometer of decision making: a template for how we will behave, a way to help keep ourselves honest. Emotional intelligence, properly understood and applied, gives every individual in a group the same understanding of what is important to bring to decision making: self-awareness, self-management, social awareness and the ability to manage relationships. In the emotionally intelligent leader and organization, integrity should trump pragmatism – which is not to say that pragmatism will not be the answer, but part of the question must be, 'does the solution have integrity?'

One of the twenty-first century's most insightful philosophers is the magnificent Professor Albus Dumbledore, Principal of the Hogwarts School of Witchcraft and Wizardry. He tells Harry Potter something compellingly true in the course of a conversation captured in *The Philosopher's Stone* (Rowling, 2007): 'It does not matter what we intend to do. We all have good intentions. What matters is what we decide to do. It is by our actions, not our intentions, that others judge us.' In this context, emotional intelligence guides our intentions, while integrity guides our actions. That is why integrity is an aspect of authenticity. Later in this chapter we will look at a very specific definition of integrity. For now, though, we need to understand better why there is too often a gap between intention and action.

Case study
Team leader Michael can happily spend hours with David discussing the business, offering a few words of advice, sharing ideas, developing the

younger man's insight and understanding. The thing is, Michael likes David and sees his potential. Michael does not like Suzanne. He finds her a bit too sharp tongued, too quick to criticize the company he admires. She puts him on the defensive. She is better with words than he is. So, while he should be developing her just as much as he develops David, he does not. He does not try as hard, does not seek her out, and does not make the extra effort. He intends to, but he somehow never manages to. Which is a pity, because as Michael's boss could tell him, Suzanne is actually the one with greater potential, the one management want to see prosper.

For many leaders the challenge to intention is temptation. There lies the perverse imperative. The canny leader prepares carefully against temptation in two critically important ways. Using emotional intelligence as a guide, the leader must be skilled at self-management. It is well documented that the emotionally intelligent can use that intelligence to manipulate and deceive, indeed to descend into actions which at their darkest can only be described as evil. Michael the team leader is far from evil, but nevertheless this dark side of EI must not be ignored or discounted. For Michael, as for all of us, the hedge against it is the individual's strongly internalized sense of integrity and values. Without it, the dark side can dominate and temptation wins the day every day. But when it is present, and using authenticity as a guide, protected by this firm grasp on personal integrity, underpinned by values, the leader is best equipped to face temptation and prevail, spending more time doing the right thing, making the right choices. It is the unprotected leader who is vulnerable and more likely to descend into poor behaviour – ultimately, for a very few, narcissistic psychopathy – in a world where one is surrounded by the temptations of power, affluence, self-indulgence, substance abuse, corruption, deceit, dissembling and so much else.

Not all leaders faced with temptation fall into darkness. Many simply stumble into gloom. They sacrifice integrity for whatever represents temptation for them – small doses of apparent power, self-aggrandisement, sniffs at wealth, the corner office, the annual award for highest achieving sales person, a swifter ascent of the slippery pole. With so much to tempt us, perhaps the wonder is not so much that so many fall but that so many prevail.

The prevailing leader will, *ipso facto,* be well versed in aspects of emotional intelligence and will likely be authentic and familiar with a life of integrity. As Neal also discusses in Chapter 6, Socrates famously claimed that *the unexamined life was not worth living*: our prototype leader will need to have examined and explored at length before developing the necessary skill in self-management and grip on values and integrity required by followers who want to be inspired and who, in times of volatility, uncertainty, chaos and ambiguity want to feel a certain confidence in the individual whom they choose to follow.

Positioning values within the lexicon of authenticity, integrity and emotional intelligence

The most influential early writer about values was probably Rokeach (1973). In his book *The Nature of Human Values* he suggested that there are a relatively small number of what he called terminal human values which act as the internal reference points which we use to formulate opinions and attitudes and which in turn inform our decisions. The challenge, as Rokeach acknowledged, was to establish what any given individual actually held as a values set – as opposed to what were merely taught or adopted values, preferred or rewarded behaviours. That challenge holds good today: a singularly dangerous assumption to make is that an individual's behaviour in any particular situation is an accurate reflection of that individual's values. Rokeach defined values as subjective lasting beliefs that certain modes of conduct or end states of existence are more desirable than others. He told us they are activated by, yet transcend any particular objective or situation. So the things that happen in the world as we experience it should regularly trigger those subjective lasting beliefs, causing us to behave in a way that is aligned with those beliefs. To act otherwise is to suggest that the situation is stronger, more powerfully persuasive than the belief. So if I have a *terminal human value* (or believe that I do) that says discrimination is wrong, then when I encounter discrimination I should speak or act against it. Simple to say – yet in workplaces where any or all of the 'isms' (ageism, racism, sexism and so forth) can be present in different and differently toxic combinations on an almost daily basis, living up to my own or the organization's values can be exhausting, frightening, challenging ... looking the other way can be a compellingly tempting alternative. Sometimes how we discover which values we truly hold dear is by finding out what happens when they are challenged.

Terminal values

Terminal values refer to *desirable end states of existence* – the goals we would like to achieve during our lifetime (such as a world without discrimination). These vary by culture and by type. Some of us pursue power or influence as an end state, or family security, wisdom, mature love, comfort, or hedonistic pleasure; others pursue knowledge or mastery of a skill, or understanding, while others endeavour to pursue a state such as peace between nations, or the eradication of disease or illiteracy or poverty, and others want social recognition or an exciting life, business success or a sense of lasting accomplishment or contribution.

Instrumental values

Rokeach's instrumental values are the preferable or supporting *modes of conduct* which are the means of achieving the terminal values. Instrumental values might include ambition, honesty, hard work or diligence, conscientiousness, obedience, self-control or restraint, creativity, positivity and so on. Rokeach helps us because he identifies the difference between a terminal value – a core subjective belief about an end state of existence – and the instrumental values or supporting modes of conduct which help us to achieve these end states of existence in which we believe so strongly. His point – that we can have too many terminal values – is well made. They determine so much about how we conduct ourselves that to have too many would be to provide ourselves with a moral straitjacket which makes every decision for us. Instrumental values are modes of conduct: for example, we can not support justice without being courageous or we can not achieve knowledge without self-discipline. The challenge for the casual observer is of course that what we tend to encounter are the individual's instrumental values. It may take a fuller, more intimate relationship to discover and understand what terminal values give rise to the need to demonstrate these instrumental values. The authentic, emotionally intelligent leader, aware of others and good at managing relationships, is well equipped to look behind behaviours to explore the driving terminal values which are the true values core of an individual.

The subjectivity of values is important to recognize, especially if one leads in diverse or multi-cultural environments. Many of us embrace terminal values around elements of our lives such as faith, tribe or nation at a very early age and as a result of prolonged exposure to others who treat the beliefs around these aspects of life not as beliefs but as facts – unassailable, unquestionable. Unexamined, adopted subjective values can represent a particularly difficult moral particularity for others to accept or to work with, not least because the owner of the mind-set does not see or understand how individualistic or out of kilter with others it may be. The result is often a mode of conduct which seems entirely appropriate to the individual but utterly inappropriate to the rest of the team. Imagine how difficult it is for an individual brought up to believe that members of a particular faith are to be mistrusted, denigrated, hounded, persecuted, even to the point of death, then to move to an environment where that same faith group is afforded equal social standing. Or imagine the difficulty in being male in a broadly misogynistic culture and then moving to lead a mixed gender team in a culture where genders are treated equally. Or moving from a culture where the old are revered to one where they are ignored.

The emotionally intelligent leader, rather than walking blindly through these realms of human emotion and interaction, must act to address the behaviour and the terminal values that drive it. But imagine how much more difficult things become if it is the leader who is behaving in a manner aligned with an unexamined, adopted moral particularity which is alien to the explored, examined and tightly held terminal and instrumental values of the team which is to be led. Or indeed if the leader's behaviour drivers – the terminal values – are examined and deeply held, but are nevertheless a minority view at least within the society or organization, team or culture where the leader is operating. The authentic leader leads better at least in part because the understanding and management of these gaps in moral particularity come more readily to the owner of the examined life.

I worked once for a leader unknowingly in the grip of a Be Strong driver. He despized all emotion, seeing it as a weakness which would, even should be, exploited. He denigrated it in others and showed absolutely no sign of it himself. He lacked empathy, lacked the insight to see the need for it. He led transactionally and firmly, and indeed with some success at least until ambiguity and complexity came knocking. His response to these challengers was to become angrier and angrier, with himself and with others. In the end the collateral damage associated with his leadership became unacceptably unpalatable. Even as he was released from his responsibilities, he cursed the organization for its weakness and lack of what he called gumption. He left us certain he was the better man and his was the better way. Little doubt he is now doing harm elsewhere.

Integrity

Goleman has a useful three step definition of integrity. He says that integrity is an ability to discern right from wrong, a willingness to act on what has been discerned and then courage to say openly that one is acting on an understanding of what is right and wrong – voicing their inner truth (Goleman et al., 2003). Sankar (2003) says integrity is a governing ethic and suggests that a strategy based on integrity holds organizations to a more robust standard. Organizational integrity is based on the concept of self-governance, but the challenge of course is that self-governance, in the face of all that might represent temptation, is demonstrably beyond all but the very best of us. Barbara Killinger (2010) says simply that integrity is doing the right thing for the right reason. She introduces the idea that integrity is other-directed, while actions driven by a lack of integrity are generally selfish or self-directed. This aligns with Michie and Gooty (2005) who define authentic leaders as being intrinsically motivated to be consistent with high-end, other-regarding values. This is important because it helps to establish the authentic leader as one whose terminal values are good values, deeply held and not merely any values deeply held. It also ensures that the instrumental values which support the terminal values will also be other-directed and therefore liable to support the integrity of the individual – values such as justice, respect and consideration.

This is not to suggest that authentic leaders cannot or should not have terminal values which are of benefit to themselves. The pursuit of knowledge for example, or family security, or mature love are all examples of such values which are positive and admirable. But it is noteworthy that even with these terminal values there is another beneficiary as well – these terminal values are not self-serving even if they are of benefit to the individual. The instrumental values which support such terminal values are also worthy and held in esteem: examples might be mindfulness, self-discipline, positive attitude and trust. Michie and Gooty (2005) are clear that authentic leaders should have both self-enhancing and self-transcending values, but will, must and should give priority to the latter. They identify self-transcending value examples as social justice, equality, liberalism, honesty, loyalty and responsibility. The associated behaviours or instrumental values they identify include treating people fairly and with respect, being open to the ideas and emotions of others, being transparent and foregoing their self-interests for the common good. For them, the authentic leader shows high consistency between values and behaviours, while the egocentric leader shows a low such consistency.

Moral capacity and courage

May et al (2003) suggest leaders are more likely to recognize moral dilemmas in the workplace if they have a heightened sense of what they describe as *moral capacity*. They mean by this a developed ability to see their role as including an ethical responsibility and a moral perspective. These authors make the point that there will be many more leaders who have the intention of acting authentically than there are leaders who actually do so – which of course is the point Rowling makes through Dumbledore. They go further though: decent people, they suggest, may have appropriate reasons for choosing not to act ethically or with integrity, including preservation. Such a dilemma is at the heart of many a professional dilemma, as well as of much fiction, as a central character struggles with the demands of the situation in the context of the integrity of the wider goal.

Courage is required to act on what one discerns as right or wrong, especially in the face of social, professional or cultural pressure. A leader may see or hear examples of 'isms' on which action should be taken, but that action against individuals may weaken, undermine or even destroy the team, making the achievement of team goals and team or individual bonuses impossible. In the face of such pressure, what team leader will stand up and condemn casual ageism, sexism, racism or other unacceptable but (to some) peripheral activities engaged in by powerful, successful or charismatic team members? May et al (2003) suggest authentic leaders 'are, quite simply, people we trust with our future' and that is a useful litmus test: what would someone I would trust with my future do in the face of an unacceptable 'ism'?

The challenge of summoning up courage in the face of the casual application of the unacceptable to our everyday lives is one thing. What happens though when actually discerning right from wrong splits otherwise like-minded individuals with shared vision and values? In the world of British politics, recent examples include positions taken on the question of the Scottish referendum and more recently the In/Out referendum on the EU. When Jeremy Corbyn and David Cameron unite against Boris Johnson, who is united with Michael Gove, who then betrays him and contests the leadership of the Conservative Party with Theresa May, while Cameron resigns and Corbyn faces a huge vote of no confidence *and all this in a single week* then the political landscape is tilted at an odd angle indeed. But in the world of business, such strange divisions are not so unusual. When there is not the underlying simplicity of the party political system, then the ambiguity and complexity of modern business life can often lead to there being many 'quite right' answers, meaning discerning right from wrong becomes more than ever a matter of subjective, divisive opinion, which in turn encourages people to act by taking entrenched positions, not least because they do not have facts from which to argue, only assertions to defend. Schisms swiftly appear, organizations become inward looking, lose focus, sacrificing traction for wheel spin until the issues can be resolved. If ever authenticity is required from leaders it is when this all-too-familiar circumstance begins to coalesce within an organization. Kanungo (2001) notes that authentic leaders are guided by explicit and conscious values that emphasize the collective interests of their organization. This once more reminds us of the other-regarding nature of authenticity.

The authentic leader acts and makes decisions not to further a personal agenda but an organizational one. If the organization's interests are ethical then the authentic leader will prosecute them tirelessly. If they are not, that same leader, through a sense of personal integrity, will challenge or quit the organization. As Thoms (2008) points out, most scholars regard integrity as a requirement of ethical leadership. Yukl (2001) found that even across cultures integrity is high on the list of essential leadership traits. A sense of ethics embraces traits such as trustworthiness, honesty, justice, principled decision making – which when rolled together with emotional intelligence both make a fair definition of authenticity and offers the foundations for a culture which might replace the mixed moral particularity of diverse teams.

May et al (2003) suggest authentic leaders must be totally immersed in their core beliefs and values and that this constitutes a fundamental sense of self-awareness. This once again cements the relationship between authenticity and emotional intelligence. This is what Covey (1999) terms principle centred leadership. He suggests that the only thing that endures over time is what he calls the law of the farm: prepare the ground, plant the seed, cultivate it, weed it, water it, nurture growth and development. His point is that there is no quick fix to behavioural problems rooted in organizational cultures or personal value sets which are inauthentic. The world works well when we pay attention to doing well what we know to be important – and we know that the foundations on which we are to build are important, and are ignored at our peril.

Exploring the gap between intention and action

As May et al (2003) suggest, the losses due to ethical corporate meltdowns and inauthentic leadership during the latter part of the twentieth century cost the US economy billions of dollars. The financial crisis of 2008/9, the reverberations from which live with us still in this age of austerity, cost considerably more, not least in terms of human suffering. Ethical failures seem to have become commonplace – to quote Libor rate fixing, FIFA World Cup scandals, mis-sold payment protection insurance, the BHS scandal in the UK, the half-truths and deceit at the heart of the Brexit campaign is merely to scratch the surface – and at their heart seems always to be unethical decision making, deceit of stakeholders, a lack of moral capacity on the part of both leaders and actors.

The answer may lie in part in the concept of errant child behaviour. Freud famously suggested that religion infantilizes us and illustrated this by comparing religion with the mother who encourages her offspring before a visit to the dentist by saying, 'Be good for the dentist, darling, and I'll give you an ice lolly.' We can see this same infantilizing at work in organizations: 'Give me the sales figure and I'll give you the bonus/car/holiday/promotion/salesman of the year award.' It is no surprise then that the recipients of this infantilizing transactional incentivizing behave in childlike ways to drive their teams over whatever line is drawn by the holder of the carrot (and sometimes stick). These behaviours may include bullying, lying or distorting the truth, manipulating individuals or groups, having temper tantrums and other manifestations of the thwarted or manipulative child. The greater the temptation, the greater the level of intensity associated with each ethical dilemma. Yet always, it seems, temptation wins. Even those leaders who intend to act authentically can fail to do so in the face of enough provocative temptation. The road to hell is paved with good intentions.

What these infantilized behaviours are not, and cannot be, is authentic. They are driven by values which are primarily self-directed, and these values have been stirred and fired up by the organization itself – the very body which in all probability proclaims elsewhere its admiration for and desire for authentic leadership. This is not good leadership, and the incidental collateral damage associated with such self-directed leader behaviour can be significant. Management must bear a large part of the responsibility, of course, because it is management which is generating the perverse temptation. This brings us back to the idea of integrity and those three steps of Goleman's. In the kind of organizational culture sketched above, for many an incentivized manager the challenge is not the discerning of right from wrong. It is the acting on what is discerned. However, as Dumbledore so deftly pointed out to Harry, it is by our actions and not our intentions that we are judged. We do not want to pave the road to hell.

Carver, author of *Boards That Make a Difference* (2006), and creator of the Policy Governance model, makes the same point when he says an organization's works, not its words, are the telling assessment of its beliefs. As Killinger points out, integrity suffers greatly when 'whatever works' (in this example, personal incentivization) is seen as acceptable. The big picture is eclipsed while myopic, short-term thinking takes charge. This thinking, often imposed from above in organizations in the form of rewarded or required behaviours, thought patterns or cultures, is the insidious enemy of authentic leadership. It encourages the shadow side of ourselves – the self-interested side, the low-end values side. This self-interestedness undermines the sort of collaborative, collegiate win/win cultures which offer some chance of stability, even success in a VUCA environment. In such an environment, where the level of challenge is invariably high, the prevailing culture is established not by that high level of challenge – because that is a given – but by the accompanying levels of support. Now, support can take many forms, but by its very nature, support is other-regarding. If the primary remuneration model in the organization encourages self-regarding behaviour, then the culture is likely to be one of high challenge coupled with low support, commonly characterized as a stressful culture, rather than one of high challenge coupled with high support, commonly termed an achievement culture. The difference between a stress culture and an achievement culture is not the level of challenge; it is the level of support. That is the responsibility of the leadership. Self-interested leaders will provide supportive leadership far less well or consistently than other-directed leaders. Organizations which create infantilizing remuneration structures very often get the culture they deserve.

Competitive versus collaborative behaviour

Another commonly found aspect of this sort of self-directed culture is the flourishing of competitive behaviour within an organization at the expense of collaborative behaviour. What happens is that individuals, who are naturally assertive and confident, become determined to get their own way within an organization. They believe that their way is the best way, and (often because they are incentivized by results) fear that if they give way to another's opinion or viewpoint, they will end up losing out on performance-related benefits. So, to their naturally high levels of assertiveness they add a low level of co-operation with others, making themselves highly competitive. In refusing to be co-operative they fail to be collaborative, creating within their teams or within their organizations an atmosphere of attrition. When such people are in positions of power and are likely to win most win/lose encounters (which is what they make every conflict or difference of opinion) the end result is often either a complete fall off in dissenting voices or opposition, meaning the end of constructive dissent, or the creation of a culture of constant friction and antagonism. It does not require infantilizing remuneration structures to create such cultures, though they help enormously; it merely requires senior figures to value assertive self-interest (lack of co-operation) over assertive collaboration (lots of co-operation). Unfortunately, in many organizational cultures, assertion is valued in the absolute, with no regard to levels of co-operation. The resulting culture and the leaders who thrive in it are inauthentic because competitiveness within an organization is inherently self-interested ('I have to win') rather than other-regarding ('We should collaborate').

In their paper 'Integrity in Practice', Steare and Jamieson (2003) say that integrity is an approach based on those shared values, attitudes and behaviours that help us to act correctly in our lives at home, at work and in society. They add that integrity also helps us to incorporate the notion of rights and duties, which we define as justice or fairness. Many management professionals are understandably ambitious and driven by a desire to succeed. Success is a measurable metric – visible to others as well as to self. But success and integrity are sometimes uneasy bedfellows. Abraham Lincoln remarked, 'I am not always bound to win but I am bound to be true. I am not always bound to succeed but I am bound to live up to what I hold to be right.' The authentic leader values integrity over success, and that in turn will colour the decision making process for that individual.

Developing authentic skills around ethical decision making

Decision making is a vital component of leadership. Ethical decision making allows the leader to be sure that decisions made are made with integrity. Our concepts of ethics have been derived from religions, philosophies and cultures. They infuse debates on topics such as abortion, human rights and professional conduct as well as how we conduct business. Generally, ethics refers to the study and development of our individual and collective ethical standards. Feelings, laws and social norms can, and often do, deviate from what is ethical – we only need to reflect on and consider what at different times has been entirely legal to understand the truth of this – and indeed what is considered ethical and socially normal behaviour can and does change over time. Ethics also means, then, the continuous effort of studying our own moral beliefs and our moral conduct, and striving to ensure that we, and the institutions we help to shape, live up to standards that are reasonable and appropriate to what we believe is due to us and from us.

Avolio et al (2009) discuss a four-part requirement for decision making which, without overtly referencing ethics, would almost certainly lead to decision making which was both sound and ethical. The critical first step is a balanced processing of objective data available for analysis alongside the subjective, values-informed sense of what we feel about the situation or circumstances. Which, if any, of our terminal values are challenged or compromised by the situation or by our planned response? Which of our instrumental values and associated behaviours will need to flex, bend or break in the face of the rewarded or required behaviours expected of us by the circumstances? Next, we need to engage with our internalized moral perspective. Our internalized standards regulate our behaviour and if this self-regulation is compromised by what we plan to do then we need to give serious consideration to our intended course of action. Are we losing our ability or willingness to differentiate right from wrong, and hence our grip on our personal integrity? Or is it perhaps our ability to act on what we perceive which is weakening? Next we need openly and appropriately to share the challenges posed by the situation and how we feel about those challenges. This relational transparency is an important aspect of our personal integrity as well as a source of reassurance for our colleagues. Finally, we need to be self-aware enough to assess the risk of behaving in a manner which undermines our integrity and authenticity and to manage that risk so that, whatever decision we take, it is one with which we can live proudly.

Values as an integrating entity

Being ethical, behaving with integrity, being conscientious, being authentic, or those behaviours which are antithetical to these positive states, all have at their centre a relationship with values. We have examined Rokeach's definition of values. We understand they are subjective lasting beliefs that transcend any particular objective or situation. We recognize terminal values which refer to desirable end states of existence and instrumental values which are the preferable or supporting modes of behaviour to help achieve the terminal values. What might help us to focus better on the importance of terminal values is to cluster together alongside a terminal value the instrumental value or behaviours that we might associate with that terminal value. One point of this exercise is to remember the importance of exploring the driving terminal value behind the more overt and obvious instrumental values. The other is to realize and understand how hard it is to lead a values-led life, and how much easier it is to claim a value and then only to have it as a preferred behaviour – one we engage with when it suits us, but not when the stakes are too high to make it attractive.

For example, the terminal value of Justice would engage us in instrumental values or behaviours around fairness and impartiality and the acknowledgement of rights and duties. Some of us have the integrity to discern right from wrong when fairness and impartiality is involved, but lack the necessary instrumental value of courage to act on what we discern. Or we discriminate because we lack or cannot consistently apply the instrumental value of self-discipline and favour those we like or find attractive. Or we lack the instrumental value of mindfulness and proceed without caution or good sense, discerning what we should do but finding ourselves powerless to do it. Or the terminal value of Excellence might engage us in instrumental values or behaviours around meeting quality standards, performing to the best of our ability and seeking to perform with merit. But do we do this consistently or only when we see reward to ourselves in doing it? Do we behave to the instrumental value when we are unobserved as much as we do when we are observed, for example? A tightly held terminal value is a hard taskmaster, and we ought not to claim such a value unless we are prepared to live within the restrictions it imposes upon us. As Hoffer (1973), the American moral and social philosopher, says, we lie loudest when we lie to ourselves and this is perhaps rarely truer than when we lay claim to a value yet ignore the behavioural requirements that value places upon us.

Research shows that a strong ethical culture creates a happier, healthier organization. Critical studies (Trevino et al., 1999) connect positive, ethical cultures to lower rates of observed misconduct; reduced pressure to compromise standards; increased reporting of misconduct to leadership; greater satisfaction with management's response to misconduct; greater satisfaction with the organization as a whole; lowered exposure to situations inviting misconduct; and increased sense of preparedness to handle situations inviting misconduct. The 2009 National Business Ethics Survey suggests that in strong ethically leaning cultures fewer employees feel pressure to compromise company standards; fewer employees observe misconduct and there are fewer incidences of every kind of misconduct; employees who observe misconduct are more likely to report it; reporters are less likely to experience retaliation; top management culture is most closely associated with improved outcomes; co-worker culture is most closely linked with rates of financial misconduct, but top management culture is associated with reporting such observations.

So what we do seem to know is that decisions and the behaviours that flow from them have a very real and powerful impact on organizational and individual activity. High performance for an organization is, to a large degree, a function of the right decisions and the right behaviours on the part of its people. Kanungo (2001) said that every organization has a purpose, and it is the desire to achieve this purpose efficiently and effectively that creates the need for leadership. If we accept that definition then the need for leaders will be with us in business for the foreseeable future, however volatile and complex that future may be. He also said that authentic leaders are guided by explicit and conscious values that emphasize the collective interests of their organization. Authentic leaders will make more right decisions and model more right behaviour than inauthentic leaders because they are, as Michie and Gooty (2005) point out, intrinsically motivated to be consistent with high-end, other-regarding values. May et al (2003) capture a similar thought when they say that authentic leaders do what is right and fair; inauthentic leaders do what is ultimately best for them. Luthans and Avolio (2003) tell us that authentic leadership is leadership where a behaviour or course of action is decided not by situational imperatives but by reference to an examined template of values and ethics.

It is not just research that tells us this. We can draw principles from the playgrounds of our youth. When life was simpler and we all wore sandals to school, what we demanded in the playground was simple: be fair, do not cheat, play hard but decent, share and share alike, tell the truth and keep your word. These rules led to the base of our values, integrity and ultimately happiness among peers. There was a virtuous circle between what we heard at home, how we behaved at school and, in time, what was expected of us in the workplace. It may be that this virtuous circle lies shattered on the asphalt nowadays, which puts far more emphasis on personal integrity – because group integrity may be a thing of playgrounds past.

Becoming and remaining authentic

If personal integrity through choice, rather than an imposed group integrity, is the way forward, it is not a way free of hazard. George (2004) warns us that to become authentic each of us has to develop our own leadership style consistent with our own personality, character, ethics and values. This is easier said than achieved, and for some of us will require significant self-examination and the development of an emotional intelligence which will allow us to build professional lives in which the adult is generally in the executive.

Self-awareness and the editing of parent tapes will be important, as will the development of self-management skills. But this is the work which will improve the quality of our leadership, moving us from contingent copers at best to leaders whose actions and decisions are congruent with the inner world of values and principles as well as the outer world of targets, legislation, competitive activity and budget management. This approach places personal values at the heart of an authentic code of conduct which will lead to predictable and consistent behaviours.

Tightly held terminal values are the ideal basis for authentic leadership. Instrumental values, which have no more status than a preferred behaviour, may be readily abandoned or ignored and while vital in helping to deliver terminal values cannot be the basis for authenticity. Any merely instrumental values on which leadership rests will probably not be sustainable under pressure. This is why the exploration of personal values is so important to the authentic leader. Authentic people are at the centre of authentic leadership and authentic leadership is at the base of positive, socially constructive forms of leadership. Authentic leaders create authenticity in followers and create a culture of authenticity within organizations.

As Bass and Steidlmeier (1999) point out, in leaders and in leader behaviour especially, predictability and consistency both reassure and motivate followers, who find the opposite behaviours unnerving, especially in ambiguous or stressful circumstances. Followers may not know what a leader will decide to do, but if they know and understand that the leader's decisions are always bound by a well understood template of ethics and values – if they believe the leader to be authentic – then they will trust that leader, however chaotic or unpredictable the situation.

In their book *The Trusted Advisor*, Maister et al (2003) introduce us to the Trust Equation. Here they suggest that we trust an individual when that individual can persuade us that they are credible, reliable and are prepared to be intimate with us – to have open and empathetic conversations, to be available for relationship building. However, the degree to which we trust any individual is not just a combination of their credibility, reliability and openness to intimacy. We then consider the degree to which we find the individual to be self-interested. The more self-interested the individual, the less we trust that individual. The perception of self-interest undermines trust. Self-interest is also the antithesis of authenticity. Authentic leaders are primarily other-regarding, and if they are ever self-interested it is in the pursuit of high-end values such as knowledge and understanding. Yet if we recall the infantilized, incentivized executive pursuing the individual bonus, what is that executive if not self-interested? Personalized incentive schemes can significantly undermine trust, because the pursuers of these personal bonuses are seen by their followers and colleagues to be fundamentally self-interested in all their decision making, which is inauthentic and generates unease.

So let us get authentic. Let us eschew self-interest and be other-regarding. Let us throw over competitiveness within the organization for collaboration – let us be assertive and co-operative. Let us be adult and emotionally intelligent, let us trust and be trustworthy, let us explore and understand our own and each others' terminal values, let us understand and value integrity. In short, let us be authentic in our leadership and our followership. It may not solve all our problems, may not remove all the volatility, uncertainty, complexity and ambiguity that our modern business world generates. But is it better than current on-offer alternatives? Surely, certainly, resoundingly so.

Chapter 5

Humanizing leadership through emotional intelligence

Kerrie Fleming

Introduction

This chapter examines how emotional intelligence offers a means of humanizing leadership and inspiring followership using the Mayer, Salovey and Caruso Emotional Intelligence Test (2002) as a canvas with which to develop self-awareness and awareness of others. The main aim is to evoke leadership behaviours which are inspiring to followers.

Case study

At the North American International Auto Show in Detroit in January 2016, VW CEO Matthias Mueller stood still at the podium amongst the media glare. The world eagerly awaited an apology from the company for the emissions cheating scandal which plagued the company in 2015. The carmaker was accused of putting forty times more pollution into the air than was allowable under US standards. The scandal resulted in the resignation of Volkswagen's CEO, Martin Winterkorn, just weeks after the EPA released its claims, followed by seismic activity on the VW board, with resignations from key people and rumblings of disquiet and dissatisfaction at how things were being run. Departing bosses lifted the lid on a company which had become autocratic in its leadership with much dissatisfaction on the ground. The revelations of how the company tampered with its emissions levels caused a ripple of disbelief across the world. The company's stock price took a hit, and it faced billions of dollars in potential fines. Volkswagen has since promised to retrofit cars with systems to limit emissions. This moment in Detroit was VW's chance to recover from the scandal which rocked the company, with a reputation steeped in reliability and longevity.

When Mueller, as leader, slight in stature, read his prepared statement, he glanced briefly at those in attendance at his audience. He once again looked down and read an apology from himself and the management team: 'We all know that we have let down customers, authorities, regulators and the general public here in America, too.' He added, 'We are – I am – truly sorry for that. And I would like to apologize once again for what went wrong with Volkswagen' (Glinton, 2016). He looked distinctly uncomfortable, almost in a hurry to read what was on the page and scurry away. The result was utter disappointment and much lamentation on a chance which was lost all through lack of true integrity and sincerity in his apology.

This crisis of management corners the perfect context in which to demonstrate some inspirational leadership skills. We all know that leadership is not what happens when the status quo is maintained but when disruptions occur. It is the excruciating time when problems arise with no obvious and immediate solutions which need to be addressed with speed and confidence. This type of leadership is not about demonstrating sparkling levels of charisma with no depth or sincerity but living and exuding honest and value-led behaviours. These behaviours occur naturally for a lucky few but for most need to be sculpted from years of awareness of self and others. This awareness usually evolves when the status quo is rudely interrupted with no obvious solution in sight. It is usually at these times of crisis when we meet leaders and enquire about their identity, brand, impact and what impression they offer when they enter and leave a room.

Our work at Ashridge suggests that these aspects of sculpting a leadership identity are the building blocks of any effective leader. These building blocks are what allows confident and consistent decisions to be made during times of stability and also in times of crisis. In the above example, Mueller appears to lack those building blocks and during a crucial time in the company's legacy, he suggests a weak and frightened figure which has been totally overshadowed by the situation. He offers a totally uninspiring example of leadership and perhaps unintentionally contributes to further damage the reputation of a brand giant in the automotive sector. His lack of sincerity leaves potential VW consumers and his half a million plus global employees disillusioned about what really happened and whether the brand which they saw as virtuous, is now shadowed by doubt and uncertainty.

Fashioning these building blocks come down to an ability to search deep within and figure out what are the values which you are led by in your life. List them. Examples might be *truth*, *integrity* and *hard work*. These values are usually visible to you as a child when you carefully observed how your parents and guardians behaved and for the most part followed their example. In some cases, you may have released the values which you were taught as they always served to make you uncomfortable or question yourself. This in itself is self-awareness in action. Evolution has bestowed a physiology upon us which offers many methods and means of reminding us when we are in precarious or dangerous environments. Our primitive brain shoots specific hormones into our bloodstream to offer us some momentum to flee or face a looming situation. This is the gift of human evolution. Most people do not notice and spend most of their lives in this state of hyper mode imagining or awaiting the next crisis or disaster. This usually happens when values or truths as we see them are compromised. If this is constant, the impact on the body and mind is enormous and manifests in debilitating illnesses which usually evolve from the search for and administration of the antithesis of this hyper state. Food, drugs, danger all offer relief, albeit short term, but continue to peddle the cycle of self-destruction. Perhaps, strange observations about the human psyche and form in the midst of seeking how to inspire leadership but ultimately important in the quest for humanizing leadership and inspiring followership.

In their paper on how to humanize leadership, Petrieglieri and Petrieglieri (2015) describe leadership activities as persistence in the face of setbacks, openness to opportunity and reducing the amount of personal sacrifice which most leadership roles tend to demand. They suggest that *inspiring* leadership is all about delivering, continuous learning, showing integrity and care, as real leadership is all about the people. This insight, although it may be accused of being ideal, certainly will encourage more followership as humans tend to respond best to those they can trust to be consistent leaders, protect their interests and help further their own ambitions. This is a very tall order for leaders. When have you ever seen the above qualities listed on a job specification for CEO or manager? Such a job advert might say:

We seek someone who is steeped in self-awareness and awareness of others. A person who shows integrity and compassion to employees and cares about their welfare and their success, someone who empowers each employee to fulfil and exceed their own and the ambitions of the company, creating a mutually successful environment which fulfils stakeholder and shareholder needs.

The big question is why not? Why are these qualities not top of the recruiters' list? It is safe to say that a lot of employees would flock to an organization if they knew that such a leader was at the helm. In reality, here is an example of a CEO role advertised from *The Guardian* newspaper jobs page in April 2016:

We seek a credible ambassador, a powerful communicator and an inclusive leader, bringing excellent strategic and business planning skills with a track record of successfully attracting funding and strategic partnerships. You will have the skills and motivation to lead and develop our services to maximise impact, putting service-users at the heart of everything we do.

Although it is just one example of such ubiquitous CEO recruitment efforts, it makes the point that business comes first, people come second. The word inclusive is used but that is the only word which would suggest that a human being is either taking the job or is leading fellow human beings. What is also fuelling such detached leadership styles is the tradition of male dominance in leadership roles which has ensured that awareness and compassion are often dwarfed by ego, hubris and short-term thinking, attributes which evidently are more rewarded by shareholders (Collinson and Tourish, 2015). This male dominance is aptly illustrated by the fact that just twenty-five of the Fortune 500 companies are run by women (Fairchild, 2015).

Consequently, a Gallup survey of 142 countries in 2015 demonstrated that just 13 per cent of employees worldwide who are engaged at work (which is one in every eight workers of a population of 180 million worldwide) are psychologically committed to their organization and are making positive contributions (Adkins, 2015). These statistics are rather alarming and although they do not offer any indication of how much this disengagement costs in revenue, one can only assert that the losses are exorbitant. The connections between poor leadership and this disconnection by employees are made in Chapter 7 of this book by Olivier and Hölscher who suggest that such employee disengagement is enhanced by poor communication and detached leadership styles. All of this data suggests that the need for humanizing leadership is greater than ever and the building blocks can be fashioned through acknowledging and developing the values which are inherent to leaders as humans. This humanizing of leaders will offer them some skills to survive in the currently volatile, uncertain, complex and ambiguous (VUCA) environments in which leaders consistently find themselves.

Humanizing leadership through emotional intelligence

Business schools are starting to understand the merits of developing self-awareness and building personal leadership brands in the midst of leadership programmes for executives. These sessions are often sandwiched between the more serious subjects of strategy, finance and operations but from our experience are the most popular in terms of engagement and long-lasting impact after the conclusion of programmes. Undergraduate business degree programmes are also offering personality testing and advocating subjects such as Emotional Intelligence (EI) as a means to enhance leadership abilities. The latest models of leadership which have emerged in the last ten years pay close attention to the symbolic behaviour of leaders, and cite the importance of inspiring followers through inspirational messages, emotional feelings, values, individual attention and intellectual stimulation (Avolio, 2007; Avolio et al., 2009; Yukl, 2006). They suggest that in order to succeed, today's organizations must encourage the development of personal competencies such as self-management, self-presentation, empathy and interpersonal sensitivity (Fox and Spector, 2000).

All of these abilities, which were absent in Mueller's presentation, are now considered mainstream teaching for cutting edge business schools. Such abilities are increasingly of interest because they deal with the recognition, regulation and expression of moods and emotions. The merits of EI as a leadership skill illustrate the continuing and necessary evolution of how leaders need to behave in order to cope with the VUCA while attending to the self and others in the midst of often frenetic environments. Emotionally intelligent leadership is an all-encompassing means of combining rationality with complementary styles of thinking, such as intuition, creativity and emotion, while encouraging insight and guiding comprehensive decision making, all very powerful when navigating their particular environments.

The academic literature offers many descriptions and research supporting the merits of EI as a means of inspiring leadership. Mathews et al (2002) describe it as temperament, character, insightfulness, self-awareness and good person–environment fit. Mayer et al (2008: 511) describe EI as the 'ability to carry out accurate reasoning about emotions, and use emotions and emotional knowledge to enhance thought'. Although there are critical questions surrounding certain aspects of evidence of EI in leadership, the majority of the empirical research validates the concept and demonstrates its importance (Brackett and Salovey, 2004; Day and Carroll, 2008; Lopes et al., 2006; Mayer and Salovey, 2002). Burgoyne and colleagues (2004) state that the key elements of leadership should include the creation of opportunities for assisting self-awareness and reflection in followers, and support the shift from individualistic notions of leadership to inclusive relational perspectives. When leaders are aware of their own emotions, they can establish stronger relationships with employees (George, 2000). These can be positive or negative in their guise.

Positive affirmations can foster trust and improve well-being because leaders are seen as role models and subsequently gain trust and respect (Avolio and Gardner, 2005; Gardner et al., 2005). All pretty useful attributes which Mueller could have benefited from in his speech. While negative affirmations may not instil such loyalty, they may generate a desperate need for leader approval which may lead to over-performance. Emotions expressed by transformational leaders can often provide blueprints for their followers on how to emotionally react in similar situations (Lewis, 2000). Gardner and Stough (2002) studied 250 high-level managers and found that EI correlated with all components of transformational leading. Transformational leaders can arouse heightened awareness in a group and de-emphasize any narrow self-interest and rationality. Mandell and Pherwani (2003) found significant relationships between transformational leadership style and EI. Other empirical research denotes EI abilities as critical in determining an individual's and an organization's success (Gardner and Stough, 2002; Mandell and Pherwani, 2003; McGarvey, 1997; Moorhead and Neck, 1995). McGarvey (1997) argues that EI is the key element that employees and leaders require to build successful organizations.

EI is described as important in assisting leaders to make good decisions about new products, markets, managing followers, and the management of certain emotions and behaviours are key determinants when matching organization values with those of employees (Gardner and Stough, 2002; Mandell and Pherwani, 2003; McGarvey, 1997). Gilley et al (2008) suggest that leaders can sabotage innovation and effective teamwork by creating hostile environments, communicating poorly, setting unrealistic expectations and being coercive. The opposite of being emotionally intelligent. Omta and Bouter (1997) suggest that if organizations are to be innovative, scientific performance goals must be met, along with the satisfaction and motivation of those who are innovating. They refer to this as socio-technical performance.

The idea of using an inherent ability, which everyone possesses to some degree, to enhance one's leadership capability is surely a novel way to manage an organization. In Whyte's (1956) classic book *The Organisation Man*, effective business people are described as logical, reasoned and rational decision makers. However, much research since then has shown that emotion is an integral part of daily life and is inseparable from the work environment (Ashfort and Humphreys, 1995; Ashkanasy, 1996). When Steve Jobs led his team in Apple, he did so with strong emphasis on emotion management. In a bizarre but effective way, he managed to instigate negative emotions which resulted in powerful innovative outcomes. Although his means were questionable in terms of fairness and morality, the final result cannot be argued with. There are of course all the other success factors at Apple to consider, but it leads to some interesting questions to current and future leaders on how they can effectively manage their own and others' emotions as a powerful means to lead their organization to success.

Using emotional intelligence

Both the academic literature and our experience as faculty and consultants suggests that EI is one sure way to try to increase leadership impact, influence and communication style with followers. Let us look at how we teach EI using the Mayer, Salovey and Caruso Emotional Intelligence Test (MSCEIT) (2002) which is an ability test to assess levels of emotional intelligence. An ability test has better or worse answers, like a traditional intelligence test, and although you will not take the test in this chapter, an illustration of its aspects will allow you to reflect on what aspects of human interaction are important to inspire leadership and why. The MSCEIT explained here is a process model of emotions and includes four abilities or branches which work together.

- The first is identifying or *perceiving emotions*, when an emotion occurs due to some event, having the ability to identify that emotion in oneself or in another person.
- The second is *using emotions* which is when the emotion is used to help pay attention to what is important.
- The third branch is *understanding emotions*, which offers some clues as to what exactly people feel and why we feel this way.
- The fourth and final branch is *managing emotions*, which considers what these emotions are trying to tell us and we then can include them in our decision-making process.

Let us now examine each branch as a means to start the process of building self-awareness and awareness of others as a means to inspire leadership.

Identifying emotions

Case study: Picking up emotional cues

Louise worked in a government strategy office. She took her job very seriously and was proud of the fact that she played a small part in the writing and publication of public policy. She had worked hard at school and university and was successful working in a well-paid job of great status which impressed her family who had high ambitions for her. Her life growing up had been an orderly and sensible affair where family managed any difficulties with great poise and silence. As the years passed, Louise realized that all of the ambitions which she had since she was young had now been achieved and she momentarily felt very proud of herself. She basked in her achievements, but over time something niggled at her. She could not quite tell what it was but this uncomfortable sensation just would not leave her . . . In her role, she managed a small team who were reasonably efficient but there was one team member, Megan, who was always bringing her personal problems to work. Louise found it most inappropriate and frowned upon such behaviour. She felt it was her duty to ensure that Megan did her job quietly and stopped disturbing the team with her latest drama. Louise decided to tackle the problem and informed Megan to get on with her job and stop bringing her personal issues into the workplace. She told Megan that she had a serious and responsible job to do but if she did not stop her nonsense Louise would report her behaviour to the senior manager. Megan became very upset and stormed out of the meeting crying, loudly stating that Louise was a cold boss and nobody liked her anyway. Louise was shocked and annoyed. She immediately went to her senior manager and reported the situation but did not receive the response she had hoped for. Her boss suggested that she spent more time listening to her team and understand how she could be more supportive as she had similar complaints about Louise in the past. Louise was stunned as she left the meeting. The uncomfortable sensation which had been niggling at her flooded back into her body. She could not understand what had just happened. Surely, she was the person who was right in this situation? How could they say she was a cold person? Was she cold? How did she feel? She honestly did not know as it had been so long since she had felt anything. It was unsettling. She went to the local café and ordered a large slice of cake. She ate it with relish and immediately felt much better.

Fleming (2016:15)

Identifying emotions should come naturally to us as humans. The amygdala, which is an almond shaped set of neurons located deep in the brain's medial temporal lobe, processes emotions and ensures that we are kept safe from prey by shooting hormones into our bloodstream when we feel fear. This has of course been tempered somewhat as society, certainly in the corporate world, suggests that emotions for the most part need to be kept private so that our fellow human beings do not bear witness to ugly outbursts of anger or tears. This has merit in maintaining a civilized and rationally focused human race but as explained earlier, physiology betrays this command by society and sometimes the emotions leak out.

As demonstrated from the example of Louise, her ability to accurately identify emotions in herself seems absent and the result was some very uncomfortable situations for her colleagues. Our work as facilitators demonstrates that the example of Louise is not uncommon. A lot of our clients, who incidentally are male, have turned off their barometer for feeling emotions due to the expectations conveyed to them by the demands of their leadership roles. As the CEO job advert example earlier demonstrates, leaders are hired to think and do but not hired to feel. When this happens, we work with clients to teach them how to feel emotions in themselves again. We encourage them to find a piece of music which means something or watch a movie which reminds them of happy times, which will evoke a feeling of happiness inside of them. We ask them to write down the emotion, how it feels, what sensations happen in the body and mind, what happens to their mood and to others around them. The purpose of which is to reawaken their body's emotional fibres which will offer them another source of data when making decisions and taking action.

The next aspect of perceiving emotions is the ability to see what is happening for others, when some leaders, overly consumed about how they are feeling, miss some stirrings of emotions within the person they are communicating with. To develop awareness of others, there are many clues which leaders can pay attention to. One indicator is body language, which includes facial expression, stance, gestures and tone. For example, a simple physical movement may indicate that someone is withdrawing from a conversation. This may be due to the fact that the subject no longer has any relevance for them, or else they do not agree with what has been said. The solution is to stop and ask some open questions as to what they think or how they feel about what has just been said. This will give them some time to assess whether they are on the right track and whether they are still engaged or not.

We also suggest that these leaders spend some time exploring their 'gut' feel in situations. This will often indicate their emotional barometer as to how comfortable or uncomfortable a situation is making them feel. Not only could Louise not pick up how she was feeling, she also failed to recognize the impact her mood was having on those around her. Good social communication requires accurate perception of content, as well as tone and non-verbal signals such as posture and facial expression. When these leaders look around, can they see who is happy or sad? How can they tell? What are they looking for? Faces usually give the first clue, then observing how people are sitting, standing and then you listen to their tone. This is not the only data they need to listen to but its existence allows them to decode emotion when only facial expression information is available. We prompt questions as to whether they can 'read' the room, detect emotions in the environment, etc. The tasks when taking the MSCEIT offer some questions around different textures, colours and designs which can often move people in different ways. Consider art, music and designs and how they communicate, for example, landscape photographs likewise have textures, patterns, and colours. As we have discussed earlier, visual information was, and is, critical to our survival.

Those leaders who have a strong ability to pay attention to how they and others are feeling are always advised to trust their initial impressions as they have a keen ability to read people initially and can label feelings accurately. We encourage them to trust their 'gut' feel about someone which suggests that they have an accurate perception of emotional data. This in essence is emotional intelligence. These leaders can walk into a meeting and easily assess the mood and emotion displays of those with whom they are interacting and accurately identify how they are feeling at those moments. Again, a useful skill which might have better informed Mueller before his speech.

Using emotions – How we feel influences how we think

Case study

Alison was a marketing manager for a medium sized firm. Although her role was in marketing, her focus was more on sales than marketing. She was an upbeat person with strong social skills, she was intelligent and possessed good analytical skills. Alison spoke eloquently about her feelings. She evidenced a lot of insight as well, except when it came to certain negative feelings. When the conversation turned to these feelings, she would become uncomfortable and change the subject. Alison tried really hard to seem cheerful and pleasant. Although Alison was comfortable feeling and expressing positive emotions and optimistic thoughts, she could not allow herself to access negative emotions, especially embarrassment, guilt or shame. She actively fought against those feelings. There was another surprising side to Alison: she had trouble generating new and creative ideas. She was very grounded, practical and concrete and did not value imagination. For a compassionate and insightful person, Alison did not have a lot of empathy for people she called 'complainers' and 'whiners'. She said that they had no excuse for focusing on the negative aspects of their lives. Alison's ability to facilitate thinking by using emotions was weak. She did not want to, and perhaps was unable to generate emotions, experience them and use them to help her think, process information, make decisions and feel empathy for people. That may work for Alison and some of her managers, but being closed off to emotion is often reflected by a rigid thinking style.

Caruso and Salovey (2004:42)

Using emotions is the ability to tap into emotional data before we think about it consciously. For example, if someone is in a positive mood they will see things differently than if they were in a more negative mood. Can an awareness of this mood to improve, prioritize or re-focus thinking in a situation? There is a large body of research on how emotions influence perception and judgement. People in different moods see and decide in part based upon that mood. Emotion and thought are intertwined, and decision making does not, and cannot, occur in the absence of emotion. If people are able to actually generate an emotion, they should be able to also generate some of these same physiological reactions. Those leaders who are competent in this area usually connect easily with others and have the ability to gain almost an intuitive insight from feelings. This suggests that they have an accurate emotional empathy for most people and emotions: they can feel the other person's pain, are flexible or open-minded and can switch point of view and feelings. These leaders have the potential to energize and motivate others as they have an ability to feel what others feel and often can feel things very deeply. This may also manifest as strong creative thinking and problem-solving abilities and leading others. They have a strong emotional imagination and a lot of emotional empathy for others which allows them to build strong connections which encourages emotional engagement.

In the example above, Alison lacked all of these skills as she was highly rational in her approach to work. As a result, she missed a lot of powerful messages or data from her team which may have impacted severely on how the business performed. The ability to use emotions is keenly associated with strong leadership and influencing abilities. Those proficient in this branch can recognize that moods and thoughts are inextricably linked and this ability really helps them to focus on what is important and can get others to do the same.

The leaders we work with lack these abilities and do not always feel what others feel or feel for certain people or certain emotions much like Alison in the example above. Their perspective on things is individually led and they may not entertain others' points of view. These practical types do not always consider the influence that emotions have on their thinking and sometimes they may have trouble feeling what others feel and may have some difficulty empathising with those around them. They block out emotions or have a hard time processing them. To develop this skill, we encourage them to notice how some people at work make them feel more energized than others. We ask for views on why they are stimulated by certain people and not others, do they share similar values or beliefs? We suggest that leveraging a good mood by bringing it to their next meeting or encounter will further create a positive mood in others around them. Good moods are contagious most of the time, as are bad moods. We suggest that they factor in the influence of their mood at work, it is contagious and can be the deciding factor as to whether people actively want to work with them or not. We encourage these leaders to become aware of how they, and others, feel, and gauge how these feelings influence decisions and judgements. This may involve more open communication, listening, observing those around them and also paying attention to moods and types of interpersonal problems which occur simultaneously and understanding why this may be the case.

Understanding emotions

Case study

Suzanne managed a twelve-person computer help desk for a large retail organization. Her department experienced a series of problems, small ones at first, but problems that were cascading into a major headache for Suzanne and for the company. One employee, Mary, was threatening legal action for discrimination, and another, George, had already filed for a work-related stress disability claim. These problems did not come as a surprise to Suzanne, because she was very aware of how Mary and George were acting, but she was very upset when Human Resources called her about Mary's discrimination complaint and she was shocked to hear that George was taking sick leave. When quizzed about the discrimination complaint, Mary indicated that she did not feel respected by Suzanne and her department peers. In a conversation with George as he packed his briefcase to leave the office, he complained over and over again about how unfairly he was being treated and how his efforts were never recognized. Suzanne had no idea where these problems originated. In fact, these two events, though unrelated in Suzanne's worldview, were based on the same underlying cause. If Suzanne could have connected the emotional dots, she would not have been surprised to learn about these problems. Here's where a what-if analysis is valuable. Her analysis should have started by asking what causes anger. The answer is that anger often rises from a sense of injustice – a feeling that we are being treated unfairly. Suzanne knew Mary and George were angry, but she did not have a clue as to why. The next step of this emotional what-if analysis is to understand how anger grows and changes, even builds over time. It can start out as a vague feeling of frustration and grow into dissatisfaction, resentment and even anger; if unchecked, it can turn into rage. Mary, a very sensitive person, performs a function that her boss, Suzanne, does not value. Such a lack of respect, although subtle, took its toll. George's need for recognition was strong, and without such recognition he felt increasingly unappreciated and devalued by Suzanne and the entire organization.

Caruso and Salovey (2002:53)

The third ability measures understanding of emotions which is the ability to reason about feelings and the information contained in them. This will allow us to figure out why a person feels a certain way and how these feelings will change over time. Suzanne would have noticed that all of the HR issues which were emerging often had very different manifestations than what was been presented outwardly. This is pretty typical in work situations. When we meet leaders who are continually complaining that their teams are ineffective, whether it is performance or attitude, we ask the leader to examine their behaviour to see if and how this might be contributing to the problem. This is not always well received but often sinks in when 360-degree feedback reports are filed and the results from the team and peers speak for themselves. When we encourage leaders to examine their ability to understand emotions, we assess how emotions arise from certain causes, develop and change in a set way. It allows us to understand a person's knowledge of emotions and how they change and develop over time: just as emotions follow a set of moves, there are simple and complex emotions. Emotions theory might not specify combinations of emotions with the accuracy of chemistry, but we know a lot about how simple emotions combine to form more complex and sometimes subtle emotions.

A good example of a deficiency in this branch of emotional intelligence is when we notice that on occasion some leaders have difficulty understanding the vocabulary of emotions. They see too many possible avenues for feelings to change, either way, may miss out on information or not consider what happens next to people on an emotional level. They have difficulty in understanding how people's feelings change over time and while they understand emotions and people, they sometimes struggle to describe feelings.

When we work with leaders to improve this skill, we suggest that they take some time to understand why or how a person is feeling the way they do. For example, when they meet an emotional response at work such as someone being angry or sad, before they react, think about what may be behind such a response. This can be difficult if it is aimed at them, but most of the time, it is not about them at all. Sometimes when people feel inadequate, or out of control, they will react emotionally to try and cope if their values or beliefs are being compromised. An emotionally intelligent person will not react to the emotion, but find out what is really going on. This may involve moving the person to a less threatening location, changing the subject until they regain composure and displaying some empathy. When they have calmed down, some gentle probing and questioning may reveal what is really going on. It can take some real confidence and bravery to put aside how their reaction has made them feel and focus on what is really going on for others. Suzanne would have benefited from exhibiting more of this behaviour with her team. Another way to develop this skill is to take some time to understand the underlying reasons behind a person's reaction in a particular situation. For example, if someone expresses distaste or puts obstacles in front of a new task or project, fear of the unknown and incompetence may be triggering their negative reactions. It may be useful to spend some time asking them open questions to prompt answers on how they really feel about doing the new task and why. They understand the causes of emotions and can predict how people will feel, as they can grasp and describe subtle emotional information. Their emotional insight is strong and they can easily understand the nuances of emotion and explain these in clear and vivid detail. They may be described by others as insightful. This is a powerful skill and one which is very useful when leading those around them.

Those who understand emotions can logically make good sense of emotions. They can speak about emotions quite easily and have a good idea about how people will react to their thoughts or suggestions. Sometimes, emotions may lack sense to them or they may not understand why people react the way they do. However, they have some keen insight into people and can figure out what will happen next in terms of how people feel. Sometimes they may have some difficulty identifying the next stage of how people will feel and may find some emotions quite difficult to predict. Effective leadership is all about adjusting their communication style depending on who they are dealing with and understanding the nuances of each person. This skill will allow them to really understand people and build strong and effective relationships with their team, peers and superiors.

Managing emotions

Case study – Underlying emotional triggers

Mike had worked in the marketing division at Rapido Tube Systems for eight years. He had a strong team who respected him and worked diligently for the division. He had spent many years with each member of the team figuring out their drivers and motivators and fashioning their ambitions to suit the requirements of the company. Mike had successfully created a high performing team who trusted him implicitly and had mutual respect for one another. He was reasonably satisfied in his job and enjoyed getting on with what needed to be done. The company recently devised a rather ambitious growth strategy to triple its sales revenue over a period of five years. This could be achieved by either acquisition or exponentially reducing costs in house. In the past month, Mike was informed by his senior team that a new manager would be arriving to help the division achieve this growth ambition. Mike's response was rather lukewarm but nonetheless he agreed to assist the new manager in whatever was needed.

When the new manager Jonathan arrived, the team greeted him with some suspicion but tried to make him feel welcome. Jonathan was an introvert and did not engage with anyone from the team and for the most part barely made eye contact with anyone from the moment he arrived. His job was to promote efficiencies for which he was valued by head office. He set an extraordinary target for the division to achieve by the end of the quarter. Mike was stunned but did not argue and presented the new demands to the team. They were horrified and said there was no way it could be done. Mike urged them along and said that they would all at least have to try. So they did. Jonathan's target of reducing spends by 12 per cent was achieved and had beaten previous records of spend reduction by 75 per cent. Mike was proud to inform Jonathan that they were all on track but Jonathan made no overt displays of gratitude and simply moved on and talked about the next quarter.

For some reason which he could not understand, Mike started to feel afraid of Jonathan. It became a preoccupation of his, mulling over the way in which Jonathan managed the meetings and it also became clear to him that the team were slightly afraid or at least intimidated by Jonathan. Mike became defensive on behalf of his team and started to feel rather helpless that this new manager was wreaking such emotional havoc amongst his wonderful team. He started to avoid Jonathan and found himself slightly palpitating while in meetings with him. As a means to regain control, he decided to confront Jonathan about the team's excellent performance stating that the he and the team had readily achieved the goals set out. Much to Mike's surprise, Jonathan agreed and suggested that perhaps Mike deserved an increase in salary. Mike was stunned but decided to take advantage of the good mood and asked for some professional development which Jonathan agreed to. Mike left the meeting feeling good but still irritated by the feeling of sheer discomfort and fear. He decided to sit down with his executive coach to discuss what was going on. When the coach started to explore with him as to why Jonathan was causing him so much upset he could not really make sense of it. In fact, when he thought about it, Jonathan had elicited a pay rise for him, which his previous manager had not done, and had sent him on a rather exclusive leadership programme which made him the envy of his peers. When they started to examine why Mike was feeling this way, the coach asked him if he could recall any person in the past who had evoked such a similar reaction. Mike thought for a moment and said 'My mother'. He surprised himself with such an answer but when they began to unravel it, Mike started to realize that Jonathan had very similar traits to his mother and he had been terrified of her while growing up. She demanded a lot from him in terms of achievements and if he did not fulfil her ambitions for him, he was studiously ignored for a period of time which was rather devastating for him as he was a child who really needed affection and endorsements that he was still a good boy.

Fleming (2016:47)

The fourth and final branch of the MSCEIT examines how people manage their emotions and those of others and use this data to make good decisions. Emotion management examines the different ways to cope with situations and looks at a leader's ability to select effective emotional strategies for themselves. There are different ways to cope with situations. Some strategies are more effective than others, and this task measures a person's ability to select effective emotional strategies to get to a certain emotional outcome in social situations. There are of course better and worse ways to handle other people. It is worth remembering that in life, some people and situations will make us feel better or worse than others. Sometimes we have no choice but to deal with and work with people who are very different to us and will evoke some real strong reactions inside of us such as was demonstrated by the example of Mike above.

Our almost primitive reaction is often prompted by a variance in values which we discussed at the outset of the chapter. The most important thing is not to ignore or suppress such feelings, but manage them in a way which works for us. If we feel angry or upset in a situation such as illustrated above, we suggest that leaders can work out some strategies which will allow them to channel that emotion into a safe and effective outlet at a later time. This may involve removing themselves from the situation when the time is right and going for a brief walk outside to breathe some fresh air. Alternatively, it is worth having a friend or acquaintance at work that they trust and can converse on any frustrations with ease. This may be a person who makes them feel good and brings their mood to a more positive place.

We always encourage leaders to have someone at work to talk with, so they are not always bringing their work frustrations home to their significant other, and upsetting them during personal time together. This could also be a coach who is independent and who can offer a means of working through certain situations and frustrations. Talking things through is the only release leaders have from their high pressure environments. In our work with those who are competent in this task, we notice that they generally stay open to emotions and are often able to choose strategies that will include this important feelings-based data. In terms of their relationships they generally stay open to feelings and encourage others to do the same. They use feelings as information to help them make reasonably effective decisions for others and can make a decision which balances both thinking and feeling abilities. However, note that they are not exempt from sometimes becoming unbalanced where their thinking overrides the emotion and leaves them making solely cognitive decisions. This can happen when they may not remain open to certain emotions which makes them feel uncomfortable or the other person's reaction may cause discomfort in them. When leaders have cracked this skill, they have the power to make highly effective decisions with an ability to blend thinking and feeling to inform their choice of decision. The final point on managing emotions is to encourage leaders to be open to emotions, even those which may be unwanted or uncomfortable allows people to make good decisions and help others to process their own feelings in order to assist them.

This was never more relevant for our opening leader Mueller, who faced a situation of great discomfort both professionally and personally. One could exhaust many chapters in this book musing on how and why VW ended up in this situation, perhaps through autocratic leadership styles, deliberate deceit, recklessness, dishonesty or just poor decision making. This is not our focus at this time. However, we do conclude that Mueller and indeed VW could have faced the situation with a very different approach using the medium of emotional intelligence. This would have allowed him to perceive his stakeholders' emotions, take and use that data to inform VW recovery strategy, acknowledge the stakeholders' dismay at being betrayed, acknowledge such betrayal and finally manage it. This might have allowed VW to turn around their reputation not through one speech but to start the process of healing relations with the world. This example demonstrates the medium of emotional intelligence as a means of underpinning strong and inspiring leadership. The four abilities, when assessed, allow leaders to easily assess what aspects of their persona and how they operate are informed by these skills. The scientific research and our experience tell us that such skills help to humanize leadership and instigate strong followership.

Conclusion

As consultants and facilitators of leadership development, we work with thousands of global leaders of varying cultures, backgrounds and industry contexts. Their diversity ensures that each has a unique skillset or offering to their role and often they have been selected due to their abilities, whether that is simply likeability, effectiveness or chance. We offer an array of tools and coaching to assist them in their demanding roles but our experience always demonstrates that the individual is the key to their own success. Their values, their awareness of self and those around them is a far superior skill in leadership than just an ability to read spreadsheets, design a strategy or send a memo updating staff on latest developments. People follow human leaders, certainly those who can lead but also those who inspire and sometimes offer a glimpse of their fallibility. These leaders have a strong self-awareness and keenly understand their values and what they stand for. They do not compromise on these values which suggests that they are tenacious, committed and honest. Emotional intelligence offers a means to capture these abilities and lead in a way which is both inspiring and intelligent in the VUCA environment.

Chapter 6

The embodied leader – character under pressure

John Neal

For decades authors as diverse as Socrates, Sun Tzu and 'Stormin' Norman Schwarzkopf examined the commonalities between the three worlds of sport, military and business. The outcomes are different but the environment and pressure is what connects them together. In Sport, Military and Business (SMB) winning really matters. Winning takes hard work, planning and nerve plus a lot of ability and a little bit of luck. Unlike some forms of art, SMB does not have a script, nobody knows what the outcome will be until the final whistle is blown. Indeed a noted quote from Bill Shankly (1913–81), the Liverpool FC manager, highlighted this when he said: 'Some people think football is a matter of life and death. I don't like that attitude. I can assure them it is much more serious than that.' In each environment success is dependent less upon resources such as the funding, equipment and numbers of the forces involved but more upon the ability of the leaders, players and soldiers to make the right decisions at the right time and under pressure. The military and sporting worlds are seen from the outside as rather directive in their leadership approach. However in our experience this is very far from the truth.

Whilst business talks about complexity and change in their environment and they offer a snappy acronym VUCA (Volatile, Uncertain, Complex and Ambiguous) the reality is that the sports and business worlds are very different. The typical tenure for a military leader is two years, maximum, and in Premier league football is now less than eight months. Results in the sports and military world are everything and failure is not acceptable. The military world has the added dimension of fatal consequences and as much as businesses face pressure it can never even be close to the pressure upon the leaders and soldiers in the military. In order to stay alive (literally in the military world) the approach to leadership development has to evolve faster than the environment in which it is applied. This chapter covers three areas for consideration based on three distinct areas which are critical to the holistic way in which humans lead – with their brain, their body and their spirit – and it is this approach which will help us understand how we can transfer the lessons from military and sport into business.

Leadership can appear easy in theory even in a book like this one. The difficulty and the challenge is the ability to lead effectively when the pressure is on, when real life meets leadership and where followers can decide by whom they wish to be led. As Binney et al (2012) suggest, great leaders don't just write about it, they actually do it; and the really great ones do it best when the pressure is on. So before we look at those three areas of leadership context (mind, body and spirit) it is critical to understand the brain and how pressure affects decision making, behaviour and leadership thinking. Let us begin with a quick trip around your brain.

Brain One is responsible for the autonomic nervous system and especially the sympathetic and parasympathetic nervous system. Sympathetic response is the fight or flight response which gets us up and going. Too little and we do nothing and get eaten. Too much and we burn out from exhaustion. The parasympathetic chemical is acetylcholine and this allows us to slow down and relax. Working together and in balance these two systems ensure that we can work at maximum brain and body capacity.

Brain Two controls the ways in which we perceive the external environment.

It is the little voice inside which says 'Yes, you can do it!' or 'What, you!? . . . no way.'

It is based upon our previous experiences, both positive and negative.

Brain Three is the big cognitive bit which is split into two halves or hemispheres and allows us to make important decisions based upon cognition.

To make this come alive for you, we can think of the brain in three simple areas. Of course it is much more complex than this but let's just try something. Raise your hand and make a fist. Imagine that your forearm is your spinal column with your fist representing your brain. Place your thumb inside your fist, like you used to when you were a small child. Now, as you look at your fist you have the three elements of the brain right in front of you. The most developed part of your brain we will call *Brain Three* and is represented by your fingers wrapped around your thumb. Your thumb inside your fist we will call *Brain Two*; this is your emotional brain which determines how you perceive the world. And finally the big muscle at the base of your thumb represents *Brain One*, the most ancient part of your brain. The three elements of your brain work together all the time and some areas are more dominant under pressure than others, so now let us examine the three levels of the brain which are helpful to understand as leaders.

Level Three (*Brain Three*)

This is the sort of thinking that you are doing right now. It is considered thinking: considering what you are reading in this book and its ideas and drills, reflecting upon how they might be used, thinking if you agree or not. You can often see people using their level three thinking. Imagine being offered a wonderful piece of cake after a meal. Your left and logical brain thinks through the calculation of calories eaten vs calories expended. The right brain thinks how good it would taste and imagines the texture and feel as you take the first bite. I bet you have seen people looking at the cake with their head going from side to side, left to right, as they consider both sides of the level-three thinking argument. It often takes a little while to come to a decision, but it is usually to eat the cake. This part of the brain works relatively slowly but allows us to be different from animals as we make choices based upon our learning from the past and our ability to imagine a future. Critically this is the part of our brain which we use to pass tests and school exams, so now you know why you hit the front and back of your head when you can not remember an answer!

Level Two (*Brain Two*)

This involves the use of emotions and is created through experiences especially when we were young. Whilst the brain is developing and especially when we are young it is known as 'plastic'. In other words, it can be moulded just like plastic. It creates pathways and roadmaps of the world which it experiences and it will take on learning very quickly and easily often through mimicking. We are very impressionable. As we get older the brain needs a little bit more stimulus to take things on board. The key to this stimulus is pressure, especially adrenalin. When you have an experience which is adrenalized, a pathway is created in the level two part of the brain. If you think back to your school days, you will often remember one teacher and perhaps one event very powerfully. Very often that event is not positive and sad but true, the most powerful memories are often negative as they involved fear and challenge and adrenalin (Thomas and Cheese, 2005). Positive memories are often less powerful because the events which created them were enjoyable, fun and the people we were with did not create an adrenalin response in us.

Level two thinking is where our perception and values live. Level two thinking is very powerful as the mental pathways are very strong. And it is just as well that we do remember negatives and avoid them. Just imagine the scenario. You are told by your parents that you should not touch the fire, but being curious and a little naughty you do so anyway. It really hurts, so just imagine if that was not enough to teach you a lesson: how many times do you want to get burned before your brain avoids the situation again? So the sad but true reality of how your brain works is that we are not designed to be happy and content. As the Australian polymath, comedian and musical genius Minchin so accurately explained, 'content and happy Homo Sapiens were eaten before they had the chance to pass on their happy and contented genes'.

Level One (*Brain One*)

This type of thinking is non-cognitive. Some would suggest that at this level there is even some role for genetic thinking. In other words, it is possible that the way in which we think is passed down through generations through our genetic code. The thinking which takes place is extremely fast, so fast in fact that we do not even know we have done it before our behaviour takes place. What do we mean by this? Well I knew that I should love my children as I have read and learned about it in all the relevant magazines and TV parenting shows (Level Three brain activity). I know that I love my children because I love spending time with them, we watch films, go to watch sports, we grunt at each other and no matter what they do, although I may not like what they have done, I always love them (level two brain activity). But on the day when each was born, when I had never met them, or spent time with them, I knew I loved each of them more powerfully than anything I had experienced before. When I see they need my help there is nothing that will stop me, there is nothing that would get in the way, not fire, danger, even death. I love them because I love them. No thinking required – and that is level one brain! Imagine if somebody barged into your children in the street and then was threatening to you and your family. When I say imagine it, I really mean it. Take your nose out of this book and take some time to just imagine a situation in which your close family are in danger or under threat. Go on, just try it.

Welcome back. As you imagined that terrible situation, did you start to become anxious and twitch a little, and become slightly uncomfortable? You knew it was not real, just your imagination, but you started to react, your body changed and perhaps you just imagined what you would be willing to do to protect your family. And if you have a strong imagination, you may have even considered hurting that threatening person, perhaps more. And of course you know that hurting another person is against the law (level three) but something inside you, deeply held in *Brain One*, said 'protect your family no matter what' and perhaps now you are a little angry. Well calm down – it is not real. Level one thinking takes place to keep us alive: it is very fast and we sometimes have no idea what we did and why we did what we did to protect our family and ourselves.

So there are three basic levels of thinking whether you are sports, military or a business leader. Your thinking will determine how you behave and the decisions which you make. To really understand how these three brains work together we have to next understand how pressure affects the activity of each area of the brain (Waller, 2012).

Leadership under pressure: the pressure effect

Pressure does not exist. It is simply in the minds of the people in that environment and reflects how they perceive what is going on around them based on their filter on the world. Without pressure nothing gets done at all. Whilst many people seek a life with no pressure, the reality of that situation is very different. Initially it sounds great: no emails or phone calls, no meetings, no deadlines, no targets, but ponder a little more. No emails or phone calls means no work, no work means no money, no house or holidays. Without meetings or deadlines, people might let you down and do their own thing; set no goals and people wander off target. The right pressure at the right level is really good for individuals. But we have a problem here, because we have not evolved fast enough for the type of pressure which we are subjected to in the modern world. We are all animals, highly evolved, but animals all the same, and our evolution into the modern world has simply not been fast enough to enable us to react in the right way to those things which cause us pressure.

When we perceive something to be a pressure or a threat, then *Brain Two* activates *Brain One*, we produce adrenalin in large enough doses to cause *Brain Three* to shut down. This means that despite all our learning and development, we end up doing the same old things, making the same errors and not *Correctly Thinking Under Pressure (CTUP)*. To understand the pressure effect, we have to first understand a little about how we have evolved and most importantly how we react when we perceive there to be a stimulus. The brain likes repetition, simplicity and clarity so let us just remind your *Brain Three* of what happens to your thinking as a leader under pressure:

So consider this . . .

If there was a lion or a tiger at the door right now what would you do?

If you have thought about it then you have never been in front of a real lion or tiger. The fact is that before you could even think, your brain and body chemistry would have changed so quickly that you would not be capable of thought. Indeed, you would not want to think, you would hopefully just react and run away, or if you could not run away then you would fight . . . if you could do neither then the final result would be to stand still. But again that would not be a choice, it would reflect the fact that you were so scared that your muscles went into tetanus where they simply will not work and you freeze, rigid and still, in the hope that the predator would not see you. Try standing very still on the street one day and you will be amazed how few people even realize that you are there.

But how does the fight, flight, freeze response relate to us in the modern world? Have you ever been in meetings all day, in an airless room with only coffee, biscuits and financial figures to stimulate you? By the end of the day you are tired, it is winter and when you get back to your car it is dark and cold. You start the car, put the heater on and start to drive. The headlights are blinding; the traffic is heavy but eventually after an hour struggling through the city you reach the motorway. You realize that you are feeling tired so you put the radio on to liven you up. Unfortunately, it is the mellow hour and they are playing the love tunes which bop along at about 45 beats per minute, your head starts to mimic the beat of the music, your mind wanders, your eyes feel heavy, your head drops and then as your neck flops down and your head hits your chin you are shot with a massive belt . . . of adrenalin. You sit up with a start, your hands grip the wheel, your eyes widen, your heart feels like it is about to leap out of your chest, the hair on the back of your neck sticks up, you begin to sweat and you can not sing along to the love tunes as your mouth is dry and your brain is fried! That is an adrenalin shock and it is designed to keep you alive.

The fight, freeze, flight response is well documented and describes how as animals the thing that used to cause us pressure in caveman days was the need to battle with animals to stay alive or to eat them. As a result, the best response was to prepare the body for physical activity, increase the heart rate, narrow the eyesight, shut down hearing, increase blood pressure and an increased supply of blood to the major muscle groups and we make a fist ready to fight. Most importantly the blood also drains away from the stomach and some people experience 'pressure induced evacuation' from the bowel. The blood also floods away from the upper cortex of the brain; the thinking part is not required as the faster core brain takes over. The adrenalin response. Do you see the similarity? Despite the fact that meetings, deadlines and emails are no physical threat to us we still respond in the same way as we used to respond to the threat from lions, tigers and bears. But in your world how often do you have to fight or run from a meeting, to become physical with a supplier who lets you down or beat the living daylights out of somebody who fails to respond in time to your important email? Hopefully never.

So why do we do it? The answer lies in the core of the brain. In order to stay alive, the core element of our brain is capable of working 80,000 times faster than the upper hemispheres. Remember your fist? The core brain is your thumb inside your fist and the muscle below your thumb. And your fingers are the upper hemispheres, or the cortex. So to make this even more real you would need to place both of your fists together wrist to wrist. This is because you have two *Brain Three* brains which work together all the time. The two hemispheres are connected by a bundle of cells called the *corpus callosum* which allows the two hemispheres to communicate and make decisions and think. Imagine thinking about how to deal with a lion or tiger: developing an effective strategy may sound like a great management process, but is simply too slow in the heat of the action. So our brain has the ability to divert blood away from the upper parts of the brain and into the faster-acting parts of the brain. As a result, we can react without thinking, to run or to fight or sometimes to freeze . . . or stay very still so that the animals will not see us. Whichever one we do, we are unlikely to make a choice about it or to think it through. We simply react, hopefully fast enough to stay alive. The core of the brain has another key function. It must be able to very quickly identify what is a friend and what is a foe. To distinguish between what we should see as fearful, challenging or fun. Dependent upon this perception we will react in different ways. Indeed, the same external stimulus may be perceived differently by different people and as a result they will react in very different ways.

Sport is a good example in this case. Imagine for a moment you are going to hit a small white ball into a slightly bigger hole, an activity otherwise known as golf. Now imagine that there are twenty thousand people watching you in action live while five million more are watching you do this on the television. If you hit the ball into the hole you will win millions of pounds but if you miss you will forever be remembered as the person who blew it. As you went through that in your imagination, certain people reading this book might shy away and others will think that it is possibly a great opportunity. Some may think, who cares? Same event, different perceptions. Those that shied away will see the event as a threat and will release larger amounts of adrenalin and their thinking brain (the upper cortex, the two hemispheres) will shut down. They are likely to panic and hit the ball far too hard or perhaps even walk away and not hit it at all. Those who perceived the situation as an opportunity and a challenge will still release some adrenalin but just the right amount to excite them and to help them to concentrate. They are likely to have a good blood flow to their thinking brain and they are more likely to hit the ball into the hole. Those people who perceived the situation to be a ridiculous activity where middle-aged, middle-class people walk around a large field hitting a little white ball as few times as possible will consider the situation to be an irrelevant exercise. These people will not care what happens with the ball, they are likely to simply close the book and move on to something which interests them. No adrenalin, no interest and no activity. So pressure does not exist in the external world, it only exists in our heads and in our perceptions of the external world.

So how does this relate to leadership? It is all about the way in which you think under pressure and make the right decisions. Popular and positive thinking suggests that we learn more from our mistakes than we do from our success and this is true – but it does not have to be this way. The reality of effective leadership under pressure is that whilst you may learn from failure you are also likely to get the sack. That is not a great learning experience. How many mistakes would you allow your leader to make before you began to become bored with the 'it's a learning experience' response? The truth is that followers want to be led well; they want their leaders to get it right nearly all of the time. The same goes for sports players, fans, soldiers and political masters. So with all the leadership development, learning and experience which is now made available to so many people, why is it that we still see so many terrible decisions being made? It is very easy to see where the decisions went wrong in the warm afterglow of reflection and with the benefit of hindsight. But that is not leadership. Leadership is carried out when you do not know the answers, leadership is most valued when there is chaos all around you and when perhaps *Brain One* and *Brain Two* are screaming at you to run away or even fight. The answer lies in the function of the brain under pressure. It is not what you know, or how clever you are, how many degrees and doctorates you have: it is all about how you use the knowledge that you have under pressure and get the decision right.

Simply, everything you read in this book will be recorded in the upper cortex of your brain. If you perceive a leadership activity to be a threat you will not be able to access that information and your leadership thinking will suffer. And there is a very simple way to determine how we perceive the outside world. It is to record our heart rate. There are two ways in which we can raise our heart rate. Firstly, we can start to exercise. As we work, our muscles demand energy and typically this is provided through aerobic respiration, the breakdown of fat and the requirement for oxygen and the output of carbon dioxide. We start to puff. Our heart picks up these changes and starts to beat faster to get more oxygen to the muscles and also to remove the carbon dioxide. This typically takes a little while, so we puff quite hard until we get our second wind and then we are fine. We can feel our heart pumping away, but it often takes a while to get going.

The second method is with adrenalin. When we are hit with adrenalin our heart rate 'spikes' and increases very quickly in order to get the blood going to the major muscles groups to provide them with the instant energy they will need to fight or run. There is a direct correlation between heart rates and perception of the external environment. If we discover that our heart rate is spiking, then it is likely that we are responding to a perceived threat and as a result our ability to think is being affected – plus of course it is very tiring. There has been research conducted within the military highlighted by Gladwell (2005) which suggests that if your heart rate increases to 135 beats per minute due to adrenalin, then the reduced blood flow to the upper cortex causes a 70 per cent reduction in the ability to think. If the heart rate rises to 175 beats per minute, due to adrenalin and not exercise, the research suggests that the reduced blood flow to the brain can be so significant that it can cause almost complete brain shut down, or as they call it 'mind blindness'. So it is simple, if you perceive an event to be a threat and your heart rate is rising above the critical level, you are likely to forget most of what we will cover in this book!

Of course, a world of no pressure would not be a great place to be (despite your dreams of an empty beach, the ocean lapping gently at your feet). You would not get up in the morning, and worse still, you would not react to the dangerous animal that just walked into your cave. But on the other hand, too many animals in your cave and too much adrenalin causes burnout. Of course as leaders we do not deal with lions, tigers and bears these days: they have been replaced by meetings, deadlines and people who annoy us. There is, however, a special place to be in terms of arousal, alertness and brain function. In sports we call this being in the 'zone'. When you are in the 'zone' you perceive the outside environment to be an exciting challenge which is perfectly met by your perceived skills and competencies; you are excited, your heart rate is elevated and your senses are at their most acute. At this point, your concentration is crystal clear, you are thinking fast and are often able to predict what is about to happen. This is also referred to as being in flow. Most importantly you are able to access all your knowledge from *Brain Three*: you recall and are able to act upon your plan and your strategy. This is a great place to be: in sport it means that you usually win, while in the military it means that you complete the mission with great success and a better chance of no deaths or injury. In business it means that you say and do the right thing, take the correct course of action, correctly predict the market, win the bid, complete the deal and deliver the solution.

Character

Because *Brain Two* controls the pressure response, we should look at an important element of leadership which is often overlooked. Skills and competencies are easier to measure than character and values, which is a great shame as under pressure it is character that counts. So what is the character of great leadership and how can it be developed for the future? Describing the character of a leader is complex and we come up against the nature and nurture argument which further bumps into personality and behaviours. We suggest that our character is a complex mix of our genes, our mental wiring based upon our personal life experiences and finally our choices around how we behave. Some is conscious and some unconscious, but character is exposed when we do not manage our emotions effectively and allow the negative and less helpful elements to override our choices. This is a really important message for those engaged in leadership development. Throw your books and theory out of the window and start to think how you can help leaders to develop the type of character and self-awareness needed to lead in their own environment and under pressure. Character is developed through experiences which are engaging, challenging and exciting but not frightening. Having created a leadership experience, it is vital to carry out some reflective practice to embed the learning even more deeply into *Brain Two* so that, when the time comes, character comes to the fore.

So what can you do to lead more effectively under pressure?

1. Self-awareness
Understanding the light and dark sides to your character enables leaders to develop insight and of course foresight to ensure that they are ahead of the game and can still think and act clearly under pressure. Self-awareness also enables a leader to recognize the sorts of environment which might cause them to shut down *Brain Three*. Consider this: if you know in advance that certain people will upset your *Brain Two* values (imagine now having a meeting with somebody who constantly eats when you are speaking to them, and worse still, eats with their mouth open) you are ready for the situation and you can adopt new ways of thinking before the meeting begins and give yourself a better chance to avoid a negative reaction which might cause you to think less effectively as a leader. It sounds trivial but these are the sorts of things that can derail your thinking – so the message is, really get to know yourself.

2. Apply your mental 'Equaliser'
This is a conceptual thinking model based upon the metaphor of a DJ who does not like the sound of a piece of music (the environment) and so can change the levels of their thinking (character framework) in order to create the music to which they can dance and be in leadership flow.

The Equaliser

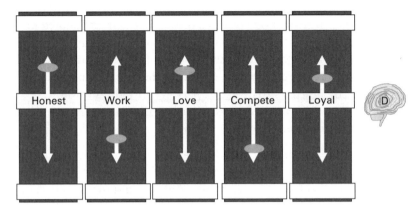

Figure 6.1 Redman.*

You will remember the graphic equaliser on your music system. The idea was that you could alter different sliders on the equaliser in order to produce the sound which you liked the best. Looking back at your own life and the key experiences you have had, what are the key values which you feel drive you? Light or dark sides. You can consider these as the names for the sliders on the equaliser. Most equalisers have six sliders but you could have anything from one or two right up to eight. You can adjust the sliders up or down at any time you like. If you feel that one value needs to be stronger in that situation, then push it up. If another value you hold needs to be pushed down then you can do that as well. Now consider a leadership situation where things went really well ... where were your sliders? And do the same for a leadership situation which did not go so well. Where were the sliders? Now consider a situation which may arise in the future. Where do you want the sliders to be?

3. The 'BLAST IT' line
This is critical and is represented by the little red dots in Figure 6.1. Whilst it is possible to suppress some values in order to create the best

---

* Note: I am indebted to an excellent and world class coach who I am proud to call a friend. Nigel Redman is a former Bath Rugby player and now works as a coach developer for the RFU and British Swimming. He created the concept of the REDMAN Equaliser.

outcome, there are certain times or events where the level to which you have to lower the value slider is simply not acceptable. This is your 'BLAST IT' line. Everybody has this line, and it is important to know where your line is, otherwise you may have an explosion or outburst which will not help you as a leader. You can discover your line level by looking back at the experiences which created your thinking at level two. Typically, when a situation or a person contradicts or shows a lack of respect for something that you think is really important or a deeply held value you will move towards the line.

Let us look at an example which happened to me recently. It had been a long day and I was standing in turn waiting to get aboard a train. I was tired and so I am sure were the people around me. We all wanted to get home and rest. As the train arrived everybody moved back to allow other passengers to leave the train. At this moment a person pushed past everybody, and dived onto the train and made straight for the only seat available. There were other people who had waited in turn, people who were tired, older people and certainly people who I felt deserved that seat more than this person. I was brought up to be polite, to let others go first and certainly not to push past people in the queue. You can imagine the outcome. I did not seek to understand this person, I did not ask any questions to consider their viewpoint, I did not reflect upon what others might think. I had reached my 'BLAST IT' line. It is not always rational and it is not always right but it is what you believe and have been brought up to believe.

So as a leader it is worth considering. What were the things that you would simply not give way on? What really matters to you? What makes you say 'that far and no further'?

The body

Because pressure is perceived in the brain but causes a reaction in the body, it is important to recognize that the two systems are synergistic and must be developed together. The physiological effects of leading under pressure affect image, posture, voice, self-esteem, resilience, recovery, fatigue, etc.

Heart Rate Variance (HRV)

We have already referred to the measurement of heart rate to understand perception. In the past seven years we have been working with a new and leading edge piece of technology known as Heart Rate Variance (HRV). The heart rate can be affected by factors other than adrenalin, such as carbon dioxide creation during exercise. Heart rate is also averaged over a minute so slight changes may go unnoticed. HRV however measures the tiny changes in the speed between each heartbeat. Using complex algorithms, it is now possible to measure which part of the brain is dominant at level one. We know that for ideal thinking and sustainable performance the body needs an equal amount of recovery to the amount of activity. When we are tired we sleep until we recover. Well, no we do not, we use an alarm to wake us up, to give us a shock of adrenalin and then to rush off to catch a train. HRV enables us to understand the balance between the autonomic nervous system, the sympathetic adrenal response and the parasympathetic relaxation system initiated by *Brain One*. We have discovered that most leaders are dominated by sympathetic response, in other words they are on the way to burnout. They get almost no daytime restfulness and their sleep patterns are much disturbed. This leads to tiredness and an inability to concentrate or think clearly when it really matters.

With this in mind, it is important to look at the strategies which leaders can adopt to ensure that they are resilient under pressure and are able to make the right decisions more often and for longer.

Coping

Practical ways are to stay fit, eat better, move more, sleep deeply and relax more. Specifically looking at the effects of challenges and supporting goals and the use of heart rate monitors to ensure health and fitness.

Confronting

'What is your greatest fear?' In the sporting and military world we do not leave the question unanswered before an important event. We discover it through training under pressure, reflective practice and brutal self-honesty. Invariably our greatest fear is a perception at *Brain Two* rather than a fact. Unless addressed, the fears we perceive can become a stress and cause us to make poor decisions and become exhausted. If confronted early fears can be addressed through training and development in order that it does not cause a problem when it most matters.

In the Moment (ITM)

A series of simple interventions leaders can apply when caught in some unexpected pressurized moments. Try taking a deep breath and holding that breath for ten seconds before slowly releasing the air. This will slow your heart rate down and your mind. You could simply stop, smile and laugh, your brain will think you are happy and start to change in very subtle ways. Distract yourself by doing something you really enjoy and enjoy doing it in the moment. As you focus and enjoy the moment, you will stop focusing upon that which irritates and upsets you. There are so many actions you could take in the area ranging from those which take many years to learn such as yoga and meditation right the way to those which take seconds, like smiling – right now – go on, try it.

Mentally Athletic Development (MAD)

This is the way in which physical movements, especially those involving fine motor control and balance, can energize and activate different elements of the brain. The specific area to activate under pressure is the area associated with visualization and imagination. When activated and developed, this area of the brain has the ability to override previous *Brain Two* perceptions. This enables leaders to see opportunity where all about them see a problem, to motivate and inspire others by creating alternative realities. Mental fitness involves the identification of key mental skills and the delivery of specific exercises and drills to deliver your potential in each of the mental skills areas. Recent research involving MRI scanning of the pre-frontal cortex of the brain has indicated that certain physical exercises stimulate specific areas of the brain – many of which are essential for clear thinking and managing pressure.

Mentally Athletic Development (MAD) training is designed to improve mental function in these key areas:

Short term memory   Decision making
Intuitive thinking   Sensory awareness
Problem solving   Creativity
Confidence   Reaction speed

Mental resilience	Detachment
Visualization	Relaxation
Effective communication	

MAD training exercises include:

Mind maps	Ambidextrous games
Use of music	Affirmations
Self-talk	Brain teasers
Puzzles	Russian skipping

You might like to try these simple exercises to determine your own mentally athletic potential:

1. Circle your right foot anticlockwise. Now with your left, write the figure 8 in the air. If you can not do both at the same time it indicates that you have poor left right brain function which is critical for pressure management and positive thinking.
2. Try to continue reading this chapter whilst listening to the discussion of the people around you. If you can not do both at the same time, it means that you are not great at multi-tasking. This means that you will struggle to think about several things at the same time, which can lead to extra stress and worry.

The spirit

Finally let us look at the spirit of the leader and the elements which may not sit in either mind or body but are essential to effect leadership under pressure. To include the word spirit in a leadership discussion may lead some people to the area of religious beliefs but that is not the use of the word in this instance. In this instance let us consider spirit to be the essence of the individual and one which, unlike the body and the mind, is difficult to measure or quantify but it is certainly present and absolutely has a significant leadership effect upon others. We can describe spirit as a layer which lies below the conscious and as such many people are unaware of it until significant pressure is applied. It is often a scary element of leadership as we just do not know what it is or how it will show itself until we are in that moment. Perhaps this explanation may help.

In my early career I was a police officer and I was called to an armed robbery at a local jewellery shop which belonged to the father of a school friend. I was excited and naively thought I could arrest the robber with ease and become a hero and make the world a safer place. On entering the building, I discovered the real world was not like the one I imagined. The robber pulled me by the collar through a locked grill, took out a gun and raised it to my face and whispered the words 'Goodbye Copper!' In that moment I was terrified and I ran backwards and jumped over a wall before he could fire his gun. But that was not spirit, it was fear, a *Brain One* reaction which kept me alive on that day.

My spirit came through in the days and weeks which followed. I battled within my own mind regarding why I had reacted in the way I had done. It did not matter a jot how many people said I had done the right thing, that I was still alive, that there were only dead heroes. My spirit beseeched me to prove myself so that I began to behave in a very different way. I volunteered for any possible opportunity to face fear, look it in the face once again and keep going. My opportunity arose when some weeks later a suspected drug dealer had to be taken to court. The Special Branch were aware that the drug dealer had three accomplices who were planning an armed escape from the court. They explained that there was a great risk in taking the drug dealer to court and asked for volunteers. I demanded that I should do it. I was driven to face the fear and do it anyway.

As it turned out, and as I stood in the dock with the drug dealer, the criminals decided at the last moment not to go for the escape. What mattered to me was that I had discovered that it was possible to overcome your fears when you are scared. I discovered that I had a spirit within me that gave me self-respect and some degree of satisfaction sufficient that I could deal with the initial robbery and move forward in my life.

So the spirit of leadership or even self-leadership is a strange concept which some people may never have the opportunity to discover because the situation may not arise or, worse still, in my case, the robber may have been a little bit faster and more accurate in their handling of a gun. Spirit of leadership is therefore an unknown within many of use which is powerful and drives us to unusual behaviours. This spirit can also draw other people to follow us, not on the basis of our values, behaviour or the way we look. It is on the basis of this powerful, sometimes invisible force. One key element in this area of spirit is the way in which you, as a leader, think about the future which may cause others to follow you. Here are some aspects which can evoke the spirit of leadership:

Motivation and inspiration. The leader's ability to motivate and inspire others to follow them based upon that certain something particular to them which can be described as above and below the line future thinking.

Above the line future. The ability to go beyond goals and objectives (below the line) to a future which does not exist (above the line). This is all about the leader's ability to think more like a child – yes, a child. When a child thinks about the future they do so in a very exciting way. They live in the moment, they mimic their heroes and their future is not bounded by their current set of beliefs. They create a mind-set which is exciting and fun, there are no limits to what they can do. Imagine a world where adults did the same. The future of course does not exist in any other place than your mind. So as a leader you have a choice to live below the line in a future of probability or go above the line to a future of possibility. Being above the line creates motivation and inspiration which can then be used to drive the goals and objectives which must be achieved below the line.

Results and legacy balance. Great leaders deliver results in the short term. Unfortunately, the leadership decisions required to deliver results in the short term are not the same as the decisions required to deliver a lasting legacy in the long term. Pressure will always drive us to short-term results, monthly and annual figures. This pressure may also cause us to think more about short-term outcomes rather than long-term legacies. Great leaders have the ability to hold these two leadership areas in both hands, in both sides of their brains and make decisions which enable the leaders to create a legacy of success.

Conclusion

In this chapter we have looked at the way in which the brain functions under pressure. We have highlighted three keys areas and looked at several approaches developed within the pressure of the sporting and military worlds which can easily transfer into the world of business. And despite all the advances in science, the HRV and the heart rate measurements, the scanning of the brain and the body, there are some simple and global truths which are still true for modern leaders. 'Orandum est ut sit mens sana in corpore sano.' 'You should pray for a healthy mind in a healthy body.'

Emerging practices in leadership development

What can be done to work with 'what is' (rather than 'what should be') in fostering talent

Chapter 7

Tackling the engagement dilemma, the role of Ego and Eco Intelligence

Sharon Olivier and Frederick Hölscher

Introduction

Through many years of working in the field of organizational consulting across diverse industries, we have been intrigued by the ways leaders attempt to engage and motivate their staff; and how their staff respond or fail to respond to these efforts. For example, we found that poor *communication* and *leadership style* were inevitably cited amongst the top three problem areas in engagement surveys, which usually comes as a shock to leaders who spend hours developing high-tech visual presentations and road shows in their pursuit of communication and employee engagement. For example: Renier, a senior leader in a large global company, once confided 'I have been complimented by my colleagues about my excellent all-staff communications notice boards and presentations, yet I scored well below average on "communication" in the culture survey.' During a debriefing of this culture survey he said, 'I am feeling disheartened and confused.' Leaders' quests for engaging their people in their pursuit of business objectives is not new, every leader or manager has to deal with this challenge 'intelligently'.

Henry Ford once was asked how he felt about making Fords; his reply, "I love making cars and enjoy every black Model T Ford that leaves the plant; my only problem is that I need *people* to build cars, and getting people engaged is a real challenge." The barriers that prevent staff from truly engaging their hearts and minds fully at work is still a hot topic in today's HR and leadership literature.

The engagement dilemma

Gallup and other surveys consistently report that work is more often dread and drudgery rather than passion and purpose. Research shows that only 13–24 per cent of employees worldwide are 'engaged' at work; productivity is at an all-time low and stress levels among employees are rising. Research also tells us that engaged employees are more productive, innovative and have less stress (Macleod and Clark, 2009). Leaders who have to deal with this dilemma often find themselves similarly de-motivated in their organizations and as a result, face a double challenge of keeping themselves as well as their teams engaged and motivated. A massive £3 billion is spent in the UK each year on leadership development, yet in a study amongst CEOs on the barriers to engagement (Armstrong, 2013) indicated that leaders feel they lack the required capabilities to engage their staff; and the Gallup studies tell us that less than 25 per cent of employees are feeling psychologically and emotionally engaged in their organizations. How is this possible given that many of the leadership programmes focus on teaching skills in engagement and motivation? Why are leadership development programmes not achieving better engagement results?

In this chapter we explore how the 'engagement' issue could be dealt with through another lens; the application of what we called 'Ego' and 'Eco' Intelligence as leadership capabilities, with specific reference to how leaders apply these 'intelligences' in a VUCA (Volatile, Uncertain, Complex and Ambiguous) world of work to engage employees. We show how using these intelligences inappropriately can lead to the kind of frustration and disappointment experienced by Renier and many other leaders who are trying to do a good job of staff engagement. In order to bring the concepts to life, we share a real-life engagement story of Sarah who recently joined a new organization and conclude by sharing six leadership practices of Eco Intelligent leadership. The aim is to encourage you to examine your own leadership experiences through these new lenses.

Ego and Eco Intelligence

The concepts of Ego and Eco Intelligence is rooted in complexity thinking and draws and builds on the work of Binney et al. (2012), Hutchins (2012, 2014), Johnson (1992), LaLoux (2014), Scharmer (2009), Scharmer and Kaufer (2013), Western (2013), Zohar and Marshall (2000, 2004) and others. Scharmer and Kaufer (2013) suggest that there are two fundamental orientations towards complexity, namely 'ego-system' or 'ecosystem' awareness. They suggest that one of the biggest challenges facing leaders today is the fundamental disconnect between 'ego-system-centric' awareness and the 'ecosystem-centric' reality.

They describe 'ego-systems' awareness as a concern for oneself, and seeing oneself as an individual in the world (self-focus), holding a belief that one can change and shape the world/business/team according to your own ideas and desires. The word 'ego' comes from the Latin and refers to 'I', 'me' and in the plural even to 'we'. The concept 'ego' is normally associated with words like self-esteem, self-importance, identity, seeing oneself as distinct and separate from the world. In using the concept 'ego', we do not necessarily draw on the Freudian use of it, although there may be some inferences.

The prefix *eco* is used beyond its common use as referring to *nature* per se. It comes from the Greek word meaning *whole house*. Scharmer and Kaufer (2013) argue that in ecosystem awareness, the *essential self* is embedded in how it expresses itself within the bigger whole. Western (2013) argues that 'Eco-Leadership' is the fourth and most current in the 'leadership discourses' over the last century, starting with the 'Controller: Efficiency and Productivity' (1900), the 'Therapist: Relationships and Motivation' (1960), the 'Messiah: Vision and Culture' (1980) and the fourth discourse 'Eco-Leadership: Connectivity and Ethics' (2000). For Western the prefix 'eco' refers to how leaders perceive organizations as ecosystems, rather than closed systems, viewing the organization as a web of connections and networks that operate like eco-systems, an 'interdependent whole' rather than a machine. He makes the point that with this view in mind, 'organisations cannot be led top-down, for an ecosystem requires nurturing not controlling' (Western, 2013: 245). We associate Eco Intelligence with concepts like interdependence, unity in diversity, synergy (as in 1+1=3), adaptability, agility, networking and emergence. As such, eco-intelligence is grounded in complex system thinking where everything is connected, and separation is regarded as an illusion (Hutchins, 2014).

In this chapter these concepts are taken into the arena of Leadership Intelligence. We define 'intelligence' as the ability of humans to adopt from, adapt to and (co)-create a lifeworld for themselves. It is suggested that leaders are *both* Ego and Eco Intelligent beings, although they have specific inclinations (due to a myriad of reasons) to lean more towards one than the other. In other words, some leaders simply have stronger ego needs than others and are naturally more orientated towards self, whilst others are more motivated by being in relation with and enabling others.

Ego Intelligence

Our ego develops from the day we are born. In his book, *Values Driven Organisation*, Barrett (2014) explains how we go through seven stages of psychological development over the full period of our lives. He says that we begin the journey by learning to *survive,* and we complete the journey by learning to *serve*. We begin our adult lives in the ego consciousness and some of us complete our life in the soul (eco) consciousness. The ego stages start with our need for *survival* (first experienced at age 0–2 years); then our need to *conform* (fit in/belong) in order to self-protect is first experienced around the ages of 2–8 years. The next stage is around our need to *differentiate* (be different and special), first experienced between the ages 8–20 years. The next phase that he calls *individuating* (typically around ages 20–30 years) signifies a transformational stage where we start to transcend our ego needs of emotional dependence and approval from the groups that we are part of. This signifies a fundamental shift from a *me* (ego) to a *we* (eco) focus. This stage takes us to a need for autonomy/mastery/self-actualization (our 40s), relatedness/connectedness which is most prevalent in our 50s and higher purpose/legacy which is most prevalent in our 60s. Because many of us do not fully transition (sufficiently satisfy these ego needs) through these early stages of our development, due to many possible reasons in our development process, these ego needs continue to play out as a part of our adult lives and often draw us and hold us back from transcending them, e.g. the need for acceptance (I am not loved), the need for self-esteem (I am not good enough or special enough or recognized enough). This obviously impacts on the type of leadership style leaders adopt, e.g. manifesting a need for security (structure), control (power) on difference (the Challenger or the Maverick).

On the positive side, our Ego Intelligence gives us our sense of identity, not only as an individual, but also as a group. Ego Intelligence sets boundaries and creates a sense of 'I am separate' from the world and other people. It helps us to project ourselves and what we value in the world, and it enables us to mould and change the world around us according to our ego needs as well as how we want to be recognized. The ego tends to defend and assert its boundaries in order to prevent others from bullying or hurting it. Many see the ego as selfish and bad. We however suggest that the ego, when used appropriately and constructively, often enables a single-minded focus to over-coming obstacles.

Ego Intelligent leaders tend to believe that it is up to them to *predict* the future and *control* the outcome, and they do well in an environment where there is less complexity and inter-dependencies, and little disagreement about the what and how of performance objectives. They have a clear sense of what they want and what they believe and are able to provide focus by articulating their needs and passions to the rest of their organization. They see themselves as *separate* to their teams in the sense of being a captain having to lead their crew towards the vision they have in mind. They often use phrases like 'it's lonely at the top', and believe that it is their job to set the direction (vision/goal/strategy), and ensure that their teams are managed to perform appropriately to achieve goals. They tend to manage and engage their teams by instituting extrinsic motivation (punishment and rewards like bonuses, awards, discipline, and training), ensuring clear job descriptions and performance contracts. They are good at appealing to staff's needs for security, belonging, status and focus (as outlined above), and are often driven by these needs themselves.

Ego Intelligent leaders rely on their own ego energy to *make* things happen, which can obviously create high levels of personal stress and anxiety for them as they blame themselves if things do not go according to plan. The metaphor of a machine comes to mind, where the leader is in control of pulling the levers and turning the dials that create a whole sequence of predictable responses within the machine (organization). The Ego Intelligent leader is able to mobilize large degrees of emotional, intellectual and social 'energy' in the pursuit of his/her objectives.

Ego Intelligent leaders address the 'need for engagement' by utilising influencing skills such as directing, persuasive reasoning or inspiration to push or pull their staff to do what they want them to do. They are often persuasive and charismatic influencers and articulate orators, able to convincingly clarify the future and the organizational direction that they intend to take. In so doing they create a sense of 'dependency' from their staff who continually strive to do those things that would please (or comply with) the 'boss'. When faced with a VUCA environment, the ego intelligent leader typically tries to bring order through imposing control.

Ego Intelligent leadership is appropriate when:

- The objectives are clearly defined, the work processes and outcomes are simple, predictable and easily measured, and where less creativity or innovation is required, i.e. low VUCA environment.
- The team or organization is facing a crisis and do not have the required information or emotional capacity to self-organize in order to deal with it.
- Teams or individuals lack the interest, capacity and/or maturity to self-manage.
- Teams are filled with insecurity and in need of a sense of direction.
- Speed or fast action is needed.
- The organization is stuck (not making headway) and requires a nudge to the next level or into a different direction.

Eco Intelligence

Like ecosystems in nature, the social ecosystem has an innate sense of interdependency and a capability to self-organize and leverage diversity. Eco Intelligent leaders tend to perceive the organization as a living organism (social ecosystem), with interdependent talents and potential synergies, and believe that it is their job to create an environment to *leverage* the strengths of the parts and the inter-dependencies. They see themselves as an integral part (as opposed to separate) of their teams. They make a shift from being the 'boss' to being a 'facilitator' of context, as a stimulator of ideas, and as a sense maker. The metaphor of a farmer creating fertile soil for the crops to grow comes to mind. Eco Intelligence has dramatic implications on leadership style. Whereas Ego Intelligent leaders often occupy and dominate the leadership space in their own capacity, Eco Intelligent leaders *share* the leadership space. As so beautifully described by Williams et al. (2012), this kind of leadership is about leadership being what emerges in the space 'between' people, and not something that is imposed by or contained in a single person. An eco-orientation encourages team members with leadership skills to step into the leadership space whenever required and the formally appointed leader becomes the one who enables and holds this space.

Because these leaders have the ability to *co-sense* and *co-respond* with their teams (Laloux, 2014), they do well in complex environments where it is difficult to predict or control the future, in that they lead from 'within the team' as it were. To do this well, they require an 'open mind', an 'open heart' and an 'open will' as Scharmer (2009) puts it. African people have a term for this, 'Ubuntu', which means 'I AM because WE ARE'; which literally means that a person is a person through other people and finds true identity in the collective mind instead of in the individual. It is this shift from 'me' to 'we' that provides a sense of fulfilment in being a part of a bigger whole.

When it comes to managing talent, the Eco Intelligent leader's style is to create a context for individuals and teams to discover and utilise their strengths synergistically with others. They focus on unleashing the talent already present in the social system rather than attempting to mould potential from 'outside' to fit their own or organizational purpose. They do this by creating a context for self-organization, self-management, accountability and intrinsic motivation. They tend to hold individuals and teams accountable for results (the what), but empower them in terms of *how* they get there, helping them to realize the importance of sharing their knowledge and skills with others in an interdependent way in order to reach goals. They encourage and recognize sharing of ideas and skills and cross-boundary teamwork. They prefer flexible job descriptions (or none at all) and value team/peer involvement in all the traditionally HR-led functions like recruitment of new team members, reviews of performance and competencies. They move from a 'people to fit jobs' to a 'jobs to fit people' orientation.

From an employee or follower perspective, this way of working implies high levels of commitment, maturity and ownership, but most importantly, a common *purpose* that pulls and holds team members together. The common purpose is usually something that is considered bigger than any one team and important to all the team members; something that motivates them intrinsically because they co-created it and found a sense of 'vocation or meaning' through it, e.g. creating a specific customer experience, supporting the disabled, or educating a certain target population. Interestingly, because Eco Intelligent leaders believe that the world is unpredictable and uncontrollable, they tend to hold the organizational purpose 'lightly', understanding that it will morph and change as the external conditions and stakeholder needs and inputs change. Laloux (2014) refers to this as 'evolutionary (evolving) purpose'; Zohar and Marshall (2004) refer to this quality as an important feature of 'complex adaptive systems'.

In order to operate effectively in a complex adaptive system, these leaders need to ensure *agility* within decision making which means that their teams have to be close enough to their customers and empowered enough to take decisions and respond rapidly to shifts and changes. Ecosystemic is thinking embraces all stakeholders, including clients, as intrinsically part of the system, allowing for co-creative, mutually influencing relationships with all stakeholders, e.g. clients and suppliers; whereas ego-orientated leaders tend to draw clear boundaries between customers, suppliers and the organization.

An IBM study of fifteen hundred CEO's (IBM, 2010) suggests that CEOs operating in increasingly complex environments tend to include clients as partners in their strategic thinking processes, i.e. bringing clients 'into the board room' as it were. Hampden-Turner and Trompenaars (2015: 182) refers to this phenomenon as an example of 'conscious capitalism' and point out that companies who are driven by a higher purpose, with leaders who pursue win-win relationships among all stakeholders, outperformed the market eight times over. Once leaders have established these principles, they tend to allow the system to *sense* and *respond*, and their role becomes that of coach and facilitator, helping the organisational ecosystem to continually evolve and grow in response to the changing external world.

Eco Intelligent leadership is appropriate when:

- The environment is complex, volatile and uncertain and there are no obvious clear answers to problems, i.e. in a high VUCA environment.
- Where high levels of interdependent actions between teams or individuals are required for success.
- Where an individual's and the team's potential for self-management is recognized and cultivated to a level where they have the maturity and capacity to self-organize.
- Where a uniting and evolving common purpose is evident or possible through a process of constructive dialogue and co-creation.
- There is a need or will to develop an organization that is less dependent on a leader, and more interested in the expression of 'leadership' at all levels.

Many may be left thinking that this that all sounds great but certainly could not work in my organization where the top team is very much driven by a 'command and control' paradigm, where management do not want to release their grip on the reigns of control. Ten years ago this may have been regarded as a 'pipe dream' in many organizations and even today there are many leaders who hold tightly onto an ego-orientation because of the sense of control it gives them. We are however discovering that more and more leaders are experiencing the benefits of applying Eco Intelligence in the workplace. The following case study is shared to illustrate how Eco Intelligence plays out in the workplace.

Case study: Eco Intelligence at work

After fifteen years as an entrepreneur and owner of her own consulting practice, Sarah had reached a stage where she felt ready to embrace the next growth curve in her career. She was tired of being the 'lone ranger' in a country that was becoming increasingly repressive. She felt ready to become part of a bigger community of like-minded people, who because of their collective capacities, were able to impact the world in a far more significant way than she was able to achieve on her own. Without realizing it at the time, she had this growing need to move beyond her own ego-system and to become part of a larger interdependent ecosystem (which completely corresponds to her age and stage of self-development discussed earlier).

Within months of realizing this need and sharing the intention with her family, an opportunity arose via a friend at a larger Corporate Consulting and Training business in Europe. A three-month process of application, Skype interviews, and a trip to Europe for a panel interview with potential colleagues followed. An important part of the recruitment process consisted of presenting some of her consulting work to a panel of eight consultants who were members of the team within which the post was advertised. Being all too familiar with typical corporate recruitment processes, she prepared a presentation with detailed content in order to demonstrate her 'vast subject knowledge' (ego focus). Five minutes into the presentation she realized that her audience was far more interested in her passion and how she was engaging with them. It became obvious that the content was merely an arbitrary container. One panellist commented, 'I sense that this piece of consulting work was far from your passion and interest, why did you choose to do it?'

It was only much later that she realized the leader (manager) of this department was not even present during the interview and that the panel members were not in specific levels or roles and had not been specifically chosen to be there, but were staff from different departments who happened to have an hour to spare on the day. It turned out that the opinions of these members of staff were highly regarded because it was felt that the most obvious decision makers are the ones who have to work with the new recruit on a daily basis. This was a beautiful demonstration of Eco Intelligence at work. Sarah was shortlisted by this team of potential colleagues and the next step was a Skype interview with the leader. During this interview she again noticed a very different approach. This leader was skilled in making her feel relaxed and establishing a genuine rapport. She sensed that the interview was as much about exploring the qualities and energy that she would bring to the team as it was about her knowledge and experience.

The feeling after that interview was one of real joy. Intuitively, the fit felt right. She felt that this could be a place which was open to co-exploring and co-developing her work further, but most importantly she sensed that she would enjoy working with, and building a significant relationship with the leader. This was an important consideration in the face of all the pending changes and loss she would experience in relocating to another country and Sarah was understandably nervous about immigrating to an unknown country and organization. All the typical 'ego' worries were present about her ability to re-establish credibility at a late age in her life, build new networks, and maintain her sense of significance and purpose. She feared that she would lose her independence as an entrepreneur by becoming part of a larger organization with rules, job descriptions, competency profiles, policies, working hours, egos and organizational politics. To her delight and surprise, these fears were not realized.

The distinction between Ego and Eco Intelligence will be used to interpret Sarah's situation and formulate six leadership attributes or practices experienced by Sarah within the culture and the leadership style of her new workplace.

1. Unleashing individual talent

Sarah was expecting a job description and a competency profile, and had assumed that she would be allocated a set number of consulting targets, and allocated specific project work. In other words, she was expecting a well-defined work environment with a clear focus, and given all the uncertainties of a new environment this could have helped her ego needs for clear definition and identity. Instead, it was explained by the leader that she needed to establish her own contribution by networking and discovering the areas she wanted to focus on. Furthermore, that over the first two months Sarah should proactively set up meetings with colleagues from various departments in order to learn about what they do and to share her areas of interest and potential contribution. The idea being that should colleagues find some resonance with Sarah, and found her potential contribution interesting or complimentary to their work, they would invite her to participate in their projects, and so with time she would build up her credibility and fill her diary.

That first meeting left her feeling a mixture of insecurity and excitement. For the first time in years she had to develop a clear and concise personal value proposition that was part of a bigger team and organizational value proposition. This was a refreshing and challenging experience for Sarah, having been a Management Consultant who pretty much said yes to every bit of work to keep her small practice profitable. It took her into a much needed path of deeper self-discovery, now as a part of a bigger whole – an UBUNTU experience as it were. This process entailed having a critical look at all the concepts she had developed and taught over the years and establishing what was most important to her. She fondly relates back to that first interview with potential colleagues where they kept digging to find her real passion and not necessarily her work experience! She had to dig deep to find and articulate her offering that was unique or different, exploring questions around 'What did she want to become known for? What difference did she want to make in the world?' The most challenging part was asking 'How could she participate meaningfully in a larger team (ecosystem), after operating on her own for so long?' In terms of our definition of intelligence, her challenge was to *adopt* from the richness of others; *adapt* her own work and lessons from the past and then *co-create* new ideas and programmes with her colleagues.

On reflection, she realized that she was being introduced to an organizational ecosystem that self-organizes through collegial relationships and networks. She was being challenged to discover and develop her unique contribution, namely her 'ego strength' within an established ecosystem. In order to do this, she had to discover and understand what others do and then to define herself (ego) in relation to others (eco) in order for the system as a whole to function effectively. This was like discovering which particular instrument one would play in an orchestra.

Sarah found this 'shared leadership' approach unexpectedly surprising and refreshing. She felt it forced her to connect to what was really important to her, to define what brought a sense of meaning and purpose to her work life, and to figure out ways to compliment others in order to achieve the purpose they all stood for, which was to become known as an organization that brought innovative and fresh approaches to leadership and organizational development. Having worked independently for so long in a highly competitive industry, the most challenging part for Sarah was an unspoken expectation that all should share their ideas and intellectual property in order to increase the knowledge of the team as a whole. In this culture, it was frowned upon to hang onto things, and to compete with or attempt to look better than colleagues. The uniqueness of each colleague was emphasized and the team had to find ways to complement each other's strengths and weaknesses. Sharing of knowledge and experience was strongly encouraged.

Regular feedback by the formal leader on how she saw Sarah's talents and strengths, and helping her to formulate her unique selling proposition (USP), and identify opportunities to express this USP within projects, with others, led to Sarah' motivation and energy soaring to an all-time high within the first three months, and she felt fully engaged.

2. Purpose and ownership

The purpose of the team did not belong to the 'bosses', and it was not communicated through documents containing vision and mission statements, and policies and procedures of how it should be implemented. Sarah discovered that although there was little evidence of a vision or mission statement, colleagues were generally motivated by the same things; wanting to fundamentally impact the learning journey of their clients (leaders) in a way that would impact positively on their organizations and their communities. She felt that her colleagues 'owned' and lived a common strategic intent, even though it was never shared by the leaders as 'the vision'. Colleagues put their hearts into their work with little regard for sticking to working hours. High levels of individual ownership meant less need for direction from the top.

This approach is distinctively different to how Ego Intelligent leaders would address the 'engagement challenge'. Ego Intelligent leaders will typically focus on getting 'buy-in', and will attempt to tell, sell and influence the team to accept the predefined vision or goals, whereas Eco Intelligent leaders will achieve 'ownership' through a process of simply living the purpose and in so doing inspiring the team to do the same. Sarah discovered the vision and mission in the hearts and minds of her leader and colleagues during her 'walk-about' in the first three months, rather than on the walls of the building.

3. Full autonomy and full support

Essentially, Sarah was set free to self-manage when she worked, how she worked and where she worked within the framework of the organizational context and calendar. She had to get on with things autonomously, with the reassurance that the leader was only a phone call away. Meetings every month were used to check in with each other and catch up on both personal and work life, e.g. debriefing client and colleague experiences; solving problems or co-discovering ways of managing difficult situations; brainstorming ideas for research, etc. The concept of full autonomy *and* full support can be misconstrued as many leaders view full support as 'being in close contact' which then feels like micro-management to the staff member. Although self-management felt very natural to Sarah, she felt that this way of working as part of a self-managed team in a corporate environment was very new and uncertain in the beginning.

One of the toughest things was getting used to the frank and open ways in which both positive and negative feedback was given. Some of Sarah's weaker areas, like her attention to detail, was brought right out in the open for all to look at and discuss. Being part of a mature team like this meant that there was nowhere to hide (which she realized she had been for years). All are expected to give developmental feedback that could be holding back the team's effectiveness. When conflict arose between team members, a process of *supervision* followed, involving an independent, skilled facilitator playing the role of coach to resolve issues maturely. The leader is not involved unless the issue involves him/her.

Autonomy and support form the foundation of a culture that enables individuals and teams to be innovative and to take risks, which is very different in a hierarchical structure where decision making is left to the leaders at the top of the structure, dictating the course of action. In contrast, an 'ego-centric' leader often finds it difficult to allow the other egos in the system to express themselves. Our ego, when out of control, can become quite persistent in protecting the outcome we believe is 'right', and this outcome then becomes an extension of our ego. Eco Intelligent leaders, on the other hand, want to explore how the other egos in the system express themselves in terms of their unique contribution and are curious in finding ways to optimise synergies for the benefit of the whole. This kind of culture does assume a certain level of maturity and capability, and may not be the best leadership style for those needing more structure and direction from the leader.

4. Deposits in the emotional bank account

One could think of humans as having an emotional 'bank account' which is either in the green or in the red. By the nature of their positions, leaders are continuously, consciously and unconsciously making deposits or withdrawals from the emotional bank accounts of their teams or individual employees. Staff in the green are feeling a sense of pride, ownership, security and engagement. Staff in the red are feeling fearful, anxious, insecure and angry, which leads to behaviours of gossip, backstabbing and blame.

Sarah's leader was particularly skilled at giving regular recognition and praise for work done and networks built, which helped Sarah to build up a positive emotional bank account and self confidence in her new role. Her leader informally discussed and promoted the skills of the various team members between each other, and ensured that other departments were kept up to date with the offerings of the people in her department, which led to a sense of pride within the team. She also found many opportunities to encourage team member's involvement in cross-departmental projects with clients.

A simple yet powerful practice was that she habitually checked in on how Sarah was *feeling* about things and not only just how she was performing. Within a short time after having started, Sarah was feeling truly supported, knowing that she was free to approach her manager at any time if she needed to talk through things causing stress and uncertainty. This kind of authentic recognition and support were deposits in her emotional bank account. Many leaders tend to think that providing information or sharing knowledge, i.e. building one's intellectual bank account, is sufficient, yet staff still continually report feeling emotionally and psychologically disengaged.

Sarah found herself intrinsically motivated firstly by the meaning and purpose derived from the work itself and secondly by the work environment and relationships with her leader and colleagues. Because her passion was ignited by the working context (structure and culture) as well as the opportunities within the work itself, keeping an eight-hour day became completely irrelevant and she now works many more hours simply because it gives her a sense of meaning and enjoyment.

5. Shared vulnerability and 'wholeness'

Laloux (2014) speaks about 'wholeness' as an important dimension of Teal organizations, and defines it as bringing one's 'whole self' to work, not just the good bits you choose to show off. We have a tendency to become masters at covering up those parts of ourselves that we do not feel proud to show, be it our insecurities or our fears. The stronger our egos' need for protection, the more we cover up, and in an ego-system this 'cover up' process starts during the recruitment interview and continues in every performance review and departmental review meeting, with staff and leaders parading their egos in order to shine more than the colleague next to them. When we ask leaders in workshops how much of their energy and team meetings are spent on this kind of 'looking good and cover up activity', they generally say 50–60 per cent, this activity is often referred as the CYA (Cover your ass) factor in team meetings!

Leaders often have a need to come across as either the saviour or the hero, the one who has the answers and who has been brought in to solve the inherent problems. In Chapter 3 of this book, Higgins et al refer to research which indicates that many employees are still looking for (and needing) such a hero to show them the way. This need would be particularly relevant for the contexts outlined earlier in 'Ego Intelligence is appropriate when'.

The leader at Sarah's workplace chose (with time) to share openly about her own strengths and weaknesses. She was prepared to show her own vulnerability. This encouraged Sarah to do the same and to bring her whole self to these discussions, not only the good parts. They were able to talk about their strengths but also their weaknesses and how to find ways to supplement weaker areas in each other. This kind of sharing is directly opposite to the 'CYA' culture in ego-systems, mostly because Eco Intelligent people believe the achievement of the team purpose depends on the strength of the ecosystems, i.e. the extent to which individuals are collaborating instead of competing, sharing and complimenting each other's strengths and weaknesses. An Eco Intelligent leader realizes that strengths and weaknesses belong to everybody, namely, 'my strengths contributes to the strength of the team and the organization as a whole and my weaknesses are a threat to all'. A team that operates like an ecosystem ensures that every part contributes its best to the bigger whole. It is much like the human body, if one part suffers; the other parts do not blame or accuse that part, but rather works together to heal that part as soon as possible.

Owning one's weaker areas without fear of rejection seems to be an important element of a mature individual who has achieved mastery and autonomy. Barrett (2014) refers to this as the developmental phase of *individuation*. It involves moving beyond one's ego needs to a place where the approval and acceptance of others is less of a motivator and is replaced by authentically knowing one's contribution and being able to say without fear 'this is me and this in *not* me'. This is a place of where we can feel emotionally free enough to be truly ourselves.

6. From leader to leadership

Sarah noticed many colleagues leading on different projects that fell into their area of expertise, not because they were appointed by the leader, but because when the occasion demanded it they had volunteered and signed up, simply because they felt they could make a contribution. Eco Intelligent leaders do not dominate and control the leadership space. Sarah soon felt that she was part of the 'leadership' as she naturally led on certain projects where she felt comfortable and competent. She felt it important to support colleagues when asked as she knew that the time would soon come where she chose to step into a lead role on a project and would want her colleagues' full support.

Conditions for Eco Intelligent leadership

For staff to be empowered to operate in this supported yet self-managed way, it is evident that some protocols or 'rules of the game' need to be clearly established:

- The 'why', or (higher) purpose must be embedded in the hearts and minds of all the team members, almost like DNA of the organization (Hampden-Turner and Trompenaars, 2015: 167).
- Leaders should focus their attention and measure the 'what'; with individuals or teams empowered to deliver in the way they feel is best (the how).
- Leaders need to create support and feedback mechanisms such as peer reviews, client reviews, debriefing after important events, and regular check-ins to enhance a culture of 'continuous learning'.
- Teams or individuals should be placed in positions where they are as close as possible to their internal or external customers, where they are enabled to make decisions and respond in the moment (agility) to the changing customer requirements.
- Essentially, it requires a different kind of 'consciousness' of how the work environment works. It requires that leaders view their organization as an interdependent complex adaptive system that can self-organize and not as a mechanical machine which needs external control to 'start and stop' and 'be fixed'.

It is important to realize that *all* of us have egos and we all experience our ego needs for security, inclusion and recognition to a greater or lesser extent. At the same time, we all also have the ability to release or tame our ego needs, and to work in a more systemic way with an eco mind-set. We all have both Ego and Eco Intelligence. We would like to position Ego and Eco intelligence as a 'polarity' that all leaders are challenged with, rather than a choice to make.

Ego or Eco Intelligence: a 'choice' to make or a 'polarity' to manage?

Johnson (1992) distinguishes between 'problems to solve' and 'polarities to manage'. Polarities refer to those 'messy or wicked', unsolvable problems where either/or thinking does not give clear answers and may result in limiting growth. The field of polarity management explores the tendency where we, as humans, have become so invested in our viewpoints of what is good or bad, right or wrong, or our perceptions of 'truth', that it blindfolds us to see the value in opposite viewpoints.

Ego and Eco Intelligence could be viewed as a polarity to be managed. Leaders have a natural tendency to lean towards one of these orientations. A leader's effectiveness decreases dramatically when he/she becomes too 'rooted' in a particular style to the extent that they are not able to flex towards the other when the situation requires it.

Ego and Eco Intelligence practices both have an upside when used appropriately in the organizational context, but both have a downside when over-done or used inappropriately at the expense of the other (see Figure 7.1). Johnson (1992) uses the 'infinity loop' to demonstrate how we often tend to get 'stuck' in one of the 'poles' and then oscillate between two opposites. We apply this principle in the polarity between Ego and Eco Intelligence.

Many HR training programmes get trapped in this 'infinity loop'. When the downside of too much control is felt, they send leaders on 'joint decision making' or 'empowerment' programmes, and so it goes on and on. This is also evident in the continuous oscillation we see between centralized vs. decentralized structures roughly every five years in many organizations. The gender issue may be regarded as another 'polarity' to manage in organizations. The key lies in a leader or organization's ability to 'hold' the polarity within a 'both-and' mind-set. Martin (2007) speaks about Integrative Thinking as a core competency of twenty-first-century leaders, which he

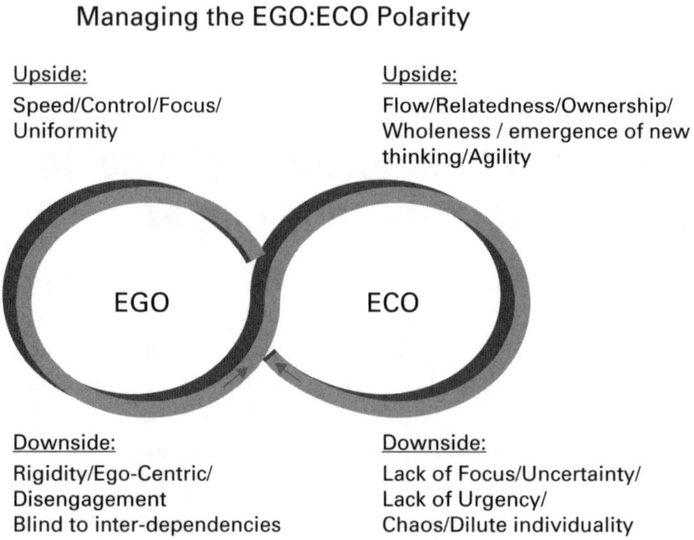

Managing the EGO:ECO Polarity

Upside:
Speed/Control/Focus/
Uniformity

Upside:
Flow/Relatedness/Ownership/
Wholeness / emergence of new
thinking/Agility

EGO   ECO

Downside:
Rigidity/Ego-Centric/
Disengagement
Blind to inter-dependencies

Downside:
Lack of Focus/Uncertainty/
Lack of Urgency/
Chaos/Dilute individuality

Figure 7.1 Ego and Eco Intelligence as a polarity to be managed. (Infinity loop concept adapted from Johnson, 1992.)

defines as the ability to hold opposing models and extract value from both.

We all have ego needs and we are all part of an eco-system. Integrative Thinking or Polarity Management cannot develop unless leaders firstly develop heightened self-awareness of their personal ego needs and orientations. This requires the ability to read a situation and to know when to rely on their ego strength but also when to 'tame' the ego and to allow the eco system to self-organize and self-manage. Constructive feedback with an open mind, an open heart and an open will prevent leaders and organizations to slip into the downside of the one or the other and being trapped in the infinity loop. We leave you with the metaphor of the human hand shown in Figure 7.2.

We believe that the most successful leaders are those with the wisdom of knowing when to use their Ego Intelligence and when to use their Eco Intelligence; who are able to effectively hold this polarity between ego and eco intelligence; intuitively knowing when to close the hand, take control, move quickly and push things forward, and when to open

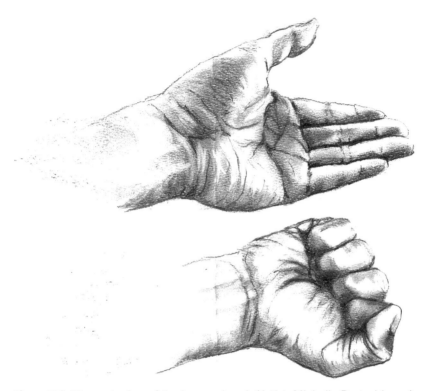

Figure 7.2 The metaphor of the human hand. (Artist: Michelle Bertschinger.)

the hand, release control, and allow the ecosystem to sense, respond and self-organize.

Case study: Next steps: The challenge of polarity?

The organization where Sarah works has recently merged with a much larger, more traditional and more commercially driven organization and a new leadership team was appointed. This merger led to an interesting dynamic within the organizational culture. A much greater focus on tighter control, top-down decisions, traditional performance measurement, clearer balanced scorecards with more specific behavioural measurements, sales incentives, and focused recording of time and results. Most of the teams have been restructured and have had to fundamentally re-look the way they do things; in other words, the organizational ecosystem has been disrupted and needs to re-organize.

The big question now is whether the ego and eco polarity can be managed in a way that maximises the value of each, or will the organization be caught in the 'either-or trap'? The answer to this question is not only for the leadership, but for all who participate in the future of the organization, which may also include other stakeholders like clients and investors. Our next interview with Sarah should be an interesting one!

Chapter 8

Appreciative Leadership

Mike Brent and Mark McKergow

Introduction

Although the word 'Appreciation' might sound feeble and weak to some, it is a vital skill for leading in a fast-moving VUCA (Volatile, Uncertain, Complex and Ambiguous) world. This chapter will start by discussing how this 'soft' skill is hard currency for tomorrow's leaders and will discuss what Appreciative Leadership is and is not, while demonstrating its use as an essential methodology in today's increasingly complex environment. We will then share some key methodologies and finish with five key practical tools. Let us begin with a caveat here. Although we strongly believe in the power of appreciation and looking at what is working, we do not necessarily feel that everything should be seen as positive. There are approaches which we might describe as 'positive claptrap', that seem to ignore any mention of what is not going well or when people are being lazy or obstructive. There are clearly times when as a leader you need to point out where things need to improve, which is fine. However, we would suggest that such methods are offered in a constructive and positive way and do not focus exclusively on what is not working.

Showing appreciation to others is a fundamental aspect of being an effective manager or leader and in developing effective relationships. The need to be valued and appreciated is a basic human need, and if managers seek successful performance from their people, they need to grasp the basic psychology of appreciation. As Olivier and Hölscher in Chapter 7 discussed the importance of employee engagement, we also believe that people have more energy and are more effective and creative when they enjoy their work, and one of the key mechanisms for this is to be valued and appreciated by their colleagues and their managers. However we believe that appreciation by their manager is the most critical. This thinking is supported by research that shows the modulation effect of positive emotions on infant growth and neurological development (Schore, 1994, 2015), and a number of studies have correlated the frequent experience of positive emotions to health and longevity (McCraty et al., 2001; Seligman, 2003).

There is reason to believe therefore that positive emotions at work – in the shape of appreciation by the manager – have a beneficial effect on both health and development. Interestingly, research also suggests that changes in emotional states are reflected in the rhythm of the heart. Studies which looked at determining which particular emotional states have the most impact found that sustained positive emotions such as appreciation, care, compassion and love clearly generate a coherent heart rhythm. This same study found emotions such as anger, frustration and fear generate a very different heart pattern, characterized by lower amplitudes and an erratic, in other words, incoherent pattern (McCraty et al., 2001).

Traditionally managers use what we might call a deficit model when dealing with situations at work. That is to say that they assume that things are a problem which they need to fix so they get into the habit of focusing on what is going wrong and what is not working, and then trying to fix it. This approach is not just limited to business. In the field of psychology there has traditionally been a focus on what is wrong with a person and what is not going well. The tendency was to look at fixing a person's problems and correcting weaknesses. Nowdays the idea that psychology should be equally interested in what is going well is gaining ground, because some things must be going well for a person, even if other things are not. In other words, we are not defining a person on the basis of what is NOT working, but rather looking at what is working. This is what gives us something to appreciate – which takes us away from the mire of well-meaning generalities and into the crunchy effective world of relationship-building and progress.

There are two approaches the Appreciative Leader can take:

1. He or she can focus on the relationship and the issue, not just the person. They would have the courage to realize that if indeed there is a problem, then they are part of that 'problem' too. They would think about how they might be contributing to the issue, and

focusing on what they could try to do differently. As the saying goes, 'If you always do what you always did you'll always get what you always got' (Henry Ford, 1863–1947). So try doing something different yourself.

2. He or she can look for some positives about the other person or persons involved. What are they doing well? When are they not a problem? What have they done well in the past? What are they doing right now that is not a problem?

Once they have established that the person is not all bad, the manager can start to build on a more positive platform and arrive at much more effective outcomes. A manager is not going to make things better by focusing on what a person does badly. In essence, they are not going to get employees into a positive frame of mind to do something about the so called problem by being negative and critical. This approach just leads to employees feeling resentful. Whether someone is at fault or not is perhaps even irrelevant. The fact is that you as leader need to understand and develop your skill in this area, so that you start to get the outcomes and results that you want.

What is Appreciative Leadership?

Appreciation is something you DO, not just something that you think about. Appreciating is done out loud, it is about noticing what is going well, what is good, useful or impressive, and then sharing it. Some of the component parts of Appreciative Leadership include the following.

Relational intelligence

Very often the real action as a leader comes from the interaction between the leader and others both inside and outside the organization. If this is the case, then the relationship becomes critical. So how can we become more skilled in our interactions and our relationships? We believe that managers and leaders need to build on their technical knowledge and develop what we might describe as relational intelligence. This involves noticing what people do well and then sharing that with the other person. It is important to be appreciative in an authentic way; the appreciation has to come from you in a genuine way rather than as some sort of gimmick or tool. So you need to reflect on what impresses you and what YOU think is useful or valuable.

There are two simple steps to appreciation:

1. *Noticing*. It is actually quite difficult to do this. You need to pay attention to what is going on around you, and focus on others rather than yourself, and see what people are doing that is good. You will need to develop appreciative eyes and ears and an appreciative instinct. It is essential to both look for and listen for what is going well, without looking to judge, criticize or evaluate. It is important to ignore the things you dislike and focus specifically on what is good. Try to create a culture of appreciation within the team and pay attention to others behaviours. Are they appreciative or critical? It is important to encourage others in the team to be appreciative too.

2. *Sharing*. It is not enough to just appreciate internally; you will need to share it with the person or persons concerned. As a manager or leader you might be thinking that they get paid for doing good work and that should be enough, but that is often not the case. What often happens is that you do not value and appreciate what is going well, but notice and criticize what is not going well. As a result, your employees never hear what you like but incessantly hear what you do not like. This does not engage or energize people.

What Appreciative Leadership is not

It is NOT a thing that is done to sugar coat the negative and make what is politely called a 'sad' sandwich. If you have not heard that expression, it is what happens when you want to be critical about someone, but sandwich the negative between two pieces of positive feedback. As you can imagine, it is not popular. In this case people are not easily fooled and of course only remember the negative feedback. It is also NOT about giving inauthentic or generalized praise. It is important when being appreciative that the leader shows the appreciation authentically. In other words, the appreciation should be genuine and not made up. There is actually no need to lie or fake it – in fact it is easier to do it properly. If you start making up and inventing the appreciation, the receivers will easily notice this and you will be worse off than before. It is better to say nothing than to just invent stuff. The humanist psychologist Rogers (2004) said that the tendency to react to any emotionally meaningful statement by forming an evaluation of it from our own perspective was the major barrier to interpersonal communication.

Why is Appreciative Leadership important?

There are a number of reasons why we feel that this type of leadership has become essential. One is that the context in which leaders operate is changing, and the second is the need for even greater levels of performance.

Context

Within this context we see two key issues: one is how to deal with more complex problems and the second is the concept of the VUCA world.

1. *More complex problems.* Leaders are now having to address what Rittel and Weber (1973) call 'wicked problems'. Probably the key definition of a 'wicked' problem is that solutions to wicked problems are not true-or-false, but better or worse. In other words, there is no one single agreed right answer to the problem. More and more of the problems that leaders face are of this kind, yet often the leader is expected to know the answer when there is no answer – only options or ideas, which can be better or worse options. In politics and strategy probably all the complex issues that are being faced are of this kind. For example, in her recent book *Hard Choices*, Hillary Clinton (2014) admits she was wrong over the conflict in Iraq and describes the current conflict in Syria as a 'wicked' problem. In other words, there is no one simple solution to it and that each potential solution might make things worse or better, but there is no way of knowing this in advance. But managers perhaps typically prefer more straightforward (or 'tame') problems, ones which have a right or wrong answer. In his classic article in the *Harvard Business Review*, Harvard professor and psychoanalyst Zaleznik (1977) argues that managers seek order and control and want to dispose of problems

before they have understood their potential significance. On the other hand, effective leaders tolerate chaos and lack of structure and are able to keep answers in suspense by avoiding premature closure. In this sense, leaders, Zaleznik argued, are more like artists and other creative thinkers than managers. Maybe the best we can do with these wicked problems is not fully solve the problem, but get to what we might call a 'good enough' resolution. Although even this can be extremely difficult since, as there are no clearly defined criteria for deciding if the problem is fully resolved, getting all the stakeholders to agree that a resolution is actually 'good enough' can be a challenge.

2. *Living in a VUCA world*. An idea which is becoming very popular in organizations now is the concept of the VUCA world which we mentioned at the start of this chapter. The concept has its origins in the US military which realized that it could not see the world in simple black and white terms any longer. In other words, there is very little certainty in the world we now face and we are moving from problem solving to facing dilemmas (or 'wicked' problems) where there are no simpler answers. The VUCA world concept has several implications for leaders: they need to move to understanding issues at a deeper level, having more patience, tolerating uncertainty and ambiguity, and engaging with it, and having a greater acceptance of diversity and challenge. The great man/heroic type of leadership is redundant in a VUCA world. The effective leader is the one who engages everyone in their organization to show leadership.

Performance

Appreciation is critical to performance. Schwartz and McCarthy (2016) suggests that a lack of appreciation is one of the five key triggers that create negative emotional reactions, which can then reduce morale motivation and commitment. The others are lack of respect, being treated unfairly, feeling that you are not being listened to and being held to unrealistic deadlines leading to less effective performance. Research from the UK's Chartered Institute of Personnel Development (CIPD, 2011) tells us that the line manager is one of the most important influences of employee engagement. Research in Ashridge Executive education in Hult International Business School shows that Generation

Y employees (born between 1982 and 2002 and who make up 35 per cent of the work force) also want to be respected and appreciated more. What does this mean in practice for managers and leaders? Based on research by Amabile and Kramer (2007), CIPD (2011), and Robinson and Hayday (2009), we have drawn up a list of ten behaviours and actions which we could promote engagement.

1. Listen
2. Value
3. Involve
4. Empathise
5. Show active interest
6. Give positive feedback
7. Recognize people's contributions
8. Show individualized interest in people
9. Show genuine care and concern
10. Respect and encourage others.

New views of leadership are appearing which place more emphasis on leading as bringing people together in an energizing environment, rather than by directing and telling. These include servant-leadership (Greenleaf, 1998) and more recently host leadership (Brent and McKergow, 2009; McKergow and Bailey, 2014).

Appreciative methods

The power of taking an appreciative stance in dealing with others is a new development in organizational and psychological thinking. Several different approaches have appeared over recent decades, each coming from different traditions or backgrounds, which arrive at similar (if not identical) conclusions. Each of these approaches would be worthy of a whole book in themselves, but we include three of them here both to raise your awareness for possible future investigation, and to draw out key messages from each. Taken together, these messages will form a powerful synthesis of the latest thinking for effective leaders. We will take a look here at three of these approaches – Appreciative Inquiry, Positive Psychology and Solution Focus.

Appreciative Inquiry

Appreciative Inquiry (AI) can be traced back to work by David Cooperrider and Suresh Srivastva in 1980. Having been invited to contribute to an analysis of: 'What's wrong with the human side of this organisation?' Cooperrider was amazed at the level of positive co-operation, innovation and egalitarian governance he saw in practice. Over the years, he and many others have developed their ideas from this initial analysis into a way of working with organizations, based on inquiring (asking questions and having conversations) appreciatively (about what is working, what is hoped for, what gives life to the organization, and so on). This is notable both for the focus of attention – on the positive – and for the methodology of developing change through conversation and dialogue, as opposed to direction and instruction.

The AI approach is founded on the impact of having conversations within an organization. These conversations are not so much about gathering information to make decisions (which is a different and valuable thing to do in the right place), but to explore perceptions and realities in dialogue, which results in new views, more energy and attractive potentials for moving forward. AI offers the hypothesis that human systems grow in the direction of what people study – therefore it is much better to search for the true, the good, the better and the possible in human systems than investigate what is wrong, what is false or what is bad.

Having grasped this central notion, AI projects stress the need to start by choosing an affirmative topic work – something the organization wants to develop in the positive (rather than something to be rid of, in the negative). This topic can then be addressed in different ways, with conversations at each stage allowing new views and connections to develop: this is not a strict process, and what happens at each stage will affect the others. The AI approach is often summarized by using what is known as the 4 D cycle (see Figure 8.1).

- Discovery – Appreciate the best of what is.
- Dream – Imagine what could be.
- Design – Determine what should be.
- Destiny – Create what will be.

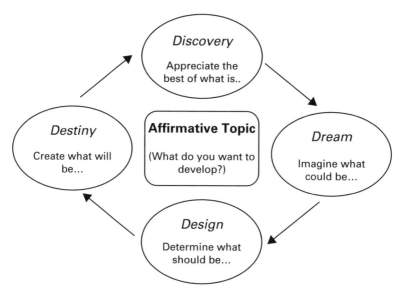

Figure 8.1 The 4 D cycle (Calabrese et al, 2015).

There is now a large AI community around the world, with many books and resources available including a large AI Commons website https://appreciativeinquiry.case.edu/. AI has often been used to take on large-scale organizational challenges, with the deliberate involvement of large numbers of people in interviewing and building change, though it can also be used to work with teams and individuals. Taking an appreciative approach can look quite simple, but can yield surprisingly good results. Let us take an example of this in practice.

Case study

John was the CEO of a manufacturing plant in the Far East and was having difficulty working with his PA, Susan. He found her over fussy, annoying and exasperating. Over time the relationship – which was a key one – became progressively worse and led to the PA becoming in John's words, 'unproductive'. John's way of responding to this situation was to focus on all the things that annoyed him, and to point out all the things that his PA was doing wrong. Unsurprisingly perhaps, this did not make things any better and the relationship was close to breaking down completely with John wondering how he could fire her. Mike suggested that John take an appreciative stance with Susan – to suspend any negative comments and reflect on what his PA actually did well. This is the first step of AI – 'discover the best of what is'.

After some time John conceded that she was very organized and energetic. So Mike asked him on the next time they met to give his PA feedback on her qualities without mentioning any negative aspects. So on his return to the plant John thanked Susan for her efforts and specifically mentioned that he valued her energy and organization. He was careful NOT to mention any negative aspects. To his surprise Susan smiled and thanked John for his comments. John then moved on a step and engaged Susan in a discussion of how they might work even better together – by 'imagining what could be' – with her. This was a very productive conversation, with both of them enjoying the conversation and noticing how often their ideas were compatible. After some time for reflection, they both committed to an action plan by 'designing what should be' and moving on to create an even better relationship. Importantly, John continued the process of focusing on Susans strengths, explicitly mentioning them, and refraining from criticism. The relation developed to such an extent that John later told us that Susan was now his best employee. John had initially been quite sceptical that the approach would work, but is now convinced that it is possible to turn round a difficult relationship using Appreciative methods.

Some key messages from Appreciative Inquiry

These are some of the key learning points from Appreciative Inquiry which can also be used more widely in building an authentic and personal approach to Appreciative Leadership:

- Words, conversations and dialogue matter. Using language skilfully is a key part of leading appreciatively.
- Finding key topics around which to develop ideas gives very useful focus – this is not about being mindlessly positive about everything.
- Engaging people widely around these key topics means that the appreciative power of conversations spreads more widely and more quickly.

Positive Psychology

The second appreciative method is Positive Psychology (PP). This is a growing field, applying the methods and tools of conventional psychology to strengths rather than weaknesses. For decades psychologists attempted to scientifically discover what caused mental illnesses and how to cure them. The positive aspect emerged in the 2000s with Seligman's books *Learned Optimism* (2011) and *Authentic Happiness* (2002) amongst others. The field is now the scientific study of the strengths that enable individuals and communities to thrive. Whereas Appreciative Inquiry shows a clear focus on the power of the conversation as a vehicle for local change, PP sets out to be scientific in a more old-fashioned way by using questionnaires and large-scale studies to build broad conclusions about what helps people thrive across many contexts. This quickly led to the emergence of 'strengths inventories' – psychometric tests which claim to reveal the user's key strengths, which make you authentic, unique and engaged. While such tests may be taken lightly, they can certainly help in beginning to think about how people operate and work together from a positive perspective.

One early book to focus specifically on how Positive Psychology might work in organizations was Buckingham and Clifton's (2001) book *Now, Discover Your Strengths*. This book was the sequel to their first book *First, Break All The Rules* and is specifically geared to using the Gallup StrengthsFinder questionnaire, itself a useful instrument for the appreciative leader. They take an interesting and provocative view of people development. Most organizations take their employees' strengths for granted and focus on minimizing their weaknesses. They become expert in those areas where their employees struggle, delicately rename these 'skill gaps' or 'areas of opportunity', and then pack them off to training classes so the weakness can be fixed. This approach is occasionally necessary: if an employee always alienates those around him, some sensitivity training can help; likewise, a remedial communication class can benefit an employee who happens to be smart but inarticulate. But this is not development, it is damage control. And by itself damage control is a poor strategy for elevating either the employee or the organization to world-class performance (Buckingham and Clifton, 2001).

This certainly offers a new perspective on the role of leaders not to run around fixing things but to focus on finding good fits between the roles to be fulfilled and the strengths of those who may fill the roles. While it may not be helpful to take too fixed a view of these strengths, there is certainly huge scope for helping people be more aware of how they work and what they bring to a team when they are at their best. Note that simply talking about strengths does not completely guarantee an appreciative stance – we can imagine frustrated managers raging that 'you're supposed to be a strategic thinker (or whatever) – you call this a strategy?' Another very interesting strand of positive psychology is Fredrickson's (2011) work on the 'broaden and build' hypothesis. Fredrickson is one of the leaders in positive psychology and has researched the impacts of positive emotions. Her findings suggest that both noticing and engaging in positive experiences not only feels good, but also broadens our ability to think creatively and expansively. This puts people into a great place to build progress and better futures. While there have been some debates about the precise figures in Fredrickson's work, the basic conclusions are surely robust and support the general benefits of an appreciative stance.

Some key messages from positive psychology

- Positive psychology gives a scientific basis for thinking that we can learn about how to thrive as people.
- Fixing weaknesses is 'damage limitation' – helping people find their strengths and use them is the route to world-class performance.
- Engaging in positive experiences and emotions broadens our ability to think creatively and widely.

Solutions Focus

Our third appreciative method is Solutions Focus (SF). While Appreciative Inquiry has its roots in large-scale interventions, Solutions Focus comes from a more intimate setting. Solution Focused Brief Therapy was created by de Shazer and Insoo Kim Berg of the Brief Family Therapy Centre, Milwaukee in the late 1970s. This discipline was itself based on Gregory Bateson and Milton Erickson's ideas on systems and language, and de Shazer and Berg had studied with members of Bateson's team at the Mental Research Centre in Palo Alto. It has become an increasingly widely used part of the leadership/management repertoire since the publication of Paul Z. Jackson and Mark McKergow's book *The Solutions Focus* in 2007.

The basis of the SF approach is that what helps to build progress towards a desired future (the 'solution') may not be related at all to what has caused things to be in a less-than-desirable present state (the 'problem'). Therefore, SF uses solution-focused questions (in particular about the better future and what is working already) and eschews problem-focused questions (about what is not working and how bad things might become). This can be seen in Figure 3.2 (the jokingly named Albert Model, after Albert Einstein) – the solution axis is not related to the problem axis.

While traditional problem-solving involves paying great attention to defining a problem and its cause, solution-building (the SF way) cuts straight to better futures and what is working.

Two important features which distinguish SF from Appreciative Inquiry are the focus on tiny details and small steps. Having people describe their better futures in tiny detail seems to help bring them

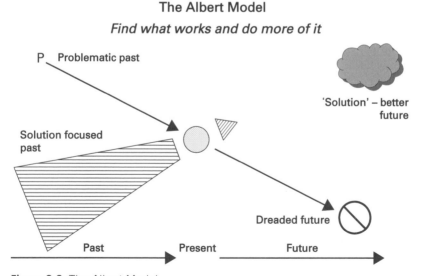

The Albert Model

Find what works and do more of it

P Problematic past

'Solution' – better future

Solution focused past

Dreaded future

Past   Present   Future

Figure 8.2 The Albert Model.

closer and make them more real. This can be achieved by using the concept of 'first tiny signs'. For example, suppose you want to engage people in terms of working better and they say that if things were better, then the team would be more productive. You can now ask 'and what would be the first tiny signs that the team was more productive?' – which will result in smaller details being discussed. Note that these are details about what is wanted – the solution, as opposed to what is wrong. When talking about possible actions, SF tends to look to small next steps (rather than big plans). The tougher the challenge, the smaller the step. These small steps can be implemented quickly (say in the next forty-eight hours) and initial feedback gained about whether to persist or find a new line of progress. If small details have been discussed already, then these may turn out to be part of some useful small steps. This has been found to be a highly effective approach in many organizational and leadership situations including coaching, appraisal, teams and strategic planning, as well as in therapy, schools, social work and other contexts. The approach looks as if it might be warm and fuzzy, but has real teeth and incisiveness when done well and has been used in many organizations, large and small, to build lasting and useful change. From Canon in Japan (Aoki, 2009), through the Austrian Parliament (McKergow, 2015), to reorganizations in semiconductor plants in Scotland (McKergow and Clarke, 2007), many managers are enjoying the positive power of SF.

Another interesting new development in using SF and other appreciative methods is Strength Based Lean Six Sigma (SBLSS). Shaked's 2014 book *Strength-Based Lean Six Sigma: Building Positive and Engaging Business Improvement* is the starting point. SBLSS uses elements from all the approaches described above, and combines them with the tools from the Lean/Six Sigma movement, which emerged from quality management and other continuous improvement processes. These tools are conventionally very problem-focused and unappreciative, but with some tweaking and rethinking they can be made into a whole new way to examine even technical and manufacturing problems as well as leadership and organizational affairs. If you are already somewhat familiar with the Lean/Six Sigma approach, this could work very well as a way to build on your skills and add another level of appreciation to your work.

Some key points from Solutions Focus
Again, these key learnings can be used more widely, in building your personal approach to appreciative leadership.

- What is wanted is not the opposite of what is wrong – so spending time analysing what is wrong may well be time wasted.
- Getting to the details by asking about 'first tiny signs' helps make the conversation more real, more grounded and more potentially action-oriented.
- Small steps, as opposed to large plans, can be an excellent way to proceed in tough, uncertain or challenging times.

How to respond constructively to others

Having looked at a number of Appreciative methods the leader can use in their everyday work, we turn now to another important aspect of Appreciative Leadership. This is building and maintaining effective relationships. We do not simply mean that this is about remaining positive when things are going badly, although this can be important. We want to specifically look at how we respond to others' good news and how this also affects our relationships. So for example if a colleague comes to you and tells you a piece of good news – let us say a promotion – you can respond in four basic ways. Gable et al (2006) suggests that you can respond either actively or passively, and you can be either constructive or destructive. All of these responses will affect the quality of your relationship, some in a positive way and others in a negative way. Let us look at the possible combinations using the framework of Active Constructive Responding (see Figure 8.3).

Active Destructive. A negative way of responding is to be destructive and this can be either active or passive. So an active but destructive, response would be to focus on the negatives and say something like, 'Oh that's a lot of work to take on! Are you sure you're ready for it?' What this is doing is belittling the other person and questioning their capacity to succeed, but under the pretence of being concerned for them. In our experience as facilitators and consultants, this is a common reaction.

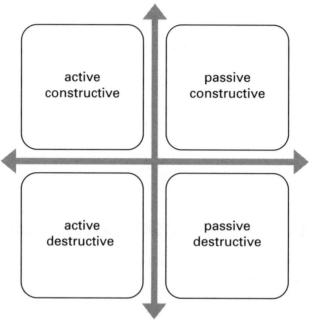

Figure 8.3 Active Constructive Responding (Gable et al., 2001).

Passive Destructive. A passive destructive response would be just to move on to a completely different subject without even acknowledging the promotion. So you might say something like: 'We need to get a move on with this report, the deadline is this afternoon...' Clearly this is not at all a recommended approach, but many of us may be guilty of using it at times, especially if we are in a rush and somewhat stressed. But we are at risk then of underestimating the emotional effect on our colleague.

Passive Constructive. Clearly one would generally want to react in a constructive way to the colleague's good news, but even then it can be quite passive. So you might say something like, 'Well done!' But then you move quickly onto another subject. This clearly shows that although you might think you have been positive, you are in fact not really that interested in what the other person has to say. And the important thing here is the person will clearly understand that you are not that interested.

Active Constructive. What we would suggest is that you use the 'active constructive' approach. So in this example you could say something like, 'That's excellent news. I know it means a lot to you!' You would then ask some open questions about the job, or the person's feelings, or their plans for the new job. Or all of these! This then demonstrates clear interest in the other, builds and strengthens your relationships and has the added benefit of contributing towards a more effective business!

It's worth reflecting on how you as a leader react to people's good news and that you train yourself to take the time to react actively and constructively.

Application tools

We believe that is important that the Appreciative leader have at their disposal a number of practical and applied tools that they can be used and applied in daily interactions.

Affirm

Affirming is a tool not used nearly enough by leaders (or indeed managers). This is a term from Solutions Focus which derives from the practice of simply giving compliments to people. Giving compliments is one of the most underrated tools in the box. Compliments in the solution-focused sense are specifically for identifying and highlighting strengths and resources. In this context, compliments are feedback on people's qualities, skills, capabilities and attitudes – based on what you have directly observed. Why directly? If you can say 'I was impressed with this – and I've seen you do it', it is incontrovertible in a way that 'I was impressed with this – which I'm imagining from something or other' is not. Compliments and praise in the workplace are, we believe, somewhat underused, so it might be helpful to show people how to use them with other members of their teams. For British managers, both giving and receiving compliments can be tricky at first – we can tend to brush them aside, get embarrassed or move swiftly on. Contrast this with common practice in the United States where compliments and praise are generally more used, and indeed might appear to be overused from a British perspective.

How to do it

The first thing is to notice something that the person has done which seems to you to be noteworthy or impressive. Then, let them know about it. There might be two parts to this:

- Thank the person for what they have done (This in itself is a powerful relationship-building strategy and is much underused).
- Expand this gratitude to further include some detail about a strength or useful personal quality, rather than an action.

This broadens the impact and brings in the idea that the person has this strength – which they may not have considered before. Then watch for the reaction. We are hoping that the person will smile (perhaps only slightly if they are British) and say thank you. That is a sign that they are somehow concurring with your judgement. Here is an example of how that might be done:

'Thank you for getting that report done yesterday.'

'It seems to me that you are a very diligent and conscientious person – it's very useful to have you in the team.'

Notice this phrase of 'It seems to me that. . .'. This is a very useful phrase. The other person can not argue so easily with something that is clearly your perspective rather than a bald statement of apparent fact. Other ways to introduce an affirm into a conversation include

I'm very impressed with your [insert specific strength].
I love the way you bring your [insert specific strength] into play at just the right moment.
The whole team owes a lot to your [strength] over the past few weeks.
I am very grateful to [name], whose [strength] is a great asset to us (said within earshot of the person concerned).

One senior manager we worked with asked us what would happen if he gave too many affirms to staff within his team. We told him it would an interesting experiment, but one which is rare in its execution.

Saying Yes . . . and

When you are asked to do something, is your natural tendency to go ahead and just 'Yes let's do it'? Or are you more reserved and cautious and usually start by saying 'No'? For us saying 'Yes' is an answer of possibility while saying 'No' is an answer of security. And in many ways it is easier to say no because the No maintains the status quo, and the security and certainty that brings. We have all seen parents dragging children round the shops where the child is continually asking for things, and the parent is continually saying, 'No, you can't have it.' It is wearing, it gets nowhere – and it preserves the status quo. When you are at work, you do not really want to act like parents to your team members do you? Hopefully, you will want to act more adult-like amongst colleagues and fellow participants to work towards goals, hopes and dreams.

So, saying 'No' all the time does not turn out to be very useful as it stops a conversation dead. It also dents whatever kind of relationship you have with the person. It is a power play – someone has come to you with a request, and you are using your leadership power to stop them. While this is OK in extremis, there are much more appreciative ways to proceed – by thinking (and saying) 'Yes . . . and'. Saying 'Yes' to someone does not mean simply acquiescing to whatever they are requesting. It means showing that you are willing to continue the conversation and explore jointly. It also helps to build, rather than dent, your relationship with the other person. When you say 'Yes . . . and', the second part of the phrase can be very useful to steer the conversation in a good direction, rather than stopping it dead. It shows appreciation of the other person, rather than rejection.

How to do it

Learning to say 'Yes . . . and' can take some practice. It is easier to do in an atmosphere of positivity and appreciation rather than one of defensiveness, where you may feel under pressure. Here are some tips about using 'Yes . . . and':

1. Take a breath before you reply (either in person or by email). Often 'No' is an instinctive reaction, while 'Yes' takes some more thought and constructiveness.
2. Think broadly. Use the moment of the breath to think about the useful possibilities that a 'Yes' might bring – to you and to others. Even if these possibilities are not at the top of your agenda right now, they may be useful in the future. And remember, you will dent

your relationship by saying 'No', as well as stopping a potentially useful development.

3. Say 'Yes ... and' and then add something to the proposal. This might be a benefit, an extra piece, or even a condition. For example, someone says to you:

> 'I'd like to investigate look at developing our widgets for the Asian marketplace.' You might be thinking 'Argh no ... stop it! We have enough to worry about with the US market.' But, saying that is not to appreciate the possibilities you are being offered. Some possible alternatives might include:
>
> 'Yes ... and we'll have to make sure it can be profitable.'
>
> 'Yes ... and you might want to talk to Carey in London about that, he's been thinking on similar lines.'
>
> 'Yes ... and that might be a good thing to discuss at next month's Executive team meeting, can you get something together to show them?'

Note that none of these are saying simply, 'Yes, that's fine, go ahead.' In each case you are steering the idea as well as offering thoughts on next steps and key priorities. By doing this you are showing appreciation and building your relationships at work – an excellent leadership move.

Scales – to help find what is working

Leaders and managers are often keen to identify what is wrong. There are all kinds of apparently good reasons for this – the search for improvement, the incisiveness of our own intelligence, the obvious inability of others to see what needs to be done. If you are identifying the faults of a machine, this is all very well. The machine does not talk back to you, go into a sulk or start planning its next career move. However, where you are dealing with people, there may be a better way – to appreciate what is working first. One neat way to do this is to use a scale from zero to ten. Ten represents everything working at its very best. Zero means that absolutely nothing is working at all. Then you can ask people where they are right now, on this scale. We find that people can sum up all kinds of aspects very quickly into a single number – 'it's at a six at the moment', for example. This sounds innocuous enough, but there are some other useful facts implied by this rating:

1. Things are not at zero – so some things must be working in some ways.
2. Things are not (yet) at ten – so there is scope for progress.
3. If a six means something (and we just said that it did), then seven, eight and five also mean something. We do not yet know what they mean, but the possibility is established.

The key thing is not to leap on to what a seven, eight or even ten might look like – but to focus instead on 'how come it's a six and not a five or lower?' This feels counterintuitive to the leader wanting to make progress, but the appreciation you are building will stand you in good stead in just a few moments time.

How to do it

First set up the scale. It is important to know what we are talking about, and what the ends of the scale mean. So for example: 'Think about how well our product is suiting our customers. Let's imagine a scale from zero to ten, where ten is that every customer is totally delighted. zero is that none of them likes it in any way at all.' (Note that the ten and the zero are both exaggerated positions – it is pretty much impossible that either of these situations happens. However, this is helpful in scaling, as it forces people away from the extremes.) Get people to say where they think the product is on the scale right now. Suppose the person you are discussing it with thinks that it is a seven right now. Move on to the next stage: 'How come it's a seven, and not a six or lower, do you think? What's working already?' The other person may be leaping on to other matters – why it is not higher, for example. But the appreciative leader will keep them focused on what is already working. It is important to build up a good long list at this point, so keep asking 'What else?' to build the answers. Then, having got a good long list, you can perhaps move onto what an eight on the scale – one point higher – might look like, or even what would be a 'perfect ten'. Either way, this talk of improvement is done with a background of appreciation, which supports and opens up the possibilities of positive change.

Suppose . . .

This is a very useful word in the leader's vocabulary. 'Suppose' is a word which invites people into a another world – one where things are a little different. Exploring this different world can illuminate all kinds of possibilities. It is a two-syllable gateway to creativity, an invitation to join in a discussion on a different basis to the usual everyday real-world need for facts and accuracy. Another way to think about this is in terms of using the term, 'What if. . . .' As in saying, for example, 'What if something was different – what would we do then?' This is a useful thing to do when the way ahead is unclear, and new ideas are needed, for example:

'What if . . . we had double the budget, what would we spend it on?'
'What if . . . we had no money at all next month, how might we keep going?'
'What if . . . we found a way to get instant customer feedback?'

These are all invitations to explore an alternative reality, to extend our thinking and to draw people together in a novel way. Some people worry that by asking 'Suppose' or 'What if', they are implying that the thing might (or even must) happen. This is of course not the case – as long as you make it clear why we are supposing something.

How to do it

It is important to be clear what we are going to suppose, and then lay it out clearly. So, in a manufacturing setting, we might invite people to:

'Suppose that this process is working perfectly . . . what would be happening?'
'Suppose we were to speed up the process by twenty per cent . . . how would it work then?'
'Suppose that everyone in the factory was working at their best . . . what would be happening then?'

All of these can be viewed from different perspectives – those directly involved, customers, suppliers, other stakeholders, finance and HR, and so on. This is not some kind of hazy 'dream' about cloud cuckoo land, it can be the first step towards initiating some major transformations – and it works best with appreciation, which brings openness and connection, rather than a criticizing mind-set with the accompanying defensiveness and resistance. This works even better after you have already appreciated what is working (perhaps using the Scale tool above).

SOAR

SOAR is the Appreciative Leader's alternative to the classic SWOT analysis. The conventional SWOT analysis looks at Strengths, Weaknesses, Opportunities and Threats – balancing positive and negative aspects. The appreciative leader will know that there is great power in the more positive angles, and might choose a SOAR analysis instead. This is often part of some kind of strategy process or market positional analysis.

SOAR comes from the Appreciative Inquiry tradition. It looks at:

- Strengths
- Opportunities
- Aspirations
- Resources.

So, rather than looking at weaknesses and threats, SOAR focuses instead on Aspirations and Resources. What do people aspire to? What do they want to achieve? What is their purpose? What gives them energy?

In addition, focusing on Resources helps us to understand people's strengths and what they do well. It seems to us that results will be better if leaders can focus on what people do well rather that wasting time on exploring areas of weakness. (Many online sources give the R in SOAR as 'Results', but we think an even more appreciative intervention can be had by looking hard at Resources first.) This is not to say that possible threats and weaknesses may not be important. However, spending too much time focusing on these aspects may be at best discouraging, and at worst distraction of attention from other much more fruitful avenues. SWOT assumes some kind of goal or direction, whereas SOAR brings aspirations – what are we trying to achieve – into centre stage at a crucial moment.

How to do it

Gather a varied group of participants and stakeholders. Let them know any information you have about the context of the organization at the moment – market conditions, results, what is going on. Then, in turn examine and discuss each aspect of SOAR:

S = *Strengths*. What is your organization doing really well? What leading positions do you hold? What excellent assets and capabilities do you have? What are the peak moments of the past period?

O = *Opportunities*. Where are the possibilities for expanding markets and/or products and services? What is happening externally that seems to be opening up new niches – for new or existing products and services? Where are there expansion possibilities or unmet customer needs? If there are major weaknesses, how can you can reframe them into opportunities?

A = *Aspirations*. What are your best hopes and dreams for the organization/team/service? What do you desire to be known for? What purpose are you serving? What is the benefit of your organization to humanity?

R = *Resources*. What do you have – particularly in human terms? What skills does your workforce possess? What knowledge do you have that others do not? What connections and contacts make your position particularly useful and interesting?

When you have looked at each individual aspect of SOAR, come back and look at the whole thing again. What is this telling you about possible new strategic directions and next steps? Where will you focus? And what will you quietly let go of, in order to concentrate in the most useful areas?

Conclusion

Appreciation is not just a soft 'nice to have', but actually is a powerful approach for leaders in the challenging situations of an increasingly VUCA world. This chapter demonstrates a multitude of methods of using Appreciative Leadership, all with varying approaches and methods. However, the aims of all methods are to evoke inspiring leadership and thus true followership. As with the employment of all methods and models of psychology in business, there needs to be an awareness and delicateness with how this is evoked. However, as discussed by our colleagues throughout this book, if appreciation is both expressed and demonstrated in a way which is sincere and authentic in its delivery, perhaps using an Eco Intelligence approach as opposed to

Ego Intelligence, then the results may prove to be substantive. As with all methods, there can be resistance to this approach, nicely encapsulated by the German – or rather Schwabian – saying, 'Nicht geschimpft ist genug gelobt' which roughly translates as, 'Not to criticize is praise enough.' However, in most places a little appreciation – placed in the right context and delivered genuinely – can go a long way towards bringing people with you, as opposed to pushing them away.

Appreciation does need conscious effort and practise – so do not worry if you do not feel you are doing it right. Keep on doing it and you will get better at it. The concept has been researched thoroughly in the last ten years or so and there is a large body of evidence pointing to its usefulness. What used to be regarded by some as 'weak' is now being seen by many more as 'sensible and pragmatic' as well as evidently effective. In particular, as younger people from the so-called millennial generation enter the workplace, the value of personal relationships and appreciation seems to be getting ever more important.

It could be argued that all leadership is appreciative leadership. It is the capacity to see the best in the world around us, in our colleagues, and in the groups we are trying to lead. It is the capacity to see the most creative and improbable opportunities in the marketplace. It is the capacity to see with an appreciative eye the true and the good, the better and the possible. There have been many scholars, practitioners and philosophers throughout the ages who have called for such approaches. The final word, we leave to them.

'Appreciation is a wonderful thing: it makes what is excellent in others belong to us as well.'

Voltaire

'Don't find fault, find a remedy.'

Henry Ford

'Life isn't about finding yourself. Life is about creating yourself.'
George Bernard Shaw

'Treat people as if they were what they ought to be and you help them become what they are capable of being.'

Goethe

Chapter 9

Leading for growth – the secrets of self-awareness and 'spiky leadership'

Patricia Hind

Introduction

When we try to pin down that crucial role of leadership we come up against a myriad of opinions, definitions and approaches. From having a vision and setting direction through to developing people and ensuring their work is meaningful – the term 'leadership' encompasses it all. However, we do know that leaders have to be good at making things happen, through other people – these seem to be the two central ideas. When developing leaders to deliver against these fundamentals the received wisdom is that, as a starting point, successful leaders need to have a good measure of self-awareness and have an ability to develop effective relationships in their teams. This chapter will explain exactly why these are truly critical issues, and extend our understanding to illustrate why good leadership is enhanced if the leaders themselves are also good team players. The chapter will firstly cover some key developments in leadership thinking, and some important research which has shaped our knowledge in the area.

Developments in leadership thinking

Perspectives on leadership have changed considerably over the years. Put simply, early thinking focused on individuals, their character traits and unique skill sets. Leadership from this perspective was about the judicious and skilful use of personal influence and from this the 'competency' view of leadership developed. A competency is defined as 'an underlying characteristic of an individual that is causally related to effective or superior performance in a job' (Boyatzis, 1982). This approach allows for the 'great man' view of leadership where leaders are those who possess special leadership competencies and traits by dint of his or her personality, and the later, behavioural view which allowed such competences to be learnt and developed through experiences. Despite holding sway for a considerable length of time, the competency model was roundly criticized.

Five of the key weaknesses identified were:

1. The simplistic way in which this approach fragments the management or leadership role rather than representing it as an integrated whole (Ecclestone, 1997; Grugulis, 1998; Lester, 1994).
2. The broad and generic nature of competencies that assumes that a common set of leadership capabilities will apply no matter what the nature of the situation, individuals or task (Grugulis, 2000; Loan-Clarke, 1996; Swailes and Roodhouse, 2003).
3. The focus on current and past performance rather than future requirements (Cullen, 1992; Lester, 1994).
4. The way in which competencies tend to emphasize measurable behaviours and outcomes to the exclusion of more subtle qualities, interactions and situational factors (Bell et al., 2002).
5. The rather limited and mechanistic approach to leadership development that often results from the mechanistic approach mentioned above (Brundrett, 2000).

Underpinning the competency approach is an objectivist view of the world that considers the worker to be separate from the work or the context of the work. The problem with this focus on objective measures is that it effectively fails to capture the subjective experience of the leadership relationship. An inevitable consequence of this approach was a strong emphasis on individual rather than collective behaviour. In response, a change in our frame of reference developed to allow for the emergence of more inclusive and collective forms of leadership, often called the 'participative' or 'distributed' leadership perspective (Bolden, 2011).

The 'participative' approach shifted thinking to a more distributed, democratic view where influence is shared. A feature of participative leadership is the seeking of input, ideas and observations from the team instead of the leader making all decisions on his or her own. This approach to leadership allows for a continuum of 'follower' input and involvement. At one end of the spectrum the leader may listen, but still retains the ultimate decision-making task. At the other end, decisions may be taken collectively, but wherever the leader sits within the range he or she acknowledges that the team may have skills and ideas that could benefit the decision-making process.

So, participative leadership involves the entire team, the leader working closely with team members, focusing on building relationships and rapport. The participatory leadership paradigm is essentially based on respect and engagement. The main objectives are to harness diversity, build community, and create shared responsibility for action. It deepens individual and collective learning yielding real development and growth and in doing so makes an assumption that involvement in decision making improves the understanding of the issues involved by those who must carry out the decisions. Other assumptions underpinning the approach include that people are more committed to actions where they have been involved in the relevant decision making and that they are less competitive and more collaborative when they are working on joint goals.

There is a key benefit of the approach in that several people deciding together make better decisions than one person alone, yet participative leadership also has its disadvantages: decision making within this paradigm inevitably takes more time, it is less effective with unskilled labour and therefore not always as inclusive as it claims and there are potential dangers when it comes to information sharing – it is not always beneficial to share all knowledge with all people.

These two hugely influential perspectives have, to a great extent, dominated leadership thinking for a very long time. Whilst different in emphasis and style, they have both, in their different ways, left the legacy of received wisdom that good leadership begins with self-awareness and is to some degree relational. For the competency model, this means that in order to deliver results leaders must understand and leverage both their own competencies and the competency profile of their team. For the participative model, leaders must know when and how far to pass decision-making responsibility from themselves to others and must be emotionally and intellectually flexible enough to allow that to happen safely and effectively.

Both perspectives rather assume that organizations are to some degree stable and discrete and that leaders within them, provided they attend to these two requirements of not behaving like a bull in a china shop, and listening to others, will ensure 'good' and effective leadership. Leadership development has focused on offering psychometric and reflective insights into personal strengths, and extensive attention to team-building skills. Although there is little depth to the standard exhortations to be self-aware, and to work well with others, these benign assumptions have dominated leadership thinking for quite some time.

Self-awareness

So, let us think about what we mean by self-awareness. Over the years, there have been many studies whose results claim to support self-awareness as the starting point for all effective leadership. One such study was conducted in 2010 by Green Peak Partners and Cornell University School for Industrial and Labour Relations. The study examined seventy-two executives at public and private companies with revenues from $50 million to $5 billion and concluded: 'A high self-awareness score is claimed to be the strongest predictor of overall leadership success' (Flaum, 2010).

The three main reasons that are cited to support such claims were:

- Executives who are aware of their weaknesses are often better able to hire subordinates who perform well at tasks in which the leader lacks excellence.
- Self-aware leaders are more comfortable with the idea that someone on their team may have an idea that is even better than their own.
- Self-awareness has a moderating effect on some of the qualities commonly associated with management and leadership such as being authoritative, decisive, forceful or even controlling. If these qualities are not moderated by a high degree of awareness as to how these behaviours are perceived and received they have the potential to easily alienate others.

The Green Peak research summary commented that 'soft values drive hard results'. It was not suggested that soft values, such as self-awareness, are a substitute for the more traditional executive skill set – which are a necessary prerequisite for leadership – but that they are an underrated, necessary complement for the long run. So whilst self-awareness is not one of those big headline leadership qualities like vision, charisma, strategic thinking or the ability to communicate effectively with many different audiences, it is thought to be a 'catalyst' that enables the high visibility traits to work.

Other evidence abounds, Sutton, a Professor of Management Science and Engineering at the Stanford Engineering School, says the best executives are willing to reflect on their own behaviour and change tactics as appropriate (Sutton, 2010). 'Good bosses are self-aware and the bad ones live in a fool's paradise,' he says. 'The good ones know what it feels like to work for them, are aware of their weaknesses and constantly make little adjustments in response to the moods and moves of the people around them, while the bad ones are remarkably clueless.'

In addition, it is often warned that many executive careers have been derailed by lack of self-awareness. Individuals feel they are all powerful and take too many risks or do not notice when actions they thought were strong authoritative leadership are actually demoralizing or when they were incapable of 'reading' how others were receiving the messages they were sending. So it is assumed that the consequences of a leader not being self-aware are alleged to be serious and career-limiting.

Yet, despite its apparently huge importance, neither the context nor the concept of self-awareness is really examined in the leadership development literature. Think about it for a moment, what does it mean? Some managers on leadership programmes think it means sitting cross-legged in the lotus position, eyes closed, humming and contemplating their inner thoughts – actions they are often reluctant to engage in! More usually, programme participants report that they think it simply means reflection on personal behaviour, and the impact that can have on others. Rarely is this important skill examined further and it is usually assumed that, for most people, the most valuable self-awareness comes from data, or feedback, that originates with colleagues, direct reports and managers. This is supposed to be the most reliable way to get an objective insight that can be used to become an ever more effective leader. Specific skill-building programmes may logically follow; but self-awareness, through the observations of others, is where the process begins. Yet self-awareness is a more nuanced concept than is often acknowledged and the term is often interpreted in widely different ways. For some it means being introspective, especially about emotions and what causes someone to be 'up' or 'down' in their outlook and behaviour. For others it means being aware of personal values and life goals. (If you discovered your house was burning, for example, what would you save?) Still others think it means being clear about the kinds of people they like and dislike and which activities bring you pleasure or boredom. For the majority, the key dimension of self-awareness, especially for those who lead organizations, is simply a clear understanding of the impact they are having on the people around them.

For such an important part of leadership, these rather vague descriptions may be too simplistic. Examining the notion of 'impact' in research into the development of effective leaders (Brook et al., 2004) indicated that key predictors of impact include much more than opportunities for constructive feedback (assisting self-awareness and reflection). There must also be demonstrable integration with organizational systems and strategy – a measure of increasing situational relevance – along with facilitation and support from managers. So simply receiving a subjective description of one's 'impact' from a colleague is probably not really exposing the heart of true self-awareness. Why must self-awareness be a complicated concept now? Well, the leadership world has changed. There have been dramatic changes in the workplace that cry out for different approaches to leadership. Alongside an increased focus on each and every individual within the organization the nature of organizations themselves has changed. To succeed today, organizations must be more aware than ever of interdependencies and networks, outsourced functions and collaboration with external stakeholders. It is this complex, externally focused system that creates competitive differentiation. Think of airline partnerships where companies who compete against each other offer joint loyalty programmes to maximize their commercial opportunities and broaden their customer base. Such collaboration, such as between British Airways and Qantas, or Etihad Airways and Air New Zealand, ensures that planes fly at full capacity and that each partner airline has access to a wide base of regular customers.

The globalization of finance and technology, the spread of privatization and deregulated markets have produced changes in the way we think about leadership. As discussed by Nixon in Chapter 2, this global information age, where careless action can cost a company its brand overnight, ensures that we have had to make a significant shift in the way we view the purpose of businesses. Leaders worldwide are embracing the concepts of corporate responsibility by reporting on their social and environmental activities, as well as their economic ones. Companies and their leaders are now monitored by many civic groups to see how they are doing on what has been termed 'sustainability'. The rising importance of this new business awareness is indicated by the fact that over 2000 companies have now signed up to the 10 principles of 'Global Corporate Citizenship of the Global Compact' launched by the UN in 2000, covering human rights, workplace safety, justice, anti-corruption ILO standards and environmental impact. Indeed, it seems that some 77 per cent of CEOs of major corporations surveyed by KPMG and the World Economic Forum in 2005 said that such higher ethical behaviour was 'vital to profitability' and continued growth.

While many of these CEOs have had a real change of heart, others have simply begun to see the practical light and decided to make changes because they make good financial sense. Studies reporting that companies with higher sustainability ratings outperform their counterparts who score lower on sustainability practices are ever more common. This seems to represent a fundamental shift that is occurring in society and business. Companies recognize they are actors in large, complex systems and need to interact in a web of relations with different stakeholder groups. Realizing corporate success requires a delicate balance of dialogue and action with groups and individuals inside and outside the organization. Leading businesses is now about balancing competing demands and engaging people in collective goals that damage neither people nor the environment. For example, Santam, a large insurance company headquartered in South Africa, has realized that explicitly encouraging sustainable business practices in the smaller companies in its supply chain not only gives the parent company significant advantages with investors, but also enhances the business success and stability of the companies it deals with down the line.

The new landscape

It is fair to say that the more connected we are, the safer, freer, and more powerful we are. But there are downsides: the more connected we are, the more dangerous it can become. Leaders will need to make the links and organize people for action – yet also protect against dangerous or dysfunctional connectivity. The skill-set required to lead in this interdependent world mirrors the complexity of the business landscape. Leaders must shift from a focus on their own position to attending to the whole. And although they will all be in positions of authority within their organization, they will not be so in the other organizations they will be dependent upon. Leadership influence and effectiveness must begin to look very different. So, leadership must look outwards as well as inwards. Organizations must consider their whole stakeholder map. The questions that matter are 'where are we giving value?' and 'where are we getting value?' and these must be applied to all stakeholder relationships as well as direct employees. This sort of self and stakeholder awareness lies outside our traditional understanding of leadership and also has implications for what we mean to be self-aware. To take another leadership metric – to be 'client focused' is frequently used as a traditional performance management measure, and is usually assessed via customer feedback, or some monitoring of repeated business. However, to truly leverage the opportunities offered by valuing and recognizing business interdependencies companies need to focus on the joint value that can be achieved through collaboration and communication. This makes information an asset, like people or property. Managing performance must encompass managing information in this new interconnected world.

Extending these ideas to our understanding of self-awareness means that our usual assumption that it is the ability to reflect on one's abilities and impact, and to manage and control one's behaviour in the light of that reflection needs to be amplified. Whilst the capacity for reflection is at the heart of self-awareness, just what this might involve has been developed in an extensive research study undertaken with the support of the European Academy of Business in Society (Wilson et al., 2006). The results of the study suggested a development of the notion of simple 'self-awareness' to one of 'reflective abilities' – a combination of emotional and intellectual capacity involving self-reflection in five areas;

1. Systemic thinking.
2. Embracing diversity and managing risk.
3. Balancing local and global perspectives.
4. Meaningful dialogue and developing a new language.
5. Emotional awareness.

1. Systemic thinking

Dealing with complexity, as all managers do today, requires the ability to think strategically, to understand the bigger picture and to appreciate the diverse networks in which an organization operates. At its simplest, systemic thinking concerns the ability to understand the interdependency of systems across the business and between the business and society.

The research suggested that systemic thinking requires a deeper understanding of both internal organizational relations and external social, economic, environmental and cultural dynamics. To be successful, managers are required to undertake a key strategic shift in the way that they view the world – they need to recognize that the company is not operating in a closed system. In addition, they are required to interpret the signals given by actors in the market and must be able to respond appropriately. There is a distinction here between systemic thinking and an appreciation of complexity such as is required in the traditional management disciplines of, for example, finance or engineering. These often call for a form of analytical thinking that seeks to understand complex situations by breaking them down into their constituent parts and analysing the impact of individual components on the problem being addressed.

However, the appreciation of social and environmental complexity (which is at the heart of systemic thinking) is simply not amenable to this type of analysis. It requires a new form of complex reflection which moves beyond the consideration of individual components and involves an analysis of the interrelations across the whole system, understanding how things impact and interact with one another at the broadest possible level.

2. Embracing diversity

The second reflective ability is to embrace diversity. Clearly at one level this is simply about building corporate teams that reflect the diversity of the societies in which they operate. Although this is considered necessary, it is not sufficient for managers to be truly responsive. Heterogeneous groups (whether based on gender, race, culture or other aspect) are better able to use their differences to appreciate the complexity of the situations in which they operate. Individuals and organizations need to respect diversity by acknowledging it, building bridges across different groups and seeking common ground without forcing consensus – respecting difference is vitally important in acknowledging diversity. However, this acknowledgement of difference is not sufficient and may simply lead to tolerance. Active reflection is needed to examine and leverage the value that may be added by using difference rather than simply accommodating it. Overall, the message was that the business decision-making process needs to structure relations which will maximize the exchange of ideas and learning across different groups – inside and outside the company.

3. Balancing local and global perspectives

The third reflective ability concerns the capacity to see and appreciate the impact of local decisions on the global stage. The organizations involved in the research were largely decentralized companies operating in many different countries dealing with a huge diversity of cultures and values around the world. At the same time, they were often striving to operate according to one set of values and beliefs.

So, this is the oft repeated dilemma of a company trying to be both global and local. The issues here are how to maintain a global framework of business values and at the same time respect local diversity and to ensure consistent operational standards while encouraging innovation and entrepreneurship in operating units. For leaders these questions must be mirrored by self-reflection into their own core values and those of the organization. Organizational values must be communicated to others in a way that helps members fulfil the organization's mission, and connects with personal values. Core values must remain stable and enduring despite differing operational contexts, but for such values-based leadership, the leader must be truly and explicitly self-aware through reflection.

4. Meaningful dialogue

The fourth reflective ability is the familiar maintenance of meaningful dialogue with others through listening, enquiring and responding appropriately. Instead of taking action along the lines of 'decides, announces the outcome and defends the decision' the process must be one of 'dialogue, deciding and implementing'. This simple description is a powerful shorthand portrayal of a much more comprehensive method of stakeholder engagement, and the key word is dialogue. The value in developing new forms of *meaningful* dialogue through reflection is that they can offer the opportunity to explore assumptions, ideas and beliefs that inform individual and organizational behaviours and actions. In this way, companies and their stakeholders can begin to explore how cultural differences between groups can cause clashes – often without an appreciation of what is occurring.

One of the key advantages of building external connections and getting engagement from others is to provide an external perspective into the business. This does not diminish the difficulties of deciding which are the appropriate issues the organization should address, and which are the legitimate external viewpoints to be heard. Reflection is needed to understand the pertinent issues at the intersection between business and societal issues and to be able to distinguish between the potential indirect impacts of the company and perhaps the core contribution it can make to society.

5. Emotional awareness

The final reflective ability is the one we usually think of as being self-awareness, but with a little more depth. Emotional awareness – described variously as empathy, perception, curiosity and the ability to use the right-hand side of the brain in decision making – is 'simply' the ability to understand the broader implications of decisions and actions on others. Emotional awareness is the ability of individuals to recognize their own and other people's emotions, to discriminate between different feelings and label them appropriately, and to use emotional information to guide thinking and behaviour. Reflection is needed to identify the interrelationships between thoughts, behaviours and emotions which are the key to operating successfully in today's business environment. All too often reactions to business decisions are not based on rational analysis but on feelings and perceptions. Frequently, when going through the decision-making process managers describe their 'thoughts' on business issues in entirely rational terms – ignoring the fact that their viewpoint is not only the product of conscious intellect but is also coloured by their feelings, emotions and desires.

Hence, it is important that managers have the ability and willingness to recognize that business decisions are not always driven by a process of economic rationality. Another element of emotional awareness is a tolerance of unusual approaches. For example, integrating corporate responsibility into an organization requires managers to go beyond the well known (and well worn) analysis of business issues. In order to deal with uncertainty and complexity they need to adopt unorthodox approaches to addressing the competing demands different stakeholder groups place on the business.

So, to be effective today's leaders must bring much more to the notion of 'self-awareness' than much of the leadership literature allows for. Successful navigation of today's complex and complicated business landscape requires leaders to extend their reflective abilities far beyond the horizons of their immediate leadership practice, and also to add a depth that goes further than a simple 'feedback' session.

Spiky leadership and team development

So, let us examine that other pillar of effective leadership – the need to be able to develop and maintain effective working relationships and ideally to create high performing teams. This is not separate from the self-awareness issues we have been discussing as, in extending our consideration of self-awareness, we have been talking of extending personal reflection in a way that has a much more 'other' focus. This is not simply a warm and fuzzy team sense of belonging and contributing, but a sharp awareness of the value of difference which speaks well to a new concept of leadership. It sounds trite, but let us be explicit here, to value difference means we are not all the same, some people are better than other people at certain things, and thus by definition, some people are worse at some things. Yet this truth is often ignored in leadership development.

Often, in development interventions there is a common misconception that CEO's and senior managers should be pretty good at everything, and indeed some expect themselves to be so. So programmes and learning interventions are designed to 'fault fix' and offer remedial help to fill in the gaps, bringing the leader up to a standard level of competence right across the board. However, our diversity perspective argues that not only can they not be good at everything, but indeed, they should not try to be. Trying to be good at everything wastes effort and takes the focus from the really important objective of developing strengths into excellence.

There is clear evidence to support this view. Research conducted by McKinsey and Egon Zehnder (2011) identified eight key leadership competences which were significantly correlated with growing business value when aligned with growth strategies. The research combined McKinsey's granular growth database – information on the growth of more than 700 companies – with Egon Zehnder international database of performance appraisals of more than 100,000 senior executives. The project examined in detail the relationship between leadership competences and revenue growth, dividing the companies into those that were in the highest percentile for revenue growth, and those that were in the lower percentile. The eight key leadership competences are clustered into three themes, all correlated with growth, with some more important to some growth strategies than others. The headline finding was not a surprise – leadership is critical to growth, but the research went on to highlight that actually, most companies simply do not have enough high quality executives. Overall, only 1 per cent of executives achieved an average competency of 6/7 or 7/7 on the eight competences and only 10 per cent had an average score of 5/7. The implication of this result is that high scoring all-round leaders are few and far between on senior management teams. However, excellence in one competency was much more frequent, so specialist expertise was quite common. Looking at the companies overall, for every competency reviewed, executives from companies in the top quartile of revenue growth scored higher than those in the bottom quartile – so these qualities matter. It is interesting to note that the leaders of the companies in the top quartile of revenue growth did not display a flat profile of strengths across all the competences, but were found to excel at only a few of the key competences, but excel they certainly did, and their companies grew strongly. The concept of 'spiky leadership' has been used to explain that the leaders most likely to drive growth are those who have real 'spikes of excellence' on some of those key competences, standing out starkly, even if they are much less strong in the others.

Now, here is where self-awareness and reflexive abilities and team building gets interesting! When relating the competences to business performance, Table 9.1 shows, in Column 1, the three clusters of competences identified. Column 2 lists those competences that differentiated between the top companies and the weaker ones and indicates to which cluster they

Table 9.1 Relating competence to business performance

Thought Leadership	Market insight; strong understanding of the market and how it affects the business	Systemic thinking Balancing global and local perspectives
	Strategic orientation; thinking beyond own area and showing complex analytical and conceptual thinking abilities	Systemic thinking
People and Organizational Leadership	Change leadership; driving change through people, transforming and aligning an organization in a new direction	Emotional awareness Systemic thinking Meaningful dialogue and developing a new language
	Developing organizational capability; developing competencies of the organization by attracting top talents and developing the team	Embracing diversity and managing risk Systemic thinking Emotional awareness
	Team leadership; focusing, aligning, and building effective groups	Meaningful dialogue and developing a new language
	Collaboration and influencing; effectiveness in working with peers or partners not in line of command	Meaningful dialogue and developing a new language Emotional awareness
Business Leadership	Customer impact; thinking about serving the customer and meeting customer needs	Systemic thinking Balancing global and local perspectives
	Results orientation; driving improvement of business results	Systemic thinking Embracing diversity and managing risk

belong. Column 3 aligns the competences with the reflective abilities discussed earlier.

It can be seen that each of the competences can be aligned with one or more of the reflective abilities in that each requires a different focus or perspective:

- The Thought Leadership cluster requires leaders to be able to use wide ranging, and often secondary, data. They need the intellectual capacity to reflect upon this and interpret the information in the light of the relevance for their own business.
- The People and Organizational Leadership cluster introduces an emotional element to the leader's skill set. Here there is the need to understand people with a view to the value they can give to the business, but also to the value they will get from the business in terms of meeting their needs motivationally as well as financially.
- The Business Leadership cluster requires that the leader really understands his/her customers and what he/she needs to do to deliver results through them, monitoring trends, grasping opportunities and minimizing risk.

However, business growth relies on all eight competences, so if leaders are rarely able to offer excellence in all of them, 'spiky' leaders, with strength in particular areas, must be capable of building up, and working within, a great team made up of other leaders with different 'spikes'. Obviously, it is great to have leaders who are outstanding in some areas, but it is clearly not great to have a senior leadership team made up entirely of people who are good in the same area. Yet many organizations recruit leaders who are 'one of us', or who can 'hit the ground running'. This often means hiring individuals who are similar to existing teams, and precludes the signing up of the necessary diverse individuals in senior teams.

In order to be comfortable relying on the expertise of others, a good deal of real and honest self-awareness is needed, acknowledging and accepting personal 'gaps' of capability. This self-awareness, combined with the determination to 'get things done' reinforces the need to have great, but different, people in the senior leadership team. Leaders must therefore develop the confidence to hire other strong people without feeling threatened. To deliver growth, spiky leaders must build a circle around them of other people who are at least as good as them, but in other areas. This leveraging of disparate skills requires leaders to bring an extraordinary degree of honesty and openness to their self-awareness. It also gives real 'legs' to the old adage that team working is a 'good thing'. It is not a just nice – to – have for businesses pursuing growth, but a diverse and complementary senior leadership team is critical for business success.

The leadership at Circle Research, a consulting and research firm, is a good example of this. The three leaders of the business have much in common – for example, they share exactly the same vision for Circle and have collectively embedded client centricity and a unique employee-based culture within the business. Their individual leadership skills, however, are quite different, but nevertheless complementary. One of the partners is particularly strong in driving forward the growth of the business, evaluating strategic options and overseeing finances; another is highly creative and applies his skills to innovative client engagement and development of the business; and the third member of the team has real expertise in people management, operational excellence and making things happen.

As David Willan, Circle's chairman explained: 'Working together for many years obviously helps because we know each others skills intimately. But we also recognize that not everybody is great about everything. And at the same time no one is particularly precious about this. So what we've come to realize is that effective leadership is about harnessing our individual strengths as opposed to expecting one person to be outstanding in all aspects of leadership. That's simply not possible.'

In addition to understanding personal strengths, organizations must also be clear about the competences needed to deliver particular growth strategies. It is not true that a solid talent bench can pull off any strategy: leadership is always contextual, and competences for success vary greatly by strategy. There are several different strategies a company might decide to implement in order to achieve growth. Let us just consider two:

- Portfolio momentum growth – market growth across existing segments.
- M&A driven growth – acquiring resources and assets.

Think about portfolio momentum growth – organic market growth across a company's existing business segments. Here we have geographic diversity, time zone differences and disparities in available local talent. The key requirement to drive this type of growth is the need to execute the strategy across far flung organizations and this needs to be embraced particularly by senior managers in the organizational layers underneath the top team. Companies in the top quartile of this growth category were highly rated in competences relating to 'dynamic people and organizational leadership: developing organizational capability, change leadership, the ability to attract and develop great employees and team leadership'. So here, strength in participative leadership is valuable, with leaders demonstrating self-awareness through, in particular, understanding diversity, and the balance between global and local awareness.

By contrast, companies pursuing an inorganic M&A-driven growth strategy need a different skills emphasis in their leadership teams. Again, the global/local balance is important, market insight and a customer centric focus – in other words, looking beyond a company's current business landscape to discern future growth opportunities. That competency no doubt supports the identification of deals, while other competences crucial for M&A-driven growth – a well-honed orientation towards achieving results and strategic thinking – help in post-merger integration, along with the ability to influence and collaborate. At most large companies, of course, there is not just one growth strategy. Most companies rely on a diversity of approaches that vary by business segment and by circumstance: at times executives might place more weight on acquisitions, while at others they focus on stealing share from competitors, for example. The McKinsey/Egon Zehnder analysis shows that high growth rates for these different strategies are associated with excellence in a range of leadership skills wielded by managers at various levels of the organization.

A spiky approach does, however, require organizations to think about leadership broadly, not just on an individual level. An unintended consequence of not recognizing the strength in 'spikiness' is that brilliance is overlooked and not built on. When a gap is seen as a 'problem' often someone is brought in to fill the gap, to 'solve the problem', instead of supporting and developing the spiky person and helping develop strong skill sets around him or her.

Conclusion

This chapter argues that, for the future, the key to effective leadership in the new paradigm is real and transparent self-awareness that acknowledges gaps, and is truly honest about strengths, even if they are limited to one or two competences. We must move from a vague, bland and uncritical assumption that 'Self-Awareness' is in place following a short peer feedback session. The concept must be interrogated and defined, as with any other necessary leadership skill. Then real team development, based on complementary skill profiles, rather than an emotional perception of synergy, can take place. However, the development needed here goes much deeper than the familiar emotional comfort zone often implied by 'team building'. This is a genuine synergy of practical and functional skills as well as relational ones. For this to be successful, leaders need to develop much sharper analysis of what they, and their colleagues, can bring to the leadership table.

Companies must accurately target their efforts to develop and recruit leaders – building true excellence in the most critical roles and competences – if these are to translate into vigorous revenue growth. The implications for companies and their leaders can be summarized in four principles for action:

- Get real and explicit about Self-Awareness.
- Focus on the leadership competences that matter most for growth and sustainability.
- Build a critical mass of excellent leaders, with diverse and complementary skills that can work as a collaborative intellectual as well as an emotionally bonded team.
- Celebrate the extremes – develop and promote 'spiky' leaders.

Author biographies

Mike Brent MA, MSc, MCMI

Mike is an Associate Member of Faculty and Professor of Leadership Practice at Ashridge Executive Education, Hult International Business School. He specializes in leadership, team-building, influencing, coaching, cross cultural management, leading change and personal development. His interests include how to foster self-awareness and creativity, and how to challenge effectively. With extensive experience as a trainer, facilitator and coach, his interventions include designing and running workshops and seminars for many organizations in Europe, Asia Pacific, the Middle East and the United States. Mike studied Sociology and Philosophy at Edinburgh University, where he gained an MA degree. He also has a Diploma in Business Studies, a Diploma in Marketing, a Masters Degree in Human Resource Development, and a Masters Degree in Organizational Consulting. Mike holds the British Psychological Society Level B qualification in Psychometric Testing, and is a licensed Neuro Linguistic Programming Practitioner. He is also trained in Solution Focus Therapy and Coaching, and is qualified in a wide range of psychometric questionnaires including MBTI, FIRO, SDI, Hogan, ESCI, SPM and CPI. He has written numerous articles and with co-author Fiona Dent has written five books on leadership, two of which were shortlisted for best practical Management Book of the Year. Mike holds both British and French nationalities and is bilingual.

Roger Delves MA (Hons) Oxon, FRSA

A Fellow of the RSA, and educated at St Catherine's College, Oxford, Roger is Dean of Qualifications and a Professor of Practice at Ashridge Executive Education, Hult International Business School. His special interests are understanding the roles of authenticity, emotional intelligence, ethics, values, principles and integrity in leadership. Roger was in 2012 voted Hult London MBA Professor of the Year by students. He has taught for Hult in London, Shanghai, Boston, New York and San Francisco. He has also taught across most of Western Europe, the

Middle East, in Turkey, Lebanon, Roumania, North America, Singapore, Malaysia, Russia, Brazil, Australia, Ghana, Kenya, South Africa and Nigeria. He co-authored a book for Pearson, *The Top Fifty Management Dilemmas – Fast Solutions to Everyday Challenges* and is co-authoring another for Bloomsbury entitled *Branded Britain*. He also contributed a chapter to the 2016 Libri book *Management Development that Works*. During Roger's twelve-year career in international advertising, he was on the London board of MB&B. He worked with P&G, GF, Mars Masterfoods, Johnson Wax, Bosch, Sony and Sterling Health. Later he was for six years Principal Consultant at a management development consultancy, and then spent six years as Programme Director in Cranfield's Centre for Customised Executive Development. He has been at Ashridge since 2008.

Kerrie Fleming B. Commerce, MBS, PhD
Kerrie is an Associate Professor of Organisational Behaviour at Ashridge Executive Education, Hult International Business School specializing in leadership development with a particular expertise in leader emotional intelligence (EI) and its practical application for individuals and organizations. She is Director of the Ashridge Centre for Leadership and is former Head of Department for the Leadership and People faculty at Ashridge. She sits on a number of academic regulatory and research committees at Ashridge. As a Client Director and facilitator, Kerrie has designed and delivered customized, MBA and Open Leadership and Management development programmes to senior executives, incorporating sessions on emotional intelligence, resilience, influencing, change management, strategy and innovation to Fortune 500 companies as well as indigenous and international organizations providing executive coaching to support managers through organizational restructuring of acquisitions, change management and performance improvement. Prior to working in executive education, Kerrie worked as a university lecturer teaching strategy, management, economics and marketing with a number of Universities in Ireland. Additionally, she worked in strategic acquisition management, account management and customer service within the European food industry. Her recent book *The Leader's Guide to Emotional Agility* published by Pearson FT was shortlisted for the CMI Management Book of the Year Awards 2016.

Jonathan Gosling BA, MBA, PhD
Jonathan is Professor Emeritus of Leadership at the University of Exeter and Visiting Professor at several prominent universities. His current research projects include a comparison of leadership development in health services around the world; leadership of agricultural reform in Colombia; the management of malaria elimination programmes in southern Africa; and multi-sector partnerships in flood defence schemes. He is active in the 'greening' of management education worldwide and is co-founder of the One Planet MBA and Coachingourselves.com. He previously worked as a community mediator.

Ian Hayward BSc Psychology, MA Org.Development, DBA
Ian joined Ashridge Executive Education as a Faculty member in 2006, having previously held senior HRD positions at British Airways and the BBC. Drawing from this experience, and with a lengthy background in training and development, his particular areas of interest are leadership, culture and organizational change. Since joining the Business School he has delivered programmes for a range of clients including: Lufthansa, Philips, Eon, the UK's Ministry of Defence and a number of organizations in the Middle East, in addition to delivering the flagship open programme, the Ashridge Leadership Process. Ian has a long association with the Ashridge Leadership Process having originally undertaken it as a participant before becoming both a Coach and Tutor on the programme. He is also Academic Director of the Executive MBA for the Creative Industries at Ashridge. As Head of Leadership Development at the BBC he launched and directed the BBC Leadership Programme, in conjunction with Ashridge, while at British Airways he was responsible for setting up and running the Senior Management Academy. In addition to his DBA, Ian has a BSc in Psychology from Southampton University and an MA in Organization Development from Loyola University of Chicago. Ian is also a Fellow of the Chartered Institute of Personnel and Development.

John Higgins MA (Cantab), MSc (Organizational Consulting)
John is a longstanding research partner of Ashridge Executive Education and tutor on the Ashridge Leadership Process. He has worked closely with the Doctorate and Masters in Organizational Change, publishing a number of books based on the experience of faculty and students – most recently *The Change Doctors: Reimagining Organizational Practice*

(Libri, 2014), with Dr Kathleen King. He is currently engaged in a long-term study into speaking truth to power with Dr Megan Reitz, their first conference paper on the subject presented at the 8th Annual DLCC at Ashridge entitled 'Being silenced and silencing others; Developing the capacity to speak truth to power'. Internationally John works with The River Group based out of Boston, helping to edit research papers based on the experience of becoming a first time CEO – he also works closely with Management Center Turkey and has recently provided editorial support to Dr Mustafa Merter, producing a book for the Anglo-American world exploring the principles and practice of Sufi-inspired psychology. John specializes in working with individuals and groups engaging with situations that require more than simple rationalization, drawing on his first-hand experience of sustained Jungian informed psychoanalysis and years of work in organizational settings. Recently he has been involved in developing sophisticated, qualitative approaches to learning and evaluation for organizational change initiatives.

Patricia Hind BSc, MSc, PhD, CPsychol., AFBPS
Patricia is Director of The Ashridge Centre for Research in Executive Development at Ashridge Executive Education, Hult International Business School in the UK. She is former Director of the Ashridge full-time and EMBA programmes, a Chartered Organizational Psychologist and a visiting fellow at Stellenbosch University in Cape Town, South Africa. She is a full-time member of faculty at Ashridge specializing in leadership development with a focus on developing effective leadership through self-awareness, improving working relationships and contextual understanding. She sits on a number of academic regulatory and research committees at Ashridge and is a client and programme director for a range of international clients. Patricia has over thirty years teaching and consulting experience in the university sector as well as in executive education. As an organizational behaviour specialist she has worked widely across Ashridge's open and customized programmes designing, delivering and managing development programmes for all levels of management. She has published widely, presented conference papers and published two books: *Management Development that Works* published by Libri in 2015, and *The Sustainability Pocketbook* in 2013. Patricia has a Doctorate in Managing without Authority, and is an Associate Fellow of both the British Psychological Society and the Academy of Management.

She is qualified to use a wide range of psychometric inventories aimed at effective individual self-awareness and development. Her current research interests are the individual implications of corporate social responsibility programmes, the development of social entrepreneurialism and the evaluation of management development programmes.

Frederick Hölscher PhD Sociology

Frederick is a director of the Civil Society Forum in the UK and works in market development and leadership development for business and civil society leadership. He is a freelance consultant, writer and guest lecturer at numerous institutions. He has been lecturing at universities and business schools for more than fifteen years. As a business owner and organizational development consultant for more than twenty-five years, Frederick has developed innovative processes for intercultural dialogue in society and in business. During turbulent times in South Africa and numerous other countries, he successfully facilitated stakeholder and employee involvement through generative dialogue to achieve sustainable business success. He has a passion for reconciling contradictions and diversities in the workplace and the boardroom, using opposing views and orientations as a platform for innovative solutions to challenges. He has developed processes and programmes that develop the ability to manage the incompatibilities facing individuals, teams and in organizations, giving birth to co-creative solutions to complex challenges. He has also introduced these insights and processes in community development as part of Corporate Social Responsibility programmes globally. The World Bank has published his case studies in 1996 as examples of best practice. He is currently conducting research in the field of Ego and Eco Leadership Intelligence, exploring how leaders can develop their capabilities to face the challenges and disruptions of an increasingly VUCA world.

Mark McKergow MBA, PhD

Mark is a consultant and author bringing new ideas into the world of organizations. He is director of the Centre for Solutions Focus at Work (http://sfwork.com), based in London, and works as an Ashridge Associate. He is also an international speaker, teacher and consultant who has brought the Solution Focused approach from the therapy room to the boardroom over the last twenty years. He is co-author of dozens of articles as well as four books including *The Solutions Focus* (with Paul

Z. Jackson) which has sold some 30,000 copies in 11 languages. He has written *Host: Six New Roles of Engagement for Teams, Organisations, Communities and Movements* with Helen Bailey (Solutions Books, London, 2014). Mark is an editor of the peer-reviewed journal *InterAction*, and is a visiting research fellow in philosophy at the University of Hertfordshire where he examines the language of coaching and therapy. He is currently developing the metaphor of leading as a host (rather than as a hero or servant), with new work appearing at http://hostleadership.com.

John Neal Dip.Sport Psych; Bachelor of Humanities
John is a Performance Psychologist who works with leaders and their teams to achieve remarkable results under intense pressure. He is an exercise physiologist, performance psychologist and Professor of Practice in Sport Business Performance at Ashridge Executive Education, Hult International Business School. He works across three industries: sports, business and the military. In the sports world John has crafted an extensive and successful career working as a performance coach preparing international and national teams and individuals for European Cups, Premier League titles, four World Cups and three Olympic Games. In business he consults with large global corporates such as Coke and Swarovski, to smaller family businesses and significant charities. In the military he works at the Defence Leadership Academy at Shrivenham and with the RAF, British Army and Navy, the British and Scottish Police service, GCHQ and the Abu Dhabi Police. John is also MD of Neal Training – Corporate Health Management. This is a small chain of Health Clubs with 30 staff and 1,500 members which maintains his pragmatic approach to performance theories. John was Wellbeing Advisor to the Royal Household for seven years. John has three grown-up sons who are all making their way in the world.

Matt Nixon
Matt is an Ashridge Associate and runs Disraeli Group, a specialist consultancy focused on leadership, reputation and legacy. He is the author of Pariahs: Hubris, Leadership and Organisational Crises, (Libri 2016). Matt has taught on Ashridge MBA and Strategic HRM programmes, and also lectured at Warwick Business School and contributed to the Daedalus Trust Hubris Project at University of Surrey Business School. Matt spent a decade in line leadership as an HR executive for Barclays, where he was Managing Director, Group Talent and Shell, where he headed up Organisation Effectiveness globally. In these jobs he played a key role

interacting with CEOs, boards and regulators as the organisations faced massive external challenges to their reputations, leadership and cultures. Previously, Matt was a partner at Towers Watson in Chicago and London, where he led the Rewards and Performance Management practice. He has worked globally for private and public sector projects for clients in diverse industry segments, including banking, hi-tech, manufacturing, regulation and museums. Matt's first degree was an MA in Classics from Christ Church, Oxford, where he was an Open Scholar. He is qualified in a number of psychometric individual and team assessment tools. He is a trustee of Demos, the think tank, and a school governor.

Sharon Olivier MA.Org. Psych.
Sharon is the Programme Director for Open Programmes at Ashridge Executive Education, Hult International Business School where she teaches, researches and consults Leadership & Team Development, particularly in Inter-Cultural Intelligence, Engagement, Polarity Management, Emotional and Spiritual (SQ) Intelligence, Talent Identification, Mindfulness, Personal Resilience and Team Resilience. Before Ashridge, Sharon spent seventeen years as a Senior Manager/ OD Consultant/Learning Facilitator/Coach/Speaker. She started her career as HR Manager in the Motor Industry, then led Human Capacity Building in a large consulting company, after which she established a successful consulting practice (Impact Consulting) in South Africa. Clients have included Audi, BMW, Land Rover, De Beers, Anglo, Sage Life, University of Johannesburg and Sasol. Sharon holds a MA in Organizational Psychology and a Management Advanced Programme Certificate. She is a Master Practitioner in NLP (neuro-linguistic programming) and a PNI (psychoneuroimmunology) practitioner. She has established a track record as an inspirational speaker at conferences and is an accredited Laughter/Levity facilitator. She has co-published a book on resilience, *Diamonds in the Dust*, and numerous conference papers on leadership and employee engagement.

Megan Reitz MA (Cantab), MSc, MRes, PhD
Megan is Associate Professor of Leadership and Dialogue at Ashridge Executive Education, Hult International Business School, teaching, coaching and consulting in the areas of organizational change, leadership, dialogue, coaching, team effectiveness and personal development. She supervises on both the Ashridge Doctoral and Masters

programmes in Organizational Change. Megan's research interests include exploring the links between mindfulness practice and critical leadership capacities, 'speaking truth to power' inside organizations and the neuroscience of leadership. Her book *Dialogue in Organizations; Developing Relational Leadership* was published by Palgrave Macmillan in 2015. Megan runs her own international consultancy practice focusing on organizational change and leadership development and is an associate of Open Mind and Witten University School of Management. She is an executive coach accredited by The School of Coaching and Ashridge. Megan joined Ashridge from Deloitte's People and Organizational Change Consulting Practice. Her business background also includes working as an analyst in a strategy consultancy called The Kalchas Group which became the strategy consulting arm of Computer Science Corporation and in supplier strategy and relationship management for both NTL and the internet start-up, boo.com. Her passion and enduring research and practice engages with celebrating the complexity and socially constructed nature of moments of 'effective' leadership in pursuit of genuine dialogue, in the service of human flourishing.

Colin Williams Dip MRS, MHCIMA, MBA
Colin Williams is Professor of Practice and Associate Director of Open Programmes at Ashridge Executive Education, Hult International Business School. He has worked at Ashridge in a variety of teaching, research, consulting and management roles for over twenty-five years and is currently Programme Director for the Ashridge Leadership Process. He has worked extensively around the world having lived and worked in France, Germany and the Middle East for ten years and taught leadership programmes in most other European countries, North and South America and Asia Pacific region. He is particularly interested in leadership in action and has been involved in two major research projects that observed leaders in action, in their specific contexts, over a number of years. He has considerable experience of leading within and across different cultures and has explored the challenges and opportunities this brings. His first career was in the hotel business where he worked for two different multi-national hotel chains. As a line manager for over ten years he became a consultant in organizational change for the next ten years and was involved in major change interventions around Europe. He has published extensively on questions of leadership, organizational change and strategy implementation.

Bibliography

Introduction

Covey, S. (1999) *Principle-Centred Leadership*. New York: Simon & Schuster.

Fletcher, J.K. (2004) The paradox of post-heroic leadership: an essay on gender, power, and transformational change. *The Leadership Quarterly* **15** (5), 647–61.

George, W. (2004) The journey to authenticity. *Leader to Leader* **31**, (Winter).

George, W. (2007) *True North*. San Francisco: Jossey Bass.

Harris, T. (1979) *I'm OK, You're OK*. New York: Harper and Row.

Killinger, B. (2008) *Integrity: Doing the Right Thing for the Right Reason*. Canada: McGill-Queens University Press.

Luthans, F. and Avolio, B. (2003) 'Authentic Leadership: a Positive Development Approach.' In K.S. Cameron, J.E. Dutton and R.E. Quinn, *Positive Organizational Scholarship: Foundations of a New Discipline*. San Francisco: Berrett-Koehler.

Michie, S. and Gooty, J. (2005) Values, emotions and authenticity: will the real leader please stand up? *The Leadership Quarterly* **16**, 441–57.

Nixon, M. (2016) *Pariahs: Hubris, Reputation and Organisational Crises*. London: Libri.

Sagnotti, L., Scardia, G., Giaccio, B., Liddicoat, J.C., Nomade, S., Renne, P.R. and Sprain, C.J. (2014) Extremely rapid directional change during Matuyama-Brunhes geomagnetic polarity reversal. *Geophysics Journal International* **199** (2), 1110–24.

Turnbull James, K. (2011). 'Leadership in Context. Lessons from New Leadership Theory and Current Leadership Development Practice,' The Kings Fund Paper. http://www.kingsfund.org.uk/sites/files/kf/Leadership-in-context-leadership-theory-current-leadership-development-practice-Kim-Turnbull-James-The-Kings-Fund-May-2011.pdf (accessed 28 July 2016).

Chapter 1

Binney, G., Wilke, G. and Williams, C. (2012) *Living Leadership: A Practical Guide for Ordinary Heroes*. 3rd Edition, London: FT Pitman Publishing.

Brittain, L.J. and Van Velsor, E. (1996) *A Look at Derailment Today in the USA and Europe*. Greensboro, NC: Center for Creative Leadership.

Carroll, L. (1865) *Alice's Adventure in Wonderland*. London: Macmillan.

Groysberg, B. and Slind, M. (2012) *Talk, Inc.* Boston, MA: Harvard Business Review Press.

Higgins, J. (2009) *Images of Authority: Working in the Shadow of the Crown.* London: Middlesex University Press.

Janssen, C. (1996) *The Four Rooms of Change – A Practical Everyday Psychology.* Stockholm: Wahlström & Widstrand.

Larkin, P. (1974) *High Windows.* London: Faber and Faber.

Owen, D. (2007) *Hubris Syndrome: Bush, Blair and the Intoxication of Power.* London: Politico's Publishing.

Pearce, V. (2014) *Focus: The Art of Clear Thinking.* London: Mercier Press.

Peterson, C. and Seligman, M. (2006) *Character Strengths and Virtues.* New York: Oxford University Press.

Reitz, M. (2015) *Dialogue in Organisations: Developing Relational Leaders.* London: Palgrave.

Chapter 2

Brown, A. (2014) *The Myth of the Strong Leader: Political Leadership in the Modern Age.* New York: Basic Books.

Christensen, C.M., Raynor, M.E. and McDonald, R. (2015) What is Disruptive Innovation? *Harvard Business Review*, December.

Culpin, V. and Russell, A. (2016) *The Wake-Up Call: The Importance of Sleep in Organisational Life.* Ashridge Report. https://www.ashridge.org.uk/faculty-research/research/publications (accessed 27 July 2016).

Danchey, A. (2011) *War Diaries of Lord AlanBrooke (1939–1945).* London: Weidenfeld and Nicolson.

Davenport-Hines, R. (2013) *An English Affair.* London: HarperCollins.

Day, A. and Power, K. (2009). Developing leaders for a world of uncertainty, complexity and ambiguity. Designing high-impact learning: translating research into practice. *Ashridge 360 Journal*, 2009/2010.

De Haan, E. and Kasozi, A. (2014) *The Leadership Shadow.* London: Kogan Page.

Economist Special Report: the Signal and the Noise, http://www.economist.com/news/special-report/21695198-ever-easier-communications-and-ever-growing-data-mountains-are-transforming-politics, accessed August 2016 or in print edition of 26 March 2016.

Edelman Trust Barometer 2014, downloaded from http:www.edelman.com/insights/intellectual-property 2014-edelman-trust-barometer/ August 2016.

Edelman Trust Barometer 2016. Retrieved from http://www.edelman.com/insights/intellectual-property/2016-edelman-trust-barometer/ (accessed April 2016).

Eggers, D. (2013) *The Circle.* Canada: Knopf.

Fine, G.A. (2001) *Difficult Reputations.* Chicago: University of Chicago Press.

Freshfields, B.D. (2012) *Knowing the Risks, Protecting Your Business*. Crisis Management London: Freshfields Report.

Freshfields, B.D. (2014) *Containing a Crisis*. London: Freshfields Report.

Furnham, A. (2010) *The Elephant in the Boardroom*. London: Palgrave Macmillan.

Garrard, P. and Robinson, G., eds (2015) *The Intoxication of Power: Interdisciplinary Insights*. London: Palgrave Macmillan.

Ghaemi, N. (2011) *First Rate Madness*. New York: Penguin Press.

Hennessy, P. (2014) *Establishment and Meritocracy*. London: Haus Publishing.

Hill R.W. and Yousey, G. (1998) Adaptive and maladaptive narcissism among university faculty, clergy, politicians and librarians. *Current Psychology*, **17** (2/3), 163–9.

Jones, O. (2015) *The Establishment: And How They Get Away With It*. London: Melville House.

Kirby, P. (2016) *Leading People*. Sutton Trust Report. http://www.suttontrust.com/research-status/2016/ (accessed 27 July 2016).

Levy, S. (2011) *In the Plex: How Google Thinks, Works, and Shapes Our Lives*. New York: Simon and Schuster.

Lieberman, M.D. (2013) *Social: Why Our Brains Are Wired to Connect*. Oxford: Oxford University Press

Maccoby, M. (2000) Narcissistic leaders: The incredible pros, the inevitable cons. *Harvard Business Review* **78** (1), 68–78.

Malkin, C. (2015) *Rethinking Narcissism: The Bad – and Surprising Good – About Feeling Special*. New York: Harper Collins.

Meadows, D. H., Meadows, D.L, Randers, J. and Williams, W. (1972) *The Limits to Growth*. New York: Potomac Associates.

Miller, C. (2016). *Harnessing Social Media Reaction to Emergency Incidents*. London: Demos.

Mishna, F., Cook, C., Gadalla, T., Daciuk, J. and Solomon, S. (2015) *Bridging the Gap: A Mixed-Method Investigation of Cyberbullying*. https://sswr.confex.com/sswr/2015/webprogram/Paper22728.html (accessed February 2016).

Morozov, E. (2013) *To Save Everything Click Here*. New York: Allen Lane.

Nadler, D. A. (2005) Confessions of a trusted counsellor. *Harvard Business Review* **83** (9), 68–77.

Nixon, M. (2016) *Pariahs: Hubris, Reputation and Organisational Crises*. London: Libri.

O'Neill, O. (2002) *Lectures on Trust*, Reith Lecture Series. http://www.bbc.co.uk/radio4/features/the-reith-lectures/transcripts/2000/ (accessed 28 July 2016).

Owen, D. (2011) *In Sickness and in Power: Illness in Heads of Government Over the Last 100 Years*. London: Methuen.

Owen, D. (2012) *The Hubris Syndrome: Bush, Blair and the Intoxication of Power*. London: Methuen.

Owen, D. and Davidson, J. (2009). Hubris syndrome: an acquired personality disorder? A study of US Presidents and UK Prime Ministers over the last 100 years. *Brain* **132** (5), 1396–1406.

Petit, V. and Bollaert, H. (2012) Flying too close to the sun? Hubris among CEOs and how to prevent it. *Journal of Business Ethics* **108** (3), 265–83.

Poole, E. (2015) *Capitalism's Toxic Assumptions*. London: Bloomsbury.

Ronson, J. (2015) *So You've Been Publicly Shamed*. London: Picador.

Ryde, R. (2012) *Never Mind the Bosses: Hastening the Death of Deference for Business Success*. London: Wiley.

Scharmer, C.O. and Kaufer, K. (2013) *Leading from the Emerging Future: From Ego-system to Eco-system Economies*. San Francisco: Berrett-Koehler.

Schwartz, Howard S. (1992) *Narcissistic Process and Corporate Decay: The Theory of the Organizational Ideal*. New York: NYU Press.

Shultz, S., Opie, C. and Atkinson, Q.D. (2011) Stepwise evolution of stable sociality in primates. *Nature* **479**, 219–22.

Smith, S.F., Watts, A. and Lilienfeld, S. (2014) On the trail of the elusive successful psychopath. *Psychological Assessment* **15**, 340–50.

Stadler, C. and Dyer, D. (2013) Why good leaders don't need charisma. *Sloan Management Review*, Spring.

Stein, M. (2013) When does narcissistic leadership become problematic? Dick Fuld at Lehman Brothers. *Journal of Management Inquiry* **22** (3), 282–93.

Twenge, J. and Campbell, S. (2008) Generational differences in psychological traits and their impact on the workplace. *Journal of Managerial Psychology* **23**, 8.

Chapter 3

Bentham, J. (2010) *The Panopticon Writings* in M. Bozovic (ed.), London: Verso.

Binney, G., Wilke, G. and Williams, C. (2012) *Living Leadership: A Practical Guide for Ordinary Heroes*, 2nd edition. Harlow: Pearson Education.

Buber, M. (1958), *I and Thou*, Smith, R. (trans), 2nd edition. London: T&T Clark.

De Haan, E. and Kasozi, A. (2014) *The Leadership Shadow: How to Recognize and Avoid Derailment, Hubris and Overdrive*. London: Kogan Page.

Fuller, R. (2004) *Somebodies and Nobodies: Overcoming the Abuse of Rank*. Gabriola Island, BC: New Society Publishers.

Groysberg, B. and Slind, M. (2012) Leadership is a conversation. *Harvard Business Review*, **1**, 76–84.

Hartley, L. (1953) *The Go-Between*. London: Hamish Hamilton.

Higgins, J. (2009) *Images of Authority: Working Within the Shadow of the Crown*. London: Middlesex University Press.

Isaacs, W. (1999) *Dialogue and the Art of Thinking Together*. New York: Doubleday.

Korzybski, A. (2003) *Science and Sanity: An Introduction to Non-Aristotelian Systems and General Semantics*. Chicago: Institute of General Semantics.

Mintzberg, H. (2006) Community-ship is the answer. *Financial Times* newspaper online edition. http://www.ft.com/cms/s/0/a3cbeade-6232-11db-af3e-0000779e2340.html#axzz4FnEeC8ly (accessed 27 July 2016).

Oshry, B. (1986) *The Possibilities of Organization*. Boston, MA: Power and Systems Training.

Reitz, M. (2015) *Dialogue in Organizations; Developing Relational Leadership*. London: Palgrave Macmillan.

Sapolsky, R. (2015) 'Our Brains Say Corporations Are People, Too.' *Wall Street Journal*, 15 October.

Symington, J. and Symington, N. (1996) *The Clinical Thinking of Wilfred Bion*. London: Routledge.

Trompenaars, F. and Hampden-Turner, C. (1993) *Riding the Waves of Culture: Understanding Cultural Diversity in Global Business*. New York: McGraw-Hill.

Williams, C., Reitz, M. and Higgins, J. (2014), Is leadership changing? *The Ashridge Journal* 360, Winter 2013/14.

Zuboff, S. (1988) *In the Age of the Smart Machine: The Future of Work and Power*. New York: Basic Books.

Chapter 4

Avolio, B.J., Walumbwa, F.O. and Weber, T.J. (2009) Leadership: current theories, research and future directions. *Annual Review of Psychology* **60** 421-49.

Bass, B.M. and Steidlmeier, P. (1999) Ethics, character and authentic transformational leadership behaviour. *The Leadership Quarterly* **10**, 181-217.

Berne, E. (1958) *Games People Play*. New York: Grove Press.

Carver, J. (2006) *Boards That Make a Difference*. San Francisco: Jossey Bass.

Covey, S. (1999) *Principle Centred Leadership*. New York: Simon & Schuster.

George, W. (2004) The journey to authenticity. *Leader to Leader* **31**, (Winter).

George, W. (2007) *True North*. San Francisco: Jossey Bass.

Goleman, D., Boyatzis, R. and McKee, A. (2003) *Primal Leadership: Unleashing the Power of Emotional Intelligence*. Boston, MA: Harvard Business Review Press.

Hannah, S., Avolio, B. and Walumba, F. (2011) Relationship between authentic leadership, moral courage and ethical, pro-social behaviours. *Business Ethics Quarterly* **21** (4), 555-78.

Harris, T. (1979) *I'm OK, You're OK*. New York: Harper and Row.

Hartner, S., Snyder, C.R. and Lopez, S.J. (2002) *Handbook of Positive Psychology*. New York: Oxford University Press, 382-94.

Hoffer, E. (1973) *Reflections on the Human Condition*. New Jersey: Hopewell.

Howell, J. and Avolio, B. (1992) The ethics of charismatic leadership: submission or liberation? *Academy of Management Executive* **6** (2), 43-54.

Kanungo, R. (2001) Ethical values of transactional and transformational leaders. *Canadian Journal of Administrative Sciences* **18** (4), 257-65.

Kanungo, R. and Mendonca, M. (1996) *Ethical Dimensions in Leadership*. Beverly Hills, CA: Sage Publications.

Kidder, R. (2005) *Moral Courage*. New York: William Morrow.

Killinger, B. (2010) *Integrity: Doing the Right Thing for the Right Reason*. Canada: McGill-Queens University Press.

Luthans, F. and Avolio, B. (2003) 'Authentic Leadership: a Positive Development Approach.' In K.S. Cameron, J.E. Dutton and R.E. Quinn, *Positive Organizational Scholarship: Foundations of a New Discipline*. San Francisco: Berrett-Koehler.

MacIntyre, A. (1981) *After Virtue: A Study in Moral Theory*. Indiana: University of Notre Dame Press.

Maister, D., Galford, R. and Green, C. (2002) *The Trusted Advisor*. London: Simon and Schuster.

May, D., Hodges T., Chan, A. and Avolio, B. (2003) Developing the moral component of authentic leadership. *Organizational Dynamics* **32** (3), 247–60.

Michie, S. and Gooty, J. (2005) Values, emotions and authenticity: will the real leader please stand up? *The Leadership Quarterly* **16**, 441–57.

National Business Ethics Survey (2009), Ethics Resource Centre. http://www.ethics.org/eci/research/eci-research/nbes/nbes-reports/nbes-2013 (accessed 27 July 2016).

Rokeach, M. (1973) *The Nature of Human Values*. New York: Free Press.

Rowling, J.K. (2007) *Harry Potter and The Philosopher's Stone*. London: Bloomsbury.

Sankar, Y. (2003) Character not charisma is the critical measure of leadership excellence. *Journal of Leadership and Organisational Studies* **9** (4), 45–55.

Steare, R. (2006) *Ethicability*. London: Steare.

Steare, R. and Jamieson, C. (2003) 'Integrity in Practice', a paper for the British Financial Service, Association in 2008.

Trevino, L.K., Weaver, G.R., Gibson, D.G. and Toffler, B.L. (1999) Managing ethics and legal compliance; what works and what hearts. *California Management Review* **41** (2), 421–9.

Thoms, J. (2008) Ethical integrity in leadership and organisational moral culture. *Leadership* **4** (4), 419–42.

Yukl, G. (2001) *Leadership Organisations*. New Jersey: Prentice Hall.

Chapter 5

Adkins, A. (2015) *What Separates Great Managers from the Rest*. Gallup Report. http://www.gallup.com/businessjournal/183098/report-separates-great-managers-rest.aspx (accessed 23 February 2016).

Ashfort, B.E. and Humphrey, R.H. (1995) Emotion in the workplace, a re-appraisal. *Human Relations* **48**, 97–125.

Ashkanasy, N.M. (1996) *Perceiving and Managing Change in the Workplace*. Management Paper Series, Graduate School of Management, University of Queensland, Australia.

Avolio, B.J. (2007) Promoting more integrative strategies for leadership theory building. *American Psychologist* **62**, 25–33.

Avolio, B.J. and Gardner, W.L. (2005) Authentic leadership development: getting to the root of positive forms of leadership. *Leadership Quarterly* **16**, 315–38.

Avolio, B.J., Walumbwa, F.O. and Weber, T.J. (2009) Leadership: current theories, research and future directions. *Annual Review of Psychology* **60**, 421–49.

Brackett, M.A. and Salovey, P. (2004) 'Measuring Emotional Intelligence with the Mayer Salovey Caruso Test (MSCEIT)' in G. Geher (ed.) *Measuring Emotional Intelligence: Common Ground and Controversy*. Happauge: Nova Science Publishers, 179–94.

Burgoyne, J., Hirsh, W. and Williams, S. (2004) 'The Development of Management and Leadership Capability and its Contribution to Performance: The Evidence, the Prospects and the Research Need.' Research Report, Lancaster University, UK.

Caruso, D. and Salovey, P. (2004) *The Emotionally Intelligent Manager; How to Develop and Use the Four Key Emotional Skills of Leadership*. San Francisco: Jossey Bass.

Collinson, D. and Tourish, D. (2015) Teaching leadership critically: new directions for leadership pedagogy. *Academy of Management Learning and Education* **14** (4), 578–94.

Day, A.L. and Carroll, S.A. (2008) Faking emotional intelligence (EI) comparing response distortion on ability and trait based EI measures. *Journal of Organisational Behaviour* **29**, 761–84.

Fairchild, C. (2015) Why so few women are CEOs. *Fortune Magazine*, 14 January. http://fortune.com/2015/01/14/why-so-few-women-ceos/ (accessed 21 January 2016).

Fleming, K. (2016) *The Leader's Guide to Emotional Agility*. London: Pearson Financial Times.

Fox, S. and Spector, P.E. (2000) Relations of emotional intelligence, practical intelligence, general intelligence, and trait affectivity with interview outcomes: It's not all just 'G'. *Journal of Organisational Behaviour* **21**, 203–20.

Gardner, L. and Stough, C. (2002) Examining the relationship between leadership and emotional intelligence in senior level managers. *Leadership and Organisational Development* **23**, 68–79.

Gardner, W.L., Avolio, B.J., Luthans, F., May, D.R. and Walumbwa, F.O. (2005) Can you see the real me? A self-based model of authentic leader and follower development. *Leadership Quarterly* **16**, 343–72.

George, J.M. (2000) Emotions and leadership: the role of emotional intelligence. *Human Relations* **53**, 1027–55.

Gilley, A., Dixon, P. and Gilley, J.W. (2008) Characteristics of leadership effectiveness: implementing change and driving innovation in organizations. *Human Resource Development Quarterly* **19** (2), 153–69.

Glinton, S. (2016) '"We Didn't Lie," Volkswagen CEO Says of Emissions Scandal.' NPR,US. Interview: http://www.npr.org/sections/thetwo-way/2016/01/11/462682378/we-didnt-lie volkswagen-ceo-says-of-emissions-scandal (accessed 28 January 2016).

Lewis, K.M. (2000) When leaders display emotion: how followers respond to negative emotional expression of male and female leaders. *Journal of Organisational Behaviour* **21**, 221–34.

Lopes, P.N., Salovey, P., Cotes, S. and Beers, M. (2006) Emotion regulation abilities and the quality of social interaction. *Emotion* **5**, 113–18.

Mandell, B. and Pherwani, S. (2003) Relationship between emotional intelligence and transformational leadership style: a gender comparison. *Journal of Business and Psychology* **17** (3), 387–404.

Mathews, G., Zeidner, M. and Roberts, R.D. (2002) *Emotional Intelligence: Science and Myth*. Cambridge, MA: MIT Press.

Mayer, J., Salovey, P. and Caruso, D. (2002) *The Mayer, Salovey and Caruso Emotional Intelligence Test, Version 2.0*. Canada: Multi Health Systems.

Mayer, J.D., Roberts, R.D. and Barsade, S.G. (2008) Human abilities: Emotional Intelligence. *Annual Review of Psychology* **59**, 507–36.

McGarvey, R. (1997) Final score: get more from employees by upping your EQ. *Entrepreneur* **25** (7), 78–81.

Moorhead, G. and Neck, C. (1995) Groupthink re-modelled: the importance of leadership, time pressure, and methodical decision-making procedures. *Human Relations Journal* **48** (5), 537–57.

Omta, S.W.F. and Bouter, L.M. (1997) Management control of biomedical research and pharmaceutical innovation. *Technovation* **17** (4), 167–79.

Petriglieri, G. and Petriglieri, J.L. (2015) Can business schools humanize leadership? *Academy of Management Learning and Education* **14** (4), 625–47.

Whyte, W.H. (1956) *The Organisation Man*. New York: Simon and Schuster.

Yukl, G. (2006) *Leadership in Organisations*. New Jersey: Pearson.

Chapter 6

Binney, G., Williams, C. and Wilke, G. (2012) *Living Leadership: A Practical Guide for Ordinary Heroes*. London: Pearson Financial Times Series.

Bolte, A., Goschke, T., Glatzeder, B., Goel, V. and von Muller, A.A.C. (2010). *Thinking and Emotion: Affective Modulation of Cognitive Processing Modes. Towards a Theory of Thinking*. Berlin: Springer.

Collins, J. (2001) *Good to Great*. Kent, UK: Random House.

Conger, J.A. (2004). Developing leadership capability: what's inside the black box? *Academy of Management Executive* **18** (3), 136–9.

D'Hondt, F., Lassonde, M., Collignon, O., Dubarry, A., Robert, M., Rigoulot, S., Honoré, J. and Gladwell, M. (2005) *Blink: The Power of Thinking Without Thinking*. New York: Little, Brown and Co.

Hersey, P. (1986) *Situational Leader*. New York: Warner Books.

Kouzes, J.M. and Posner, B.Z. (2010) *The Truth about Leadership*. California: Jossey Bass.

Lepore, F. and Sequeira, H. (2010) Early brain-body impact of emotional arousal. *Frontiers in Human Neuroscience* **4** (33), 1–10.

Maier, S.F. and Watkins, L.R. (2010) Role of the medial prefrontal cortex in coping and resilience. *Brain Research* **13** (55), 52–60.

McEwen, B.S. (2012) Brain on stress: how the social environment gets under the skin. *Proceedings of the National Academy of Sciences* **10** (2), 17180–5.

Pease, A. and Pease, B. (2001) *Why Men Don't Listen and Women Can't Read Maps.* London: Orion Books.

Thomas, R. and Cheese, P. (2005) Leadership: experience is the best teacher. *Strategy and Leadership* **33** (3), 24–9.

Thompson, C.P. (1985) Memory for unique personal events: effects of pleasantness. *Motivation and Emotion* **9**, 277–89.

Waller, L. (2012) *Leadership Development Evaluation: An Ashridge Market Report.* Ashridge Business School Report, August.

Chapter 7

Armstrong, A. (May 2013) *Engagement Through CEO Eyes.* Ashridge and Engagement for Success Research Report.

Barrett, R. (2014) *Values Driven Organisation.* Oxford: Routledge.

Binney, G., Wilke, G. and Williams, C. (2012) *Living Leadership: A Practical Guide for Ordinary Heroes,* 2nd edition. Harlow: Pearson Education.

Hölscher, F. (2009) *Diamonds in the Dust: Crafting Your Future Landscape.* Johannesburg: Congruence Publishing

Hampden-Turner, C. and Trompenaars, F. (2015) *Nine Visions of Capitalism: Unlocking the Meanings of Wealth Creation.* Oxford: Infinite Ideas Limited.

Hawkins, P. (2011) *Leadership Team Coaching: Developing Collective Transformational Leadership.* London: Kogan Page.

Hutchins, G. (2012) *The Nature of Business: Redesigning for Resilience.* Dartington: Green Books.

Hutchins, G. (2014) *The Illusion of Separation: Exploring the Cause of Our Current Crises.* Edinburgh: Floris Books.

IBM (2010) *Capitalizing on Complexity: Insights from the Global Chief Executive Officer Study.* IBM Report. http://www-935.ibm.com/services/us/ceo/ceostudy2010/ (accessed 28 July 2016).

Johnson, B. (1992) *Polarity Management: Identifying and Managing Unsolvable Problems.* Massachusetts: HRD Press Inc.

Laloux, F. (2014) *Reinventing Organisations: A Guide to Creating Organizations Inspired by the Next Stage of Human Consciousness.* Brussels: Nelson Parker.

MacCleod, D. and Clarke, N. (2009) *Engaging for Success: Enhancing Performance Through Employee Engagement: A Report.* Department for Business, Innovation and Skills www.bis.gov.uk first published July 2009. London: BIS/Publishing.

Martin, R. (2007) How successful leaders think. *Harvard Business Review*, June.

Scharmer, O.C. (2009) *Theory U: Leading From the Future as it Emerges*. San Francisco: Berrett-Koehler Publisher.

Scharmer, O.C. and Kaufer, K. (2013) *Leading From the Emerging Future: From Ego-system to Ecosystem Economies*. San Francisco: Berrett-Koehler Publisher.

Stacey, R. (2012) *Tools and Techniques of Leadership and Management*. New York: Routledge.

Taylor, S. (2005) *The Fall: The Insanity of the Ego in Human History and the Dawning of a New Era*. Hants, UK: John Hunt Publishing Ltd.

Western, S. (2013) *Leadership: A Critical Text*. London: Sage Publications.

Zohar, D. and Marshall, I. (2000) *Spiritual Intelligence: The Ultimate Intelligence*. London: Bloomsbury Publishing.

Zohar, D. and Marshall, I. (2004) *Spiritual Capital: Wealth We Can Live By*. London: Bloomsbury.

Chapter 8

Amabile, T. and Kramer, S. (2007) *The Progress Principle*. Boston: Harvard Business Press.

Aoki, Y. (2009) Creating a workplace where we all wanna go every morning! Workplace climate change at Canon FineTech Inc. Japan. *InterAction* **1** (2), 103–19.

Ashridge and MSL Group (2014) The Millennial Compass – Truths about the 30-and-under Generation in the Workplace. Retrieved from http://www.scribd.com/doc/211602632/The-Millennial-Compass-The-Millennial-Generation-In-The-Workplace. (Accessed 28 July 2016).

Brent, M. and McKergow, M. (2009) No more heroes. *Coaching At Work* **4** (5), 44–8.

Buckingham, M. and Clifton, D.O. (2001) *Now, Discover Your Strengths*. New York: Simon and Schuster.

Calabrese, R.L., San Martin, T., Glasgow, J. and Friesen, S. (2015) *The Power of Appreciative Inquiry 4-D Cycle in a Non-AYP Middle School*. Retrieved from http://www2.education.uiowa.edu/archives/jrel/Calabrese_0803.htm (accessed 9 December 2015).

Childre, D. and Martin, H. (2000) *The Heart Math Solution*. New York: Harper One.

CIPD (2011) *The Coaching Climate Survey*. Retrieved from http://www.cipd.co.uk/hr-resources/survey-reports/ (accessed 28 July 2016).

CIPD (2013) *Learning and Talent Development Survey*. Retrieved from http://www.cipd.co.uk/hr-resources/survey-reports/ (accessed 28 July 2016).

Clinton, H. (2014) *Hard Choices*. London: Simon and Schuster.

Cooperrider, D.L. (2005) *Thought Leaders: David Cooperrider And Appreciative Inquiry* (interview with David Creelman). http://www.hr.com/en/communities/

human_resources_management/thought-leaders-david-cooperrider-and-appreciative_eacwmnbn.html (accessed 2 December 2015).

Cooperrider, D.L. and Whitney, D (2005.) *Appreciative Inquiry: A Positive Revolution in Change.* San Francisco: Berrett Koehler.

Fredrickson, B. (2011) *Positivity.* London: One World Publications.

Gable, S.L, Gonzaga, G.C. and Strachman, A. (2006) Will you be there for me when things go right? Supportive responses to positive event disclosures. *Journal of Personality and Social Psychology* **91** (5), 904–17.

Greenleaf, R. (1998) *The Power of Servant-Leadership.* San Francisco: Berrett Kohler.

Grint, K. (2005) *Leadership: Limits and Possibilities (Management, Work and Organisations).* New York: Palgrave Macmillan.

Honoré, S. and Paine Schofield, C.B. (2012) *Culture Shock: Generation Y and Their Managers Around the World.* An Ashridge Business School Report. Retrieved from http://www.ashridge.org.uk/getattachment/Faculty-Research/Research/Current-Research/Research-Projects/Culture-Shock-Generation-Y-andtheir-Managers-Arou/Gen-Y-Report_Nov2012_FULL_lores.pdf (accessed 27 July 2016).

IBM (2010). 'Capitalising on Complexity: Insights from the Global Chief Executive Officer Study'. Downloaded from http://www-935.ibm.com/services/c-suite/series-download.html (Accessed 27 July 2016).

ILM and Ashridge (2015) *Attract, Grow, Engage: Optimising the Talents of an Age-diverse Workforce.* Institute of Leadership and Management/Ashridge Business School Guide.

Jackson, P.Z. and McKergow, M. (2007) *The Solutions Focus: Making Coaching and Change Simple.* London: Nicholas Brealey Publishing.

Losada, M. and Heaphy, E. (2004) The role of positivity and connectivity in the performance of business teams. *American Behavioural Scientist* **47**, 740–65.

McCraty, R. and Childre, D. (2004) 'The Grateful Heart: The Psychophysiology of Gratitude'. In R.A. Emmons and M.E. McCullough (eds) *The Psychology of Gratitude.* Oxford: Oxford University Press.

McCraty, R., Atkinson, M., Tiller, W., Rein, G. and Watkins, A. D. (1995) The effects of emotions on short term power spectrum analysis of heart rate variations. *American Journal of Cardiology* **76** (14).

McKergow, M. (2007) *Solution Focus Working.* London: Solutions Books.

McKergow, M. (2015) From diagnosis to dialogue in Organisational Development: an interview with Susanne Burgstaller. *InterAction* **7** (2), 104–10.

McKergow, M. and Bailey, H. (2014) *Host: Six New Roles of Engagement for Teams, Organisations, Communities and Movements.* London: Solutions Books.

McKergow, M. and Clarke, J. (2007) *Optimising the Organisation: Restructuring at Freescale Semiconductor, in Solutions Focus Working: 80 Real-life Lessons for Successful Organisational Change.* Cheltenham: Solutions Books, 93–103.

Olivier, S. and Hölscher, F. (2016) 'Achieving Coherence as a Leadership Capability in a VUCA environment' (unpublished manuscript).

Paine Schofield, C.B. and Honoré, S. (2015) *Don't Put Baby (Boomers) in the Corner: Realising the Potential of the Over 50s at Work*. An Ashridge Business School Report.

Paine Schofield, C.B. and Honoré, S. (2015). *A New Generation: The Success of Generation Y in GCC Countries*. An Ashridge Business School Report.

Rittel, H. and Weber, M. (1973) Dilemmas in a general theory of planning. *Policy Sciences* **4**, 155–69.

Robinson, D. and Hayday, S. (2009) *The Engaging Manager*. Institute of Employment Studies Report, 470.

Rogers, Carl (1951) *Client Centred Therapy*. London: Constable.

Rogers, Carl (2004) *On Becoming a Person*. London: Constable.

Schore, A.N. (1994) *Affect Regulation and the Origin of the Self: The Neurobiology of Emotional Development*. Hillsdale, NJ: Lawrence Erlbaum Associates.

Schore, A.N. (2015) *Affect Regulation and the Origin of the Self: The Neurobiology of Emotional Development*. Oxford: Routledge.

Schwarz, T. and McCarthy, C. (2011) *The Way We Are Working Isn't Working*. New York: Simon and Schuster.

Seligman, M. (2002) *Authentic Happiness*. London: Nicholas Brealey Publishing.

Seligman, M. (2011) *Flourish. A New Understanding of Happiness and Well-being*. London Nicholas Brealey Publishing.

Seligman, M. (2011) *Learned Optimism*. New York: Vintage.

Shaked, D. (2014) *Strength-based Lean Six Sigma: Building Positive and Engaging Business Improvement*. London: Kogan Page.

Srivastvas, S. and Cooperrider, D. (1990) *Appreciative Management Leadership; the Power of Positive Thought and Action in Organisation*. London: Williams Custom Publishing.

Tierney-Moore, H. and Fiona MacNeill (2014) *Appreciative Leadership: Delivering Difference through Conversation and Inquiry*. Chichester: Kingsham Press.

Zaleznik, A. (1977) Managers and Leaders: are they different? *Harvard Business Review*, May/June, 67–78.

Zaleznik, A. (1992) Managers and Leaders: are they different? *Harvard Business Review*, March/April.

Chapter 9

Bell, E., Taylor, S. and Thorpe, R. (2002) A step in the right direction? Investors in People and the learning organization, *British Journal of Management* **13**, 161–71.

Bolden, R. (2011) Distributed leadership in organizations: a review of theory and research. *International Journal of Management Reviews* **13**, 251–69.

Boyatzis, R.E. (1982) *The Competent Manager: A Model for Effective Performance*. New York: Wiley.

Brook, C., Burgoyne, J.G. and Pedler, M. (2004) Time for action. *People Management* **10** (24), 46.

Brundrett, M. (2000) The question of competence; the origins, strengths and inadequacies of a leadership training paradigm. *School Leadership and Management* **20** (3), 353–69.

Cullen, E. (1992) A vital way to manage change. *Education* **13** (November), 3–17.

Ecclestone, K. (1997) Energising or enervating: implications of National Vocational Qualifications in professional development. *Journal of Vocational Education and Training* **49**, 65–79.

Flaum, J.P. (2010) *When it Comes to Business Leadership, Nice Guys Finish First*. Green Peak Partners/Cornell University.

Grugulis, I. (1998) 'Real' managers don't do NVQs: a review of the new management 'standards'. *Employee Relations* **20**, 383–403.

Grugulis, I. (2000) The Management NVQ: a critique of the myth of relevance. *Journal of Vocational Education and Training* **52**, 79–99.

Lester, S. (1994) Management standards: a critical approach. *Competency* **2** (1), 28–31.

Loan-Clarke, J. (1996) The Management Charter Initiative: a critique of management standards/NVQs. *Journal of Management Development* **15**, 4–17.

McKinsey & Co. and Egon Zehnder Intl. (2011) *Return on Leadership – Competencies that Generate Growth*. https://www.egonzehnder.com/files/return_on_leadership.pdf (accessed 29 August 2016).

Sutton, R. (2010) *Good Boss, Bad Boss: How to be the Best and Learn from the Worst*. New York: Business Plus.

Swailes, S. and Roodhouse, S. (2003) Structural barriers to the take-up of higher level NVQs. *Journal of Vocational Education and Training* **55** (1), 85–110.

Wilson, A., Lenssen, G. and Hind, P. (2006) *Building Responsible Leadership*. The European Academy of Business and Society, Research Report, July 2006.

Wood, M. (2005) The fallacy of misplaced leadership. *Journal of Management Studies* **42** (6), 1101–21.

Zaleznik, A. (1977) Managers and leaders: Are they different? *Harvard Business Review*, May–June, 67–78, 17.

Index